Phippy

Phippy

A biography of Jonathan Wathen Phipps/Waller

Eye-surgeon to King George III

Ruth Hayward

BREWIN BOOKS

BREWIN BOOKS
56 Alcester Road,
Studley,
Warwickshire,
B80 7LG
www.brewinbooks.com

Published by Brewin Books 2014

A CIP catalogue record for this book is available
from the British Library.

ISBN: 978-1-85858-521-5

Printed in Great Britain
by Gomer Press Limited.

Contents

Acknowledgements

This biography arose directly from the Warwickshire County Record Office's imaginative initiative "Outside the Box", designed to involve the community in bringing the Waller Collection to life. Thanks to Alaina MacGregor's drive and enthusiasm in managing the project, it was hugely successful: 2,500 people participated, or became aware of the archives – a truly tremendous achievement. As a volunteer transcriber and researcher, I was galvanised by Alaina, then ably and sensitively guided and supervised by Neil Bettridge and Helen Arbon. Heartfelt thanks are due to all three, and to Warwickshire's archives and historic environment manager Sam Collenette for her unfailing support and encouragement, and for permission to quote liberally from the Waller letters.

I am grateful to Her Majesty Queen Elizabeth II for granting me access to the Royal Archives and for her kind permission both to quote from Queen Victoria's Journal and to reproduce portraits from the Royal Collection. My research visits to Warwick, Windsor, and to numerous other record offices and libraries have been made a pleasure by the courtesy and helpfulness of the staff I have encountered. The following repositories have kindly permitted me to quote from their archives: the Dorset History Centre, both East and West Sussex Record Offices, the Centre for Buckinghamshire Studies, the Cornwall Record Office, the Bodleian Library in the University of Oxford, and the Richmond upon Thames Local Studies Collection. I am sincerely grateful to them and to the custodians of pictures I have been licensed to reproduce. It was a great pleasure to meet Mr and Mrs Ken Biggs at their delightful house, Camerton Court, and I much appreciate their kind permission to include photographs from that visit in my illustrations. I am also indebted to Mrs Kathleen Dando of Camerton for generously welcoming me to her home and sharing her knowledge of the Jarrett family history. My publishers Alan and Alistair Brewin have been generous with their time and advice; they have responded to numerous queries with tact, patience and good humour, for which I thank them most warmly.

Writing is a solitary task and I would not have coped without the invaluable support of my sister and brother-in-law Gwyneth and Grahame Castor, who have encouraged me at every step of the way. They made me aware of the Waller transcription project and I was able to join in, via email, from Surrey or (frequently) from further afield; they drove me around Warwickshire to the haunts of the Wallers and Wises, to the Record Office, and to my publishers, providing hospitality and stimulating conversation on every flying visit; they read all my drafts, demonstrating a matchless ability to enhance a sentence with a mere tweak – a semi-colon here or an inspired choice of adjective there; they generously undertook the proofreading with all the necessary painstaking attention to detail. I am hugely indebted to them, and cannot thank them enough. Their daughter Helen very kindly gave me a full day's "tutorial", sharing her experience of writing history and preparing manuscripts for publication. I greatly appreciate the interest she and her sister Harriet have taken in the book's progress. To my immediate family go very special thanks for support of a different kind, grounding me in the present when my mind was wafting through the Georgian decades. They provide me with the buoyancy of spirits and peace of mind that comes from understated but constant affection. This book is dedicated to all seven of my boys: my husband, my sons and my grandsons – Charles, Carlos, Raphael, Thomas, Jonathan, Edward and William.

Prologue

History at first hand with a *frisson* of eavesdropping – what could be more satisfying than private letters as a biographer's source material? No editors, no hindsight, no bias, no spin: just voices from the past expressing their own thoughts in their own words, with an undeniable stamp of truth. When dozens of letters are carefully preserved in a family for nearly two hundred years, they clearly have a tale to tell; when many are intimate confidences of kings and princes, the tale is all the more extraordinary. Royal and family letters recently discovered in the Waller Collection at the Warwickshire County Record Office furnish a rare glimpse of court and private life from the 1790s to 1850, an exciting and colourful period in English history, virtually unscathed by the revolutionary fever on the Continent. The very word "Georgian" conjures up an era of elegance, mellow stone, classical proportions, powdered wigs, silks, buckles and lace, not to mention an expansion of geographical and scientific horizons. Into this world, (Jonathan) Wathen Phipps/Waller – Phippy to his friends – was born, and his story has survived via the Waller letters. Those of us who helped to transcribe them had the daunting task of deciphering hundreds of pages, sometimes in a minuscule script, sometimes very faded, sometimes even cross-hatched. But the letters turned out to be astonishingly vivid and personal, and soon it was possible to get to know the writers and recipients as real people, with news and gossip to relate, heartfelt emotions and identifiable traits of character to convey.

The family letters span three generations and most were addressed to Phippy's son, Thomas Wathen Waller, whose postings to diplomatic missions in The Hague, Paris, Constantinople, Athens and Brussels occasioned a frequent exchange of news with his anxious father and siblings. As a young man far from home, Thomas cherished the letters which kept him in touch with his family; in later life his was the role of anxious father, reading and re-reading a further batch of letters, his 18 year-old son's personal chronicle of the Crimean War as seen from the "Camp before Sebastopol". Thomas was also custodian of a rare and exceptional bundle of papers, candid private letters from royal dukes and princesses to his courtier father.

(Jonathan) Wathen Phipps, later known as Sir Wathen Waller (1769-1853), was appointed oculist to George III at the age of twenty-six, and became a life-long friend and confidant of three of the king's sons: Prince George (as Prince of Wales, Prince Regent and King George IV), Prince William (as Duke of Clarence and King William IV), and Prince Ernest (subsequently Duke of Cumberland and King

Ernest Augustus I of Hanover). Wathen emerges from the Waller collection as its main protagonist and dominant personality: a strong, confident and spectacularly upwardly mobile *paterfamilias*, juggling a thriving and demanding career with the ups and downs of family events and relationships. Numerous letters written by him, to him or about him, reveal his preoccupations, foibles, even private moments of self-doubt and fatigue, against a backdrop of court and political affairs from 1796 to 1853. Somewhat paradoxical in character, Wathen was clearly driven by vanity and ambition, but he also strove to live up to the strict religious principles ingrained in his mind from childhood, and was fearful of divine retribution, if he or his children were to stray from a righteous path. As a young man, dazzled by the opulence of the Court, he relished the status his royal appointment afforded him. Quite unexpectedly his good fortune went further when several princes and princesses of his own generation, charmed by the likeable newcomer, took him into their confidence as a special friend. The ties of affection proved genuine and durable; in middle age Wathen valued them above any material considerations. He stands out among his contemporaries on account of these unlikely relationships, though he has been afforded scant attention by historians of the period; at most, there has been a passing reference in some accounts of the later Hanoverians. This book tells his remarkable story.

Wathen lived a long and eventful life, surviving to the age of eighty-three. Only four of his seven children reached adulthood, a not untypical ratio for the times, but all four married, and he was grandfather to their nineteen offspring. The roles of courtier and father were interwoven throughout his life and encompassed two distinct social spheres. Whilst Wathen moved in royal circles, surrounded by splendour and extravagance, his children were only minor gentry – well educated, extremely presentable, but constantly worried about money and the practicalities of life. The Waller letters allow us to eavesdrop on intimate accounts of the births, marriages, deaths, joys and anxieties in their lives and those of the families they married into, the Wises, Jarretts and Langford Sainsburys. Already well established in his career by the 1790s, Wathen also saw more than half of the nineteenth century. He was born in the 32nd year of the reign of George III, to whom he dispensed treatment and advice on his failing eyesight. By the time Victoria became Queen he already considered himself old, but he lived for another fifteen years. His attention was mainly focused on his public and private commitments, but he was nevertheless aware of the bigger picture: the French Revolution (he was in Paris in July 1789), the Revolutionary and Napoleonic wars, and, closer to home, the "madness" of King George III, the Regency, the earliest railways – gradually replacing stage coach travel – and the agricultural and industrial revolutions. Political preoccupations in his time included Catholic emancipation, the first Reform Act, and the abolition of slavery. In art, architecture, literature and music

Neo-classicism gave way to Romanticism. Wathen witnessed the magnificent heyday of Carlton House and its subsequent demolition, the building of Regent Street, and the enormous expansion of the capital city where he was born and where he died.

Most of the letters in the Waller Collection date from the 1820s and 1830s, so the earlier part of Wathen's life and career has been derived from less personal sources, lacking the impact of unedited private letters. The difference is stark and underlines what a rare privilege it is to have an opportunity to make contact with historical characters and events without intermediaries. To cite just one example: Prince Ernest, best known as the Duke of Cumberland, has been depicted as a thoroughly disreputable criminal and ogre by most of his contemporaries and many later historians. Yet no-one could accept such a one-dimensional image after reading his letters to Wathen, characterised as they are by his overwhelming honesty, his good intentions, his complete lack of pretension, and the warmth of his appreciation of his friend, affectionately addressed as "Dear Phippy". The two men became so close that it was Wathen's custom always to have a dinner provided "such as the Duke may sit down to, as he comes very often, and unexpectedly." Whilst Wathen is the central character in this narrative, Ernest has a crucial secondary role to play. The lives of the two men ran in parallel, their comfortable friendship lasting for more than half a century. To Wathen, Ernest entrusted a secret which remained virtually undiscovered to this day, escaping the notice of Professor Aspinall (who edited the letters of George III and George IV), as well as all of his biographers. It has been possible with a modicum of detective work to make sense of some mysterious enclosures in letters sent to Wathen from Hanover in the late 1830s, and to uncover a previously unknown dimension in the life and character of the much-maligned royal Duke.

Nearly all of the letters surviving in the Waller Collection were retained by their recipients, as might be expected; consequently Thomas's own "voice" is absent, and his story is revealed via the letters from his father and sister Anna (Jarrett). The royal correspondence is also overwhelmingly one-sided: most numerous are the letters from Prince Ernest, who spent more time abroad than his siblings and so relied on the mail to keep him abreast of affairs at home. Several of his brothers and sisters also wrote frequently to Wathen. Princess Sophia, in tiny semi-legible handwriting, fretted for years over her deteriorating eyesight and her lack of independence; when eventually freed from the role of dutiful daughter and able to set up her own household, she joyfully sent Wathen shopping for porcelain in Paris. Many of the surviving notes from William concern invitations to dinners and balls (often involving his illegitimate FitzClarence children); in addition they include a letter of recommendation for Thomas as he embarked on his diplomatic career. Princess Mary (the Duchess of Gloucester) in her latter years kept Wathen in the forefront of her social circle – constantly inviting him to call at her London residence (Gloucester House), or to stay at Bagshot Park, her country home. More than once she put into words her gratitude for his friendship and care for her father King George III, and brothers George IV and William IV. Although Wathen considered the Prince of Wales/Prince Regent/George IV "one of the most affectionate friends man ever possessed", not a single letter survives from this long-lasting relationship and it is likely that their correspondence was deliberately destroyed at George's request.

Of Wathen's own letters to his royal friends only two examples survive. He kept a copy of two particularly sensitive letters he wrote in the summer of 1830. Both were addressed to William IV. The first, describing in detail the final hours and minutes of the life of George IV, will take its chronological place in the narrative; the second, written a month after King William's accession to the throne, serves to demonstrate at the outset the overwhelming sense of duty and responsibility Wathen felt towards his royal friend. He deliberated about it for some time and consulted Princess Sophia, William's sister, about the wisdom of sending it. Wathen faced a most delicate dilemma. Although William was his friend, he was also his monarch, and Wathen was worried about the excitability he was displaying. It reminded him of George III's erratic moods and behaviour, which he had witnessed at first hand. How was he to alert His Majesty to the possibility that he might go mad like his father? As a friend, he felt he had to do something, even at the risk of losing favour with the King and banishment from Court circles. It was crucial to find the right words, and strike the right tone. Wathen drafted his letter with the utmost care, explicitly justifying his temerity as an "imperative duty", and creating a masterpiece of obsequiousness, affection and tact. The Princess gave her approval and it was delivered. Then he held his breath.

"28 July 1830. I scarcely know in what words to address your Majesty, but an imperative duty, resulting from that fidelity I owe your Majesty, & from that affection which your Majesty's long continued & gracious kindness demands, jointly compel me to lay my opinion at your royal feet. Next to my wife & children, my late royal Master [George IV] was the dearest object of my heart, & in that humble heart, your Majesty held the next place, & indeed, so mingled did I consider the duty I owed to both, that in faithfully serving the one, I ever considered myself as equally obeying & respecting the other. With these still existing feelings, I could not close my eyes in peace if I neglected at once presenting my opinion to your Majesty; & altho' amidst the adulation of a new Court, the voice of truth may sound harshly, & I may even incur the severe displeasure of your Majesty, yet you are still too dear to my heart, for me not to venture the risk of even that worst misfortune, when I think your Majesty's own happiness & welfare is at stake. If the very short remainder of my days pass in obscurity & neglect, it is of small consequence, but the health, life & peace of the Monarch of England is of vital importance to my country & to millions, & the consciousness of having discharged my duty to your Majesty, who I have even hitherto dared to think & feel my friend, will support me, even under your Majesty's displeasure, tho' I certainly acknowledge that the trial would be equal to my late irreparable loss.

The state of excitement in which your Majesty has past [sic] this last month, has been carefully observed, & silently watched by my anxious eye, & I venture now to incur your Majesty's anger, by saying, that if continued, will certainly & shortly, either convey your Majesty to that silent abode to which your Majesty so lately followed your dear Brother, or else, not improbably confine you, like your lamented father to a solitary Room in Windsor Castle. May I entreat your Majesty, to call to mind, what dire effects, even the minor excitements at the Admiralty soon produced, & how narrowly your Majesty then escaped the consequences. Forgive then Sire, & ponder my presumptuous attachment, that dares to breathe this opinion in your royal ear; & having thus discharged what I considered an imperious duty, I will only add, that whilst my heart continues to vibrate, it will still glow with the strongest attachment & loyalty towards your royal person, & to its last pulsation remain your Majesty's most faithful & devoted servant & subject

JWWaller" [1]

The reply came swiftly, from the King's private secretary. The letter had been received exactly in the spirit intended:

"My dear Sir Wathen,

The King yesterday put into my hands the letter you addressed to him on the 28th Inst[ant] and desired me to thank you for it as he could not find time to write himself. He observed: 'He is a kind affectionate creature'. I have since read the letter and with great satisfaction and a thorough sense of your honest & honorable character & conduct; and I am assured that the admonition, altho' unreserved, has not been ill received, nor thrown away…" [2]

Wathen had shown great audacity in offering unsolicited advice, highly personal in nature, to a King, but it had been gratefully accepted and, moreover, heeded. The King calmed down, adopted a more regal demeanour, and his seven-year reign was thereafter unblemished by inappropriate behaviour. So utterly transparent and well-intentioned was Wathen's motivation that William immediately knew that his friend had his interests at heart. Too often surrounded by flatterers and sycophants, kings and princes have few trustworthy intimates – genuine, disinterested friends. In turn the three royal brothers, Ernest, George and William, all came to recognise in Wathen a man of rare nobility of character whose notion of friendship extended way beyond the norm. As a friend had he not watched over Ernest day and night after an assassination attempt, nursed and comforted George IV in his last painful months of life? Indeed it was he who held the King's hand as he took his final breath and to whom George addressed his dying words: "My dear boy, this is Death." From the moment William heard from Wathen's lips that he was King, he also depended on his friend's presence at his side. A week into the new reign, Wathen was obliged to cut short a journey to Hampshire for his elder daughter's wedding, "as the King does not like me to be absent from him at present." Just as he had been essential to Ernest and to George, Wathen had become the indispensable confidant of King William.

Notes
1. Warwickshire County Record Office: CR 0341/26, JWW to William IV, 28 July 1830.
2. WCRO: CR 0341/27, C Naylor to JWW, 31 July 1830.

Author's note regarding names, spelling and punctuation
Unfortunately for the biographer, and confusingly for the reader, four people in this story share the same name, Wathen, so some explanation is required at the outset to pre-empt exasperation. The protagonist, (Jonathan) Wathen Phipps (later Waller), was named in honour of his step-grandfather, the surgeon and oculist Jonathan Wathen, whose surname he used as his first name throughout his life (though it was his middle name). His elder son, Thomas Wathen Waller, also used his middle name as a first name, so a letter beginning "Dear Wathen" might be intended for father or son. Clearly it is impossible to use exactly the same name for both of them without causing endless confusion and complications, so – reluctantly (because no-one actually called him Thomas) – I have decided to use the son's first name to make his identity instantly recognisable. The fourth Wathen is the fifth baronet, Sir Wathen Arthur Waller, mentioned in the Epilogue.

When quoting from eighteenth- and nineteenth-century sources I have usually kept original spellings, but have sometimes modified the punctuation and removed unneeded capital letters so that a passage reads more naturally.

PHIPPS/WALLER FAMILY TREE

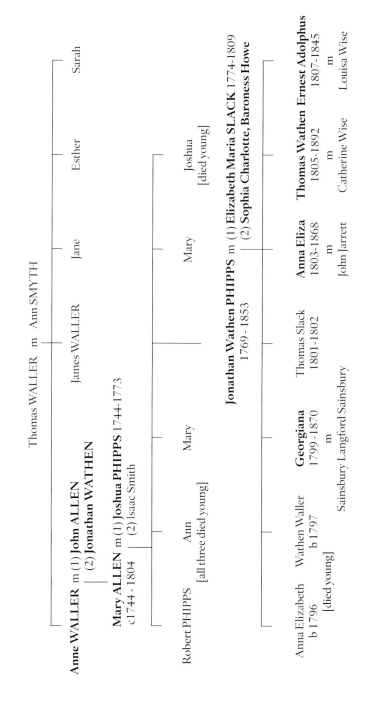

Thomas WALLER m Ann SMYTH

Anne WALLER m (1) **John ALLEN**
　　　　　　　　 (2) **Jonathan WATHEN**

James WALLER　　　　Jane　　　　Esther　　　　Sarah

Mary ALLEN m (1) **Joshua PHIPPS** 1744-1773
c1744 - 1804　　　 (2) Isaac Smith

Robert PHIPPS　　Ann　　Mary　　Mary　　Joshua
　　　　　　　[all three died young]　　　　[died young]

Jonathan Wathen PHIPPS m (1) **Elizabeth Maria SLACK** 1774-1809
1769 - 1853　　　　　　　　 (2) **Sophia Charlotte, Baroness Howe**

Anna Elizabeth　　Wathen Waller　　**Georgiana**　　Thomas Slack　　**Anna Eliza**　　**Thomas Wathen Ernest Adolphus**
b 1796　　　　　 b 1797　　　　　 1799-1870　　　 1801-1802　　　 1803-1868　　 1805-1892　　　　　　 1807-1845
[died young]　　　　　　　　　　　　 m　　　　　　　　　　　　　　　　　　 m　　　　　　 m　　　　　　　　　　　 m
　　　　　　　　　　　 Sainsbury Langford Sainsbury　　　　　　 John Jarrett　　 Catherine Wise　　　　 Louisa Wise

Chapter 1

Family background, upbringing and education

"[to] my dear Grandmother … I owe not only every comfort I enjoy in this life but every prospect I look forward to in another…her injunctions ever those of her God, & inforced by parental anxiety & parental affection, & praised be God, they have not been lost upon me…"

Jonathan Wathen Waller

In later life Wathen liked to refer to himself by his full array of titles: Sir Jonathan Wathen Waller of Braywick Lodge, Berkshire, Baronet and Knight Grand Cross of the Royal Hanoverian Guelphic Order, and Groom of the Bed Chamber to His late Majesty King William the 4th. With these titles he began his Will in 1845. They provide clear pointers to his character: here we have a worldly man, avid for advancement, wealth and status, and confident in the highest echelons of society. He was able to invite all the royal family to dine at his country mansion, yet he was born into a modest non-conformist family of no more than middle-class status. To achieve such an elevated position he must have had skill and good fortune but especially charm and charisma. Wathen became a close friend and confidant of four kings (George III, George IV, William IV, and Ernest Augustus I of Hanover), as well as the Princesses Sophia and Mary, daughters of George III. Away from the Court he played a quite different role: that of a loving but demanding and critical father, mindful of his Christian duty and determined that his children should uphold the faith to merit eternal salvation.

Wathen's surname at birth was Phipps. His family background is complicated by untimely deaths, second marriages, inter-marriages and name changes. Realising that after his death some difficulties might ensue if his origins were not clearly understood, he left an explanatory memorandum[1] plus copious detailed pedigrees.[2] It is unlikely that Wathen remembered his father, Joshua Phipps, who died when he was only three, but he cherished a small remembrance of him: a touching love poem written by Joshua to his wife on the occasion of their marriage in 1764.[3] In the same year, Princess Augusta, elder sister of George III, married the Duke of Brunswick with all the lavish ceremony the royal house could muster.

In the poem – copied by Wathen into his Commonplace book under the title *My Father to my Mother* – Joshua expresses his contentment with a far simpler union:

Let Brunswick's Duke the fair Augusta boast
With all her princely Train & costly Store,
Pregnant with Rapture quit Britannia's Coast
And land triumphant on the Belgic Shore.
At all their mighty Bliss & gaudy Shew
I envy not, nor in the least repine,
Give me the greatest Blessing here below
And let me call the lovely Mary mine.

Joshua's "lovely Mary" was the daughter of John Allen and his wife Anne, née Waller. (Jonathan) Wathen Phipps, the fourth of their six children, was born on 6 October 1769. The family lived at the time in Leadenhall Street, and later in All Hallows Lane, Upper Thames Street, in the East End of London. As the parents were 'dissenters', all of the children were baptised at Goodman's Field Presbyterian Church, Stepney. The three eldest, a son followed by twin girls, lived only a few weeks. Their father, still in his twenties, died in January 1773 shortly after the birth of his sixth child (also named Joshua). The baby barely survived him. Only Wathen and his younger sister Mary lived beyond infancy. In his Will, Joshua describes himself as an Iron Founder. It would seem that he was the owner or manager of a business, as his legacies indicate a well-educated man with a comfortable standard of living. He left £1000 – a very substantial sum of money – to be invested for his son Wathen, and £700 each for Mary and the baby Joshua. The children were to come into their inheritance at the age of twenty-one, or on marriage if sooner. Meanwhile the interest would provide for their maintenance and education. Other bequests provide a glimpse of the family home: Joshua's father, Robert Phipps, was to have "a Mahogany Library desk which stands in the Compting House", his sister, Elizabeth Maria Phipps, "a walnut desk and bookcase which stands in my closet", and his uncle by marriage, James Waller, a solar microscope and "my refracting telescope". There were specific bequests of several books, including to his mother-in-law, Anne Wathen (formerly Allen and née Waller), Stackhouse's *History of the Bible*, and six volumes of the works of Dr Isaac Watts, the non-conformist hymn-writer and theologian. Joshua's father, Robert Phipps, was to survive his son by only two years, and he also left legacies for his grandchildren, £1000 apiece to be invested until they came of age. Sadly, despite their handsome financial provision for him, neither his father nor his grandfather Phipps was a physical presence or even a faint memory in Wathen's childhood, and in later life he changed his family surname, preferring to be identified with the Wallers, the family of his maternal grandmother.

It was to the care of that grandmother, Anne Wathen, and her second husband, the surgeon Jonathan Wathen, that the children, (Jonathan) Wathen Phipps and his sister Mary, were entrusted after Joshua's death. Mary may have lived partly with her mother and her new husband, Isaac Smith, the non-conformist hymn-writer and precentor of Ayliffe (now Alie) Street Chapel whom she married in 1773, when Mary was only two.[4] Wathen writes of his grandmother, Anne, with great affection, gratitude and respect in some surviving family letters. He does not mention his mother at all. In an Indenture drawn up to establish the business partnership of Jonathan Wathen and James Ware in 1778, provision is made for part of the profits to be given to Jonathan Wathen Phipps and Mary Phipps, share and share alike, in the event of Jonathan Wathen's death during the seven-year term of the partnership. At its start both children were under ten and it is clear that their grandmother and step-grandfather had assumed responsibility for them. They had evidently been influential in Wathen Phipps' life right from his birth, as his parents chose to name him after his step-grandfather, though they could not have known that Anne and Jonathan would become his surrogate parents. The Wathens were very conscious of their rank in society as part of a middle class which needed to earn a living.[5] However, by commissioning a Chinese porcelain dinner service decorated with the Waller and Wathen arms entwined, they indicated their comfortable financial situation, and showed an awareness of pretensions to gentry status among their ancestors – a lesson not lost on young Wathen.

From an early age Wathen heard and read numerous sermons. Decades later when writing to his grown-up children about religious faith and observance he would unconsciously adopt the rhetorical tone, style and vocabulary of the non-conformist preachers of his youth. What is more, a profound fear of divine retribution and the Day of Judgment never left him. He was brought up in a family much influenced by the Wesleyan movement, and 'Salvation' was the watchword. His great-uncle James Waller had accompanied the hymn-writer Charles Wesley on several preaching tours, and on one of these he had met and married Charles's sister-in-law, Elizabeth Gwynne.[6] Aunt and Uncle Waller were second only to Anne and Jonathan as influential figures in Wathen's childhood world. His formal education took place at a boarding school, the fashionable "Hackney School for the sons of gentlemen", otherwise known as Newcome's School, where a modern education (including science) was on offer in a semi-rural setting, a healthy environment with abundant playing fields.[7] The school was in its heyday. It had opened in 1685 and had established its reputation under the leadership of its second headmaster Dr Henry Newcome, a classical scholar and a diehard Whig, who was succeeded by two of his sons and a grandson. Peter Newcome, the third headmaster, was a notable scientist and a Fellow of the Royal Society. The third and fourth Dukes of Devonshire sent their sons there (including Henry Cavendish);

the diarist Thomas Creevey was a pupil in Wathen's day, and 60 MPs were former pupils of the Newcomes. (The much-nurtured art of public speaking evidently bore fruit in later life.) School plays were notable social events, and it is said that 100 carriages would arrive bringing eager parents and guests to see the latest production. Many of Wathen's fellow pupils went on to Cambridge, but it was decided that he would become a surgeon like his step-grandfather, and the route to this profession (unlike that of physician) was apprenticeship.

Naturally Wathen would serve his apprenticeship under Jonathan Wathen, who in his youth had been apprenticed to his older brother Samuel, a general surgeon, and later physician (MD Aberdeen, 1753) and obstetrician, listed as man-midwife to Queen Charlotte in the *Royal Annual Kalendar* for 1766.[8] Jonathan and his partner, James Ware, took on as apprentice the sixteen-year-old Wathen Phipps in 1784, becoming jointly responsible for his board and lodging, as well as for teaching him their craft of surgery. Of Wathen's seven-year period of study there is little direct evidence, apart from a quite unexpected comment contained in a letter written some sixty years later and dated 28 February 1848,[9] four days after the abdication of the French King Louis-Philippe. Wathen, by now an old man, expresses fear and panic about the violent uprising then taking place in Paris – bringing horror and consternation to every face: "I feel it deeply as it brings to my recollection all I witnessed at Paris in July 1789." So he had actually been present at the start of the French Revolution! We are left wondering how Wathen, at the age of 19, came to be in Paris. Was he alone? If not who was with him? Was he on holiday or pursuing his studies? Was he accustomed to travelling abroad? All we have is a tantalisingly brief glimpse of a major historic event through a young man's eyes, from a copy of a letter he wrote at the time: "Paris, 13 July 1789. Every Man, Woman & Child wore green cockades. All the Armourers' Shops had been plundered during the night and those who could not procure firearms, swords or bayonets have fastened knives & steel blades to long poles."[10] Evidently he returned home unscathed, though deeply shocked, and completed the term of his apprenticeship. He wrote a lengthy poem entitled *Lecture Room at Guy's Hospital 1790* (current whereabouts unfortunately unknown) identifying various students, including himself. After two terms of seven years the Wathen-Ware partnership was dissolved and young Wathen became his step-grandfather's junior partner, leaving James Ware free to set up his own separate practice. Eighteen months later, at the age of twenty-three, Wathen married his nineteen-year-old cousin, Elizabeth Maria Slack, daughter of Thomas Slack, a prosperous sugar refiner, and his aunt Elizabeth Maria Slack (née Phipps).

Although Jonathan Wathen came from a Gloucestershire family prominent in the wool trade, he had spent most of his adult life in what we would now call the East End of London, a desirable location in the eighteenth century from many points of view. It was the merchants' quarter with some elegant town houses, terraces and squares, as well as smaller, poorer housing. Trade and manufacturing were carried on side by side in a bustling work-centred environment, with ships regularly unloading raw materials from far-flung lands. Horses were ubiquitous and it was not unusual to see farm animals in the streets; milk was delivered by milkmaids wearing the traditional wooden yoke across the shoulders linking two churns. Among the predominant businesses were silk-weaving, sugar-refining and cloth-making, and there was, and still is, a bell foundry in Whitechapel. The overcrowding, disease and poverty which gave the East End its reputation as a slum area was yet to come a hundred or so years later. In the eighteenth century there were more fields and open spaces than we might expect, as well as numerous churches, chapels and churchyards. It was also the heart of London's medical world, with St Bartholomew's and the London hospitals close at hand, and St Thomas's and Guy's just across the river. Noteworthy apothecaries, such as the Quakers Sylvanus and Timothy Bevan, were conveniently nearby. With their more famous relations, the Barclays, they became partners in a banking enterprise formerly known as the 'Black Spread Eagle'(the family name and logo remaining instantly recognisable to this day). Then, as always, there was plenty of crime in London, and Jonathan and Samuel Wathen were from time to time called as expert witnesses in Old Bailey trials.

The Wallers had been an East London family for at least a couple of generations. Anne's father, Thomas Waller, had been granted the Freedom of the City in 1712 and was buried at St Dunstan's in Stepney in 1731. In bringing up her grandson, Anne looked to her only brother, James Waller, for moral support. Wathen was fortunate to belong to an outward-looking family with far from parochial horizons, either geographically or intellectually. James, a wholesale lace merchant, did business in Antwerp and Brussels. His partner, Edward Bridgen, had inherited land and property in America and was prompt in recognising the commercial opportunities afforded by transatlantic trade. Wathen's close relations were highly literate, with a wide-ranging curiosity. They valued books, read and wrote a great deal, frequently turning their hand to poetry on all manner of topics, from the profound to the trivial. In his 'Commonplace book' the young Wathen preserved numerous verses, including a light-hearted poem[11] written by 'Westley' – presumably Aunt Waller's brother-in-law Charles Wesley. It conjures up a charming vignette of a game of Quadrille (a fore-runner of Bridge) played by Uncle James Waller, his wife Elizabeth and their respective sisters, Anne Wathen and Rebecca Gwynne – a scenario frequently witnessed by Wathen, no doubt. The game *almost* provokes a rare falling-out among the players. Music also formed part of the routine home entertainment. James and Elizabeth's nephews, Charles Wesley junior and his brother Samuel, both became professional musicians and composers. They performed in concerts from an early age, rather like Mozart and his sister, whose contemporaries they were.

When Wathen was born in 1769, all members of his family and social circle lived within a few miles of Devonshire Square, Bishopsgate, where his step-grandfather had established himself as a surgeon in the 1750s.[12] By 1778, when Jonathan Wathen went into partnership with James Ware, he was living at Bond's Court, Walbrook, and Ware boarded with him there. The family was solidly established in the local community, close to the non-conformist chapels of Pell Street, Stepney, Ayliffe Street and Goodman's Fields, as well as the dissenters' burial ground at Bunhill Fields where Wathen's father and his older siblings were buried. Thomas Slack, who had married Wathen's aunt Elizabeth Maria Phipps (and was the father of Wathen's cousin and bride, Elizabeth Maria Slack), carried on his thriving sugar refining business in Gravel Lane (close to Petticoat Lane and Devonshire Square). The surge in demand for sugar from the 1770s onwards made Thomas a fortune, enabling him to acquire an address in Bloomsbury Square and a country retreat, Braywick Lodge, in Berkshire: "a handsome mansion with a small but picturesque park".[13]

The circumstances of Wathen's upbringing clearly led to his choice of profession, if indeed choice came into it. His apprenticeship and subsequent absorption into Jonathan's practice must have seemed to all concerned a logical and natural progression, and he had much to be grateful for – far more than he could possibly have foreseen as a young man, since his role of surgeon-oculist was to bring him influential contacts and unimaginable social advancement in a very short space of years.

Of course surgery in the twenty-first century differs vastly from the profession of Wathen and his step-grandfather. In their day three categories of professionals shared the responsibility for delivering health care: physicians, surgeons and apothecaries, each with a distinct role, educational background and status in society.

The elite group were the university-educated Physicians, learned men who were paid for their knowledge, observations and judgement – in short for diagnosis and advice. They might recommend a change in diet, perhaps rest, or alternatively fresh air and exercise; increasingly they advised a period of sea-bathing or taking the waters at one of the new spa towns. They could prescribe remedies, but they neither performed surgery, nor dispensed the medicines and drugs they prescribed. They were regulated by the Royal College of Physicians, an academic body established in the reign of Henry VIII to maintain standards. If graduates of Oxford or Cambridge, they could become Fellows (FRCP), but with a degree from elsewhere, such as Scotland (like Samuel Wathen and other dissidents who were at that time inadmissible to Oxbridge), they had to be content with a Licenciate (LRCP).

Surgeons, on the other hand, were craftsmen, non-graduates and less highly regarded than physicians, although they too were required to undergo a lengthy period of training. Theirs were practical skills to be learned by precept and example, while apprenticed to an experienced practitioner whom they could observe and assist. In addition they were expected to attend a course in Anatomy (including dissection) and Surgery, at their own expense, under senior surgeons at London teaching hospitals, and to study individual case histories by "ward walking". James Ware, who wrote a detailed account of his student days in London in 1773-1777,[14] was probably exceptionally conscientious. He enrolled on additional courses in Chemistry, Physic (Medicine) and Midwifery whilst a "walking pupil" at St Thomas's. He observed operations, delivered babies and, as was customary, dissected corpses retrieved from the gallows. From 1745 when the Surgeons separated from the Barber-Surgeons' livery company, their regulatory body was the Company of Surgeons (granted a Royal Charter as the Royal College of Surgeons in 1800). It was in 1745 that Jonathan Wathen began his apprenticeship with his brother Samuel, who in turn had served an apprenticeship in the 1730s in Bristol (where he had become one of the earliest followers of John Wesley). No doubt Jonathan, once qualified, managed the Devonshire Square practice while his brother took his Scottish degree in medicine. Samuel Wathen was among the first to be "disfranchised" from the Company of Surgeons in 1753 (for the substantial fee of 40 guineas), in order to become a Licentiate of the Royal College of Physicians in 1756. It was not permitted to be a member of both professional bodies at once. The difference in roles is underlined by the required equipment in each case. Physicians needed little more than a stethoscope and a watch, but a surgeon was obliged to possess a wide range of surgical instruments. He was expected to set bones, lance boils, dress wounds, apply ointments, poultices and plasters, remove cysts and occasionally limbs, and most commonly of all to perform bloodletting in a variety of ways.

The third group of professionals consisted of Apothecaries, frequently consulted over all manner of medical matters, but whose role – strictly speaking – especially in the eyes of physicians and surgeons, was to be tradesmen. They obtained supplies of exotic and mundane plants, minerals, and animal matter (mainly insects) in order to concoct a wide range of medicines, pills and potions which they dispensed to the public according to the prescriptions presented to them. They were well educated, Latin being a requirement before apprenticeship, and regulated by the Society of Apothecaries. Over time they increasingly felt tempted to produce their own patent medicines and to make recommendations to the patients who consulted them, but physicians (for internal disorders) and surgeons (for external complaints) guarded jealously the privilege of prescription. In practice the neat divisions set out above were rarely properly observed, as patients, especially the poor, could scarcely be expected to pay fees to several different specialists. In an effort to bring the three branches together and diminish the competitive spirit between them the Medical Society of London was founded in 1775 by a Quaker physician, Dr Lettsom, who specified that all qualified professionals were welcome as members.

Jonathan Wathen and his brother Samuel made a comfortable living from the practices they had built up, and true to their religious principles involved themselves in charitable movements and good works. It is not surprising to find them both listed as Governors for Life in William Dodd's 1776 publication: *An Account of the Rise, Progress and Present state of the Magdalen Hospital for the Reception of Penitent Prostitutes [founded 1758]*. The book contains statistical information plus anecdotes and letters from several of the grateful young women taken into the hospital and rehabilitated. Samuel also worked for more than fifteen years at the City Lying-in Hospital, an institution set up in 1750 "for the reception and delivery of the pregnant wives of seamen and soldiers, also those of industrious mechanics and of the laborious poor, and pregnant widows of poor persons recently deceased".[15]

In the papers surviving in the Waller collection, there is barely a mention of Wathen Phipps' training as a surgeon. Ware's detailed account is therefore all the more valuable, as an approximate guide. Wathen's apprenticeship may have been less broadly based, as both Jonathan Wathen and James Ware began their careers as general surgeons, dealing with a wide range of problems. By the time they went into partnership together they had decided to specialise in ophthalmology; in the terminology of the times, they had become "oculists". To emphasise and publicise the clear new focus of the practice, James Ware published in 1780 the first of many academic papers: *Remarks on the ophthalmy, psorophthalmy and purulent eye*, to which he appended twenty-five detailed case studies of his own and Jonathan's patients. Then in 1785 Jonathan published an essay that was to have far-reaching significance: *Dissertation on the theory and cure of the Cataract, in which the Practice of Extraction is supported, and that Operation in its present state is particularly described*. The operation was to become the speciality of both Jonathan Wathen and James Ware, and would make the reputation and fortune of Wathen Phipps.

Throughout their careers James Ware and Jonathan Wathen published numerous academic papers, thereby achieving international recognition as pioneers in a new branch of surgery. So what contribution did Wathen Phipps make to the plethora of Wathen-Ware publications? Surprisingly just a single essay – a meagre amount in comparison with his elders; his *Dissertation on the Treatment after the operation for Cataract* [1792] was added to the second edition of a 1781 booklet by Jonathan Wathen on *Fistula Lachrymalis*. The paper was issued within a year of his joining the practice, and he probably saw it as the first of many. It did contribute to his standing and reputation, but his fame spread mainly by word of mouth. By treating some hugely influential patients he was drawn into fashionable circles as a "celebrity" doctor. Soon he had no need to seek to enhance his reputation or acquire an authoritative voice through writing – nor did he have time to do it. Five years after qualifying as a surgeon Wathen Phipps had obtained the most prestigious post in his field. On 20 April 1796 the Lord Chamberlain appointed him "Oculist to the Royal Household".

Notes

1. Warwickshire County Record Office (WCRO): CR 0341/234, CR 0341/235/1 (reference numbers beginning CR 0341 indicate items in the Waller Collection).

2. WCRO: CR 0341/271/2.

3. The poem was copied by Jonathan Wathen Phipps into his Commonplace book, WCRO: CR 4436/1. The Princess Augusta mentioned here would become the mother of Princess Caroline, bride of George IV, her cousin.

4. The main beneficiary of Isaac Smith's Will was Elizabeth Blunt, daughter of his step-daughter, Mary (née Phipps).

5. Thomas Waller, Anne's father, John Allen her first husband, Joshua Phipps her son-in-law, and Thomas Slack – Joshua's brother-in-law and Wathen's eventual father-in-law, were all members of Guilds and Freemen of the City of London, and were based in Stepney, Spitalfields, and thereabouts.

6. James Waller accompanied Charles Wesley on preaching tours in Cornwall, Worcestershire and elsewhere in 1748-50. During their travels they stayed with the Gwynne family of Garth, Breconshire and Ludlow. Charles married Sarah (Sally) Gwynne on 8th April 1749, and James was married to Sarah's sister Elizabeth Gwynne by Charles Wesley in Ludlow on 4th December 1750.

7. WCRO: CR 0341/327/24, Jonathan Wathen Waller to Thomas Wathen Waller, 28 February 1848.

8. This was the year in which Princess Charlotte, the Princess Royal, was born.

9. WCRO: CR 0341/327/24, JWW to TWW, 28 February 1848. Wathen had known Louis-Philippe during his exile in Twickenham, and had visited him in Paris after the defeat of Napoleon – see Chapter 5.

10. Extract included in the description of a Manuscript Book of Sir Jonathan Wathen Waller, sold at auction by Stride & Son of Chichester in 1996. The green cockades were rapidly superseded by cockades in the more famous "tricolore". The poem written on a Lecture Room at Guy's Hospital 1790 is in the same book. The current whereabouts of the book is not known.

11. WCRO: CR 4436/1, p 36:

Quadrille Party
With Discontent in half their faces
Three different Ladies took their places
[i]One Beau they had and only one
Perhaps they better had had none
His Brow was knit, his Voice grew strong
He strove to prove that each were wrong
Declar'd none knew so well the Game
[ii]As he – a worthy skilful Dame
Sat half affronted by his side
Such Declaration shock'd her pride
Her Conscience told, it told her true
The Game as well as he she knew
[iii]Anna she sat in fix'd Amaze
E'en Discontent had mark'd her Face
[iv]Eliza's placid Brow alone
Remain'd untainted with a Frown
If Cards were first design'd t'amuse
This Party sure mistook their use
By their Example warn'd I will
Fly to my Books, my Work, my Quill
To any thing but play Quadrille.

Wathen's footnotes:
i) My Uncle Waller
ii) My Aunt Gwynne
iii) My Grandmother
iv) My Aunt Waller.

12. During her marriage to John Allen, Anne (née Waller, later Wathen) lived in Petticoat Lane, Spitalfields, in a freehold property John had inherited from his father Henry, a Merchant Taylor. Devonshire Square was close by and the surgeon Jonathan Wathen evidently knew John Allen, perhaps as a patient, as he witnessed his Will, drawn up in 1759. John died the following year, and on 8 June 1761 Anne Allen and Jonathan Wathen were married at St Katherine's by the Tower.
13. Kerry, Charles, *The history and antiquities of the hundred of Bray*, 1861, p 82.
14. Surrey History Centre, Woking: 1487/103/1, Ware, James: *Journal of Transactions while in London, 1773-77* and 1487/103/2, *General Notes and memorandum during my stay in London, 1775-1777*.
15. Low, Sampson, *The Charities of London*, 1850, p 29.

Chapter 2

A fashionable oculist
in the West End

"I am sure you would be pleased with the manner I have mentioned you as my best friend and a person whom I esteem'd not only from gratitud [sic] *but respect for the most valuable & uncommon qualities of mind and heart."*

Georgiana, Duchess of Devonshire

The parish church of Bray, Berkshire, close to Thomas Slack's Braywick Lodge, was the scene of Wathen Phipps' marriage to his cousin Elizabeth Maria Slack in 1793. Soon afterwards they began their life together in an unfamiliar but exciting environment, setting up house in a part of London given over mainly to leisure and entertainment rather than to trade and labour – the elegant and rapidly developing West End. Cork Street, in Burlington Gardens near Piccadilly, was in the heart of the district favoured by the *ton* – the Society of the day – and anyone who was anyone was to be found within a mile or two. The aristocracy strove to outdo each other with ever grander and more palatial mansions: Devonshire House, Spencer House, Marlborough House and so on. King George III held court at his official residence, St James's Palace, while his private homes were Kew Palace, Buckingham House (also known as the Queen's House), and a country estate at Windsor. A rival court frequently assembled at Carlton House, the lavishly furnished and continually re-furbished home of the Prince of Wales which stood between the Mall (then a walk rather than a road) and Pall Mall. Wathen was probably influenced in his choice of location by the cluster of other miscellaneous "doctors" established in Cork Street, which was becoming the Harley Street of its day. Though not home to the grander echelons of the gentry and nobility, it was a sought-after address for people of some substance, including several dowagers and officers' widows, and had been much favoured a decade or so earlier by those wishing to offer a service to the seriously wealthy and influential – tailors, peruke makers, apothecaries, etc. A few specific residents are named in surviving documents. One was the miniaturist and Royal Academician, William Wood, the Georgian counterpart of today's society photographer. He was greatly in vogue and was the Phipps' next door neighbour.[1] Wood became godfather to Wathen's son, Thomas Wathen, and gave him a present of a miniature portrait of his sister Anna, soon to be followed by one of himself. He also painted Mr and Mrs Phipps and their elder daughter, Georgiana, methodically noting all the names and materials used in his record of work completed.

As an "oculist" Wathen proved an immediate success. He had devised a surgical instrument – a "gold hook" for use in the couching[2] and removal of cataracts, and he made his name as a skilled practitioner in these operations. That is not to say that every operation had the desired effect, but success outweighed failure enough for Wathen to prosper – and often the joy and gratitude of the patient was boundless. Who would not be impressed by a man capable of preserving or restoring sight? From time to time patients were moved to express their gratitude in verse, as was a Surrey clergyman, Charles Jasper Selwyn, who not only dedicated a poem to Wathen and Phipps, but preserved the tumour they had removed in a glass bottle mounted on a pedestal engraved with further verses in Latin. The preamble reads as follows,

"To Jonathan Wathen
and
Jonathan Wathen Phipps
Professors and Practisers
Of an Art
The most wonderful in its Operations
The most beneficial in its Consequences
And
The most important in its Uses
Of any
Which the ingenuity of the present Age
Has brought so near to Perfection
This Offspring of Gratitude
For it claims no other Merit
Is
Affectionately addressed
By their truly obliged
And
Very faithful humble servant
Charles Jasper Selwyn"

and the poem begins in this fashion:

"Wathen and Phipps my honor'd Friends
Who with the tend'rest Skill
Correct the eyes impeded Use
And cure each visual ill
To you I owe it under God
When Sight was well nigh gone
That its dark clouds are near dispers'd
Its darkness almost flown…"[3]

continuing in like manner in stanza after stanza.

Given the literary habits of the times, it is perhaps not surprising for a parson to express his delight and gratitude by composing verses in the vernacular and also in Latin. More unexpected, but equally heartfelt, are the *Lines written by a Poor Woman at Winchester on the Recovery of her Sight*. The unnamed woman begins her poem with an elaborate metaphor sustained over four lines, clearly attempting a piece of sophisticated rhetoric worthy of the occasion and the emotions which inspired it. By the end she has abandoned such devices, and her thoughts, naively expressed, are all the more touching in their simplicity and sincerity:

"To that bless'd Spring from whence all Blessings flow
I offer up my Thanks as Tribute due
I praise the Fountain so I can't exclude
The healing Stream its Share of Gratitude
So great a favour can't unheeded lie
Should I be silent sure the Stones would cry
O blest Alternative my dismal Night
Turned to bright Day, my Darkness into Light
Which bless'd Event more fully must express
Than can my Tongue or Pen my Thankfulness
What can I say, alas my Wit too small
To speak his Worth, he is above it all
I'd call him worthy, but fear to call him so
Lest I should wrong him by a name too low
I would say something but I can't say what
Say all that's good in Man and he is that."

The unrivalled reputation of Wathen and Phipps brought them to the attention of King George III's fifth son, Prince Ernest Augustus (later the Duke of Cumberland), who had been wounded in active service and left with chronic eye problems. In 1796 he summoned the celebrated oculists. For Wathen this was a consultation with momentous consequences. Despite the difference in their rank and social standing, the two young men liked and respected each other immediately and an unlikely friendship grew up between them. It was to last for half a century.

The prince had sustained his injuries while serving as a cavalry officer in the French Revolutionary Wars (at Tournai in Flanders in May 1794); a cannon ball had glanced past his left arm and eye. He had been allowed a brief period of recuperation in England that summer – his first visit home in eight years. His sister Princess Augusta (accustomed to seeing maimed officers at church in Portsmouth) thoughtlessly remarked to her mother: "how lucky it is that Ernest is just come so seasonably with that wound in his face – I should have been quite shocked else, not to have had one little bit of glory."[4] After four months Prince Ernest had rejoined his regiment – though the injured eye had not improved and soon he feared he would lose its sight completely. What he needed was professional advice and treatment, but for months on end the king refused him permission to return home a second time,[5] fearing he would ally himself with his brother George, the wayward Prince of Wales, with whom the monarch was on the bitterest of terms. Finally the king relented, and in mid-February 1796 Ernest arrived at Carlton House. The Prince of Wales was greatly disturbed to find that "his left eye is shockingly sunk, and it has an amazing film grown over it."[6] Ernest immediately put himself under Wathen Phipps' care. A period of rest was recommended, so he retired to live quietly at his old childhood home on Kew Green. Meanwhile Wathen kept his patient under observation, waiting for the right moment to remove the cataract – timing being a crucial element in achieving a successful result.

It is almost certain that Prince Ernest recommended his friend to his father, the King. In April 1796 when Wathen was appointed oculist to the Royal Household, he was required to attend to eye problems or diseases suffered by any member of the royal family. Apart from King George and Queen Charlotte there were seven surviving princes and six princesses, all but the Prince of Wales unmarried. It was soon apparent that the family was uncommonly susceptible to eye disease, and that their misfortune could only prove beneficial to Wathen. As for Prince Ernest, months and years went by, but the right moment to operate never occurred. Oculist and patient eventually had to admit that the sight of the left eye was irretrievably lost. This negative outcome might well have caused their close friendship to wither, but it was to last for the rest of their lives.

With the endorsement of the Royal Family, Wathen immediately became the oculist of choice for those who could afford the best of everything. When Georgiana, Duchess of Devonshire, suffered an acute, agonising and protracted bout of eye disease beginning in July 1796, it was, of course, Wathen who was summoned. Before long he was treating twice daily the hugely influential Duchess, who had been the ultimate fashion icon and undisputed queen of the *ton* in 1770s and 1780s. Six letters from the Duchess survive in the Waller Collection. There were evidently others, as some are numbered but there are gaps. All of them are about money. One, undated but apparently written in haste at "11. Wednesday", requests an instant loan, (not for the first time it seems): "Dear Phipps, I hope you are at home & not gone to bed. Will you with your accustomed goodness send me a draft for £20 for tomorrow. I will pay you tomorrow or next day – God bless you."[7]

Vagueness about repayment similarly extended to payment of Wathen's professional fees. Despite the Duke's undoubted wealth, Georgiana was always in debt. She was a compulsive gambler and also kind-hearted and generous, having assumed responsibility for her sister Harriet's debts as well as her own.[8] During her severe illness she needed intensive treatment and seems to have monopolised Wathen's time for several months. No doubt he expected a substantial remuneration. An anecdote related to John Cam Hobhouse, later Lord Broughton, some years after Georgiana's death, is entirely credible, and indicates that Wathen may have been somewhat disappointed: "Mr Phipps was sent to Chatsworth to operate upon the Duchess' eye. He stayed there some time, and at parting received from the Duke a fee of a thousand pounds. Just before he stepped into his carriage, a message from the Duchess brought him to her bedchamber. She hoped the Duke had done what was handsome by Mr Phipps. The gentleman protested 'Yes, and more than handsome.' 'It is an awkward thing,' continued Her Grace, 'to ask, but really I am at this moment in immediate want of such a sum, and if you could, Mr Phipps?' What could the oculist do? He produced his thousand pounds, took his leave and has never heard of his money from that day to this."[9]

Prompted by guilt at the evident displeasure of Mr Wathen (step-grandfather Jonathan) over the non-receipt of fees which were due to the partnership, Georgiana went through the motions of attempting to pay: "you have attended me 7 months now almost twice a day – however let us say 6 months twice a day. This at your usual price would be £365 – independant [sic] of this you have liv'd here for two months & I know for a mere cataract case you have 100, which only takes you 10 days – tell me honestly then what sum I shall name to the Duke, 500 – 600 – 700 – name the sum. To pay you what I feel to owe you would be impossible but I only mean to clear to the present moment & then we will go on & I will fee you regularly every week, & you will allow me by & by, when I am sure there will be [even] greater improvement, to add the present my gratitude will engage me to?"[10] In a subsequent letter Georgiana talks of having made an arrangement with her bankers, Coutts, to pay her debt to Wathen in case of her death before her promised instalment plan is complete. At the same time she makes it abundantly clear that he is being promptly and very adequately paid in her own characteristic fashion: "I am sure you would be pleased with the manner I have mentioned you as my best friend and a person whom I esteem'd not only from gratitud [sic] but respect for the most valuable &

uncommon qualities of mind and heart."[11] In 1799 the Duchess was true to her promise of an added present when she stood godmother to Wathen's first child to survive infancy – named, of course, Georgiana.

While a cataract operation was relatively straightforward for Wathen and took a matter of minutes (apart from after-care), dealing with infection and inflammation before antibiotics were known was a matter of trial and error, and the standard treatments were based on various unproven hypotheses. In December 1796 Georgiana's mother described her daughter's condition as follows: "the inflammation has been so great that the eye, the eyelids and the adjacent parts were swelled to the size of your hand doubled, and projecting forward from the face…. The eyelids are still much swelled and scarred with the leeches…. The eye itself… is still more horrible." [12]

At that time a great deal of store was set by maintaining a balance of bodily fluids. It was thought that illness was caused by an excess of fluid, and consequently purging and bloodletting were usually tried first. Sometimes blood was obtained directly from a vein but more usual methods were wet cupping[13] or the application of leeches. Georgiana suffered all manner of excruciating treatments; one of the most horrific and distressing was blistering. Her sister Harriet wrote: "It was thought necessary to perform a most painful operation on her. Applying causticks behind the ears and a blister to the back of her neck for four hours. I never saw anything like the agony she suffer'd."[14] Blistering or vesication was brought about to "draw off abundant humours" and to demonstrate the principle of counter-irritation, in other words:"to establish a degree of inflammation or irritation on the surface of the body and thus to substitute a mild and easily managed disease for an internal and intractable one, on the principle that two sets of inflammation cannot be carried on in the system at the same time."[15] Once blisters formed they were maintained and not allowed to heal, sometimes for weeks on end. With a cruel and perverse kind of reasoning it was thought that deliberately creating additional painful areas might help existing infection and inflammation to subside.

The Duchess did eventually recover from her illness without losing the sight of her eye, but she was disfigured and thereafter wore a lock of hair in a convenient curl covering part of her face. Her energy and vitality were much subdued and for a year or two she became almost reclusive, quite the opposite of her former extrovert and hugely sociable *persona*. Whether Wathen's treatments contributed to her recovery is doubtful. It seems more likely that they increased her suffering immeasurably, but she retained her goodwill and indeed gratitude towards him. The warm relationship built up between them during her severe illness lasted for the rest of her life. She even felt able to trust him with arranging for the care of a "little unfortunate creature"[16] – presumably an orphan she had decided to sponsor – and in several of the letters she sends small sums for the upkeep of the child,

Patience. Addressing him as "my dearest Phipps" in 1801 she writes: "I am more anxious than I can express about Mrs Phipps and your son and besides I want to know millions of things concerning you – I send you £20 for Patience and £50 I am miserable at having deprived you of so long…." [17]

The mention of Mrs Phipps is a very rare occurrence in the letters in the Waller Collection. Elizabeth's life can only be guessed at, but it cannot have been happy in the early years of her marriage. Whilst Wathen was forging ahead with his career, networking with ease among the great and the good, his wife was coping with a series of pregnancies and infant deaths. A daughter, Anna Elizabeth, and a son, Wathen Waller, baptised at St James' Piccadilly in 1796 and 1797 respectively, lived only briefly: Anna died aged four, and Wathen at three months. Another child, Thomas Slack Phipps (b. 1801), the son mentioned in Georgiana's letter, lived for fifteen months. Four children were to survive childhood: Georgiana (b.1799), Anna Eliza (b.1803), Thomas Wathen (b.1805) and Ernest Adolphus (b.1807). Such was Wathen's standing at court by the time this fourth surviving child was born that he was able to prevail upon two royal Dukes, Ernest of Cumberland and Adolphus of Cambridge (in person), plus two Princesses, Sophia and Mary (by proxy), to accept the role of godparents to the boy.

The Duchess of Devonshire was not alone in having money problems. Indeed it is remarkable how often the subject of money crops up in relation to Wathen's patients, correspondents (even royal ones) and family members. In 1804, the Duke of Sussex's small daughter was a patient, and a sad little letter written by her mother sheds some light on the family's difficult circumstances at the time. The background is as follows: on 4th April 1793, George III's sixth son, Prince Augustus (not yet Duke of Sussex), and Lady Augusta Murray were married by an Anglican priest in Rome, without his father's permission. They returned to England and were married again, just in case anyone doubted the first marriage, this time at St George's, Hanover Square (5 December 1793). A son, named Augustus like his father, was born on 13th January 1794. In the same year the marriage was declared void, as it had taken place in contravention of the Royal Marriages Act (1772), the Sovereign's approval not having been sought or given. The couple continued to live together for several years, ignoring the annulment, and a daughter, Augusta Emma, was born in 1801. In that year the offer of £12,000 and the title Duke of Sussex persuaded Prince Augustus to abandon his family and conform to his father's wishes. His wife, as she considered herself, was devastated, and reduced to a life of comparative hardship. Already deeply in debt when her daughter needed treatment for an eye infection, Augusta appealed to William Pitt for help. A settlement of some kind had been promised; all she wanted was an advance to see her through her immediate difficulties, so she wrote to Pitt's private secretary:

"Dear Mr Adams,

My little girl's eye has what Mr Phipps calls a blight. She is at Ramsgate as I am here [in London], which makes me miserable. As I think there may be some delay in settling everything <u>finally</u>, would Mr Pitt allow Mr Huskisson to advance me only £1000 to enable me not merely to go to Ramsgate but to pay off every expence [sic] there. My girl's eye is to have leaches [sic] etc, and unless she is sitting on my lap she will not suffer them on. Pray, my dear Mr Adams, don't laugh at my request. You have no idea of the many miseries I experience not only on account of my debts, but at being absent from my children, especially at a moment when one of them is suffering a great deal, and likely to suffer more…" [18]

Augusta did get to Ramsgate, as the diarist and Royal Academician Joseph Farington[19] saw her at a Ball there on 11 August 1804, and complained to his diary that she was wrongly calling herself the Duchess of Sussex. She settled with her children in Ramsgate and was always known in the town by that title (although the establishment had denied it to her).

On the first of October 1804, John Cunningham Saunders, a surgeon employed as Demonstrator of Anatomy at St Thomas's hospital, published a proposal to set up a London Dispensary for curing diseases of the eye and ear. Not to be outdone, Wathen came up with a similar plan, though confined to eye disease, and was able to proceed more rapidly than Saunders by playing two trump cards. He decided to base his case on the sad plight of hundreds of soldiers and sailors who had returned from serving their country (in the Napoleonic wars in Egypt) suffering from trachoma – potentially blinding tropical conjunctivitis. An epidemic had been raging since 1798, and many came home blind. Surely they deserved a specialist hospital to cater for their needs? And who better to sponsor such a hospital than the King and Queen themselves? A channel of communication was conveniently available to Wathen in the person of his friend, Prince Ernest, now Duke of Cumberland, who on 12 December 1804 addressed his father in these terms: "… My own sufferings with my eyes make me the more desirous to assist in alleviating those of my fellow creatures who are not like myself blessed with the means of attempting to preserve one of the greatest and most precious gifts of the Almighty, **sight**. Should you, Sir, give your Royal countenance to the plan set forth in the enclosed paper, your example will give it sufficient weight to be immediately undertaken with success, & I shall rejoice in the belief that it has pleased the Almighty to make me the humble instrument towards the relief of a thousand distressed beings & that I have served Phipps, who has attended me assiduously over a number of years, by procuring him your Majesty's protection, which will give him the credit of becoming the promoter of this charity……"[20]

The response was immediate and Wathen was able not only to name his institution the **Royal** Infirmary for Diseases of the Eye, but also to claim that its foundation dated from 1804. This was a significant coup for Wathen. The hospital would be the first of its kind, as Saunders did not open his, The London Ophthalmic Infirmary, until 25 March 1805. So furious was Saunders at being outplayed that he took out advertisements to proclaim that he had been the originator of the idea although he was perceived as merely a "humble copyist".[21] The damage was done, however, as far as Saunders was concerned. With this (undoubtedly imitative) project Wathen had succeeded in enhancing his credentials as a benefactor of the poor, and had raised his profile in society once again. The two salient traits in his character, good-heartedness and ambition, could not have been better displayed.

Notes

1. William Wood, portrait miniaturist, lived at 8 Cork Street (and Wathen Phipps at No 6). *Transactions of the Society Instituted at London for the Encouragement of Arts, Manufacture and Commerce*, Vol. 24 p 497, 1805. In 1807 Wood exhibited at the Royal Academy "a drawing of Miss Anna Phipps, of Cork Street, when about 4 years old, on yellowish vellum, which Wood gave to her brother [Thomas] Wathen Phipps, who was his godson, on January 10th,1807, and whose portrait at the age of 3 he painted a little later as a companion work." From *The Miniature Collector, a guide for the amateur collector of miniatures*, by George C Williamson 1921, p 169. See also National Art Library, pressmark 86 KK 3-6, re Wood's Phipps family miniatures.
2. Couching: the process of dislodging or depressing a cataract, without removing it.
3. WCRO: 4436/1, Jonathan Wathen Phipps' Commonplace book. The poems from patients are from p 245 and p 44.
4. Hemlow, Joyce, *The Journals and Letters of Fanny Burney*, Oxford 1972-84, Vol 3, p 182.
5. Willis, G M, *Ernest Augustus, Duke of Cumberland, King of Hanover,* London, 1954, p 47. In September 1795 he had written to his father, begging for permission to come home to consult Dr Wathen.
6. Willis, G M, op.cit. p 50.
7. WCRO: CR 0341/213, Duchess of Devonshire to Wathen Phipps, undated, c 1797.
8. WRCO: CR 0341/219, Duchess of Devonshire to Wathen Phipps, 1798. "As with you I need have no reserve I will tell you that all the money I have had or could raise has been employ'd to enable my poor sister's family to wait for the arrangements that are to take place."
9. Hobhouse, John Cam, later Lord Broughton, diary entry for 28 March 1814 in *Recollections of a long life,* Broughton Holograph Diaries, Berg Collection Vol 2, p 202.
10. WCRO: CR 0341/215, Duchess of Devonshire to Wathen Phipps, undated, c 1797.
11. WCRO: CR 0341/216, ditto, September 1799.

12. Foreman, Amanda, *Georgiana, Duchess of Devonshire*, London 1998, pp 299-300.

13. Wet Cupping: Cups are applied to the skin to bring the blood to the surface, then the skin is punctured so that the blood can flow.

14. Foreman, Amanda, op.cit. p 305.

15. Waring, E J, *Practical Therapeutics*, 1866, observation 2949.

16. WCRO: CR 0341/214, Duchess of Devonshire to Wathen Phipps, c1800.

17. WCRO: CR 0341/217 ditto, 1800.

18. Whyman, John, *Aspects of holidaymaking and resort development within the Isle of Thanet, with particular reference to Margate, c 1736 to c 1840*, published in *Dissertations on Economic History*, 1981. Whyman quotes from Letters to Pitt, Dacres Adams Papers, TNA 30/58, Bundle 7, Part III. Letter 75.

19. *Farington Diary*, Vol II, pub 1923.

20. Aspinall, A: *The later correspondence of George III*, Vol IV, p 257, Letter 2980.

21. Saunders, John Cunningham, *Letter to the Committee* p xvi, in preface of *A treatise in some practical points relating to diseases of the eye*, published posthumously 1811.

Chapter 3

Royal patients

"Mr Phipps gives us hopes and is to return again next Sunday. He says it must take time and by avoiding dusty roads, great lights, and above all not overstraining the eye, he hopes to see great amendment in a short time."

Queen Charlotte, 4 August 1805

By the summer of 1805, George III had been on the throne for nearly forty-five years. He had succeeded his grandfather George II in 1760 at the age of twenty-two; his father, Frederick, Prince of Wales, had died nine years earlier, when only forty-four. The monarchy had skipped a generation. When the young King George III married, he chose a "suitable" German Protestant Princess, Charlotte of Mecklenburg-Strelitz. The couple produced 15 children (two of whom, Octavius and Alfred, died in infancy). Although George was destined to be known to posterity as "Mad King George", he had been rational and lucid for most of his reign. (A period in 1765 gave cause for concern and a more serious episode of illness including "derangement" took place in 1788. The possibility of a Regency was discussed, but the King recovered and the plans were shelved. Some symptoms of mania occurred in 1801 and 1804, but were fairly short-lived.) In the main the King insisted on being a "hands on" monarch, dealing with his own correspondence and even drafting letters himself. But June 1805 was a turning point. Suddenly George III's sight deteriorated to the point where he was almost blind. Wathen Phipps was soon in attendance.

The Home Secretary, Lord Hawkesbury, wrote to his father, Lord Liverpool, on 28th June: "I am sorry to inform you that a complaint which the King has had for some time in his eyes is become within the last few days very alarming; he has not been able to see with one eye for some time, but the other is now nearly as bad, and though he can see to write, he is unable to read the notes we are obliged to send him. Phipps has seen him and has privately declared it to be a cataract on both eyes; he says he can cure him but that the operation cannot be performed until he is quite blind. The king does not yet know his real situation but he will be informed of it in a few days. I should add that Phipps says there is no danger whatever in the operation, that he never knew an instance of its failing, and that it is as safe for a person of eighty, as for one of twenty. The general health of the King is remarkably good at present, and his spirits less affected than I should have thought possible. His situation will however for some time be a most lamentable one. I only wish it may give him some sedentary habits."[1]

Wathen made frequent trips to advise and treat the King at Weymouth, where George was spending the summer months to enjoy sea-bathing on his doctor's advice, as was his custom. The patient was optimistic that his sight would not be permanently lost, but in mid-July he accepted the appointment of a private secretary, Lieut. Col. Herbert Taylor[2], to help with his correspondence and official papers. At about that time the King wrote (to Lord Hawkesbury) one of the last letters that he was to attempt unaided. Hawkesbury's biographer described it as follows: "the writing is scarcely legible; the signature and part of the postscript absolutely undecipherable from the way in which the one is written over the other, while the confusion of the first sentence shows how unable the writer was to read what he had said." It read: "The King cannot refrain from the pleasure of acquainting Lord Hawkesbury that an accidental inflammation in the worst eye, with the remedies ably used by Mr Phipps, has proved of great advantage to the use of that eye. Mr Phipps says that he had a similar instance the last year with the eyes of Lord Melbourne, where a cataract had been expected, but had since completely disappeared……. P.S. We have just received……Lord Nelson has destroyed…enemy. Heaven has granted us this success. George R' ".[3] The news of Nelson's naval triumph was greeted with rapture, but a far more decisive victory at Trafalgar would be celebrated some months later, though marred by the Admiral's death.

While a vestige of sight remained, the King and Queen retained some hope of improvement, and on 3 August 1805 the Queen wrote to Lady Chatham: "You will I am sure rejoice to hear the dear King's eyes are much better. The inflammation which we had reason to fear not only much abated, but hath proved the means of dissolving the skinn [sic] which threatened the cataract. Mr Phipps gives us hopes and is to return again next Sunday. He says it must take time and by avoiding dusty roads, great lights, and above all not overstraining the eye, he hopes to see great amendment in a short time."[4]

In his epic drama of the Napoleonic wars, *The Dynasts*, published a century after the events, Thomas Hardy mentions Wathen's membership of the royal entourage at Weymouth. There is a scene set in "King George's watering place, South Wessex, in a red-brick residence known as Gloucester House", in which the king discusses the war with his Prime Minister Pitt, subsequently inviting him to join the royal party, consisting of "many friends of mine". The King then names half a dozen people including "Mr Phipps the oculist, not the least important to me. He is a worthy and a skilful man. My eyes, he says, are marvellously improved in durability as I know them to be in power." [5] For Hardy to have put these words in the mouth of the sovereign, Wathen's reputation in Dorset must have long outlasted his own times. It is true that the royal family had great faith in Mr Phipps, setting great store by his advice. The usual treatments (leeches etc) may not have brought about any genuine improvement, but his reassurances did much to maintain the morale of the King. All the same not everyone thought so well of him. He had his detractors – but so did everyone in an age where gossip, criticism and invective were daily currency: in conversation, cartoons, verses and all manner of scandal sheets. Wathen escaped quite lightly. The politician, George Canning, commented in a letter to his wife: "Poor old Nobbs [George III] is losing his eyes – a cruel case – really a most moving and afflicting one. As yet the disease is not yet out of reach of a cure, I hope – but he has Phipps to attend him, in whom I have no confidence. I wish I could persuade them to call in Ware. Phipps is a coxcomb and frequents Devonshire House. The Duchess is under his care now for <u>her</u> eye, so I found from Lady Bessborough [Harriet, sister of the Duchess of Devonshire] whom I saw yesterday – and of course has the best intelligence of poor Nobbs's progress – and what with that communication, and what with the Prince &c. &c. &c. I cannot help wishing that poor Nobbs's eyes were under other hands. It will be a serious difficulty – if he should really lose his sight – besides what one feels for him – a serious difficulty in public business. Indeed there are difficulties enough on all sides – and how we are to get through them is more than I can guess."[6] Despite his fading sight, the King managed to struggle on, keeping a reasonable grasp on the affairs of state for about five more years. He may have had one of his eyes couched in 1807. The testimonies found are contradictory, but in that year there was no summer visit to Weymouth.

For all his frailty and now infrequent appearance in public, King George remained popular with his subjects in whose eyes his role as constitutional monarch was favourably contrasted with Napoleon's increasingly despotic demeanour. In 1807, Wathen, apparently without compunction or any sense of impropriety, sent "a little of the King's hair" as a keepsake to a Miss Walter (or Waller?), one of his "poetical" friends. In these lines from her poem written in response to this gesture, she appoints herself spokeswoman for the nation – elaborating the prayer at the heart of the patriotic song "God save the King", later to be adopted as the national anthem.

> *"While Britain's Monarch makes our Hearts his own*
> *Protects our Commerce, Liberty and Laws,*
> *And lives the Prop of our religious Cause*
> *Long may he live, Oh hear all bount'ous Heav'n*
> *Long may he to the Nation's Praise be given."*[7]

During the winter of 1809-1810 Wathen was called upon to operate on his friend Ernest's remaining good eye. It was a risky business, of crucial importance to the Duke and a pivotal moment in Wathen's career. There were a few days fraught with suspense, but the outcome was fortunately successful, as the Duke explained in a letter sent from St James's Palace on 11th February 1810 to the Duchess of Richmond in Dublin. After thanking her for her enquiries he continued: "thank God…alarmed as I was for the first 48 hours of becoming totally blind – from the unwearied and unremitting attention of Phipps I have entirely recovered the sight as you will perceive from this letter."[8] The two men had been on friendly terms for well over a decade, but the restoration of his sight enhanced Ernest's respect for Wathen to whom he felt a life-long debt of gratitude.

Celebrations for George III's Golden Jubilee began at the start of his fiftieth year as King, on 25th October 1809, and events were organised throughout the country with huge popular support. Sadly the King, now almost blind, was unable to take an active part, and for him 1810 was far from happy. His second son, Frederick, Duke of York, was obliged to resign as commander-in-chief of the army after a scandal: his mistress, Mary Anne Clarke, had been selling army commissions for cash. George's youngest and favourite daughter Amelia was ailing very painfully, with a tubercular condition plus erysipelas, and was not expected to recover. Then in the early hours of 31st May, his fifth son, Ernest, Duke of Cumberland, was seriously wounded. Opinions differ to this day as to what exactly happened. Was Ernest the victim of a failed assassination attempt by his valet Joseph Sellis, who subsequently committed suicide, or did the Duke murder Sellis and then injure himself to create a cover story? The coroner's inquest unanimously accepted the first version, but some said the jury had been rigged. The possibility that the Duke was a murderer has blackened his reputation ever since that night. As recently as 2002 John Wardroper[9] published a biography entitled *Wicked Ernest* setting out the evidence against the Duke and confidently asserting his guilt. Earlier biographers G M Willis[10] and Anthony Bird[11], take a different view, with Bird attempting to vindicate a man generally considered 'damnable', but probably much maligned. This is not the place to review the arguments and witness statements yet again; it is in any case impossible to know who was telling the truth. What concerns us here is Wathen's part in the story and he had a major role to play.

On 30th May 1810 Prince Ernest Duke of Cumberland had spent much of the day at the Royal Naval Asylum, a school for orphaned children of naval personnel, recently established at Greenwich. In the evening of the same day he had attended a concert and had gone to bed at about one o'clock in the morning. The attack took place an hour or two later. When word reached Wathen that the Duke of Cumberland was wounded, he rushed round to St James's Palace and took charge of the situation. Everard Home and Sir Henry Halford, royal surgeon and physician respectively, had been summoned during the night, and had dressed the wounds. Home later attested that the pulsation of the brain had been visible. The attacker had wielded the Duke's own razor-edged cavalry sabre, and the first two blows to the head might have proved fatal had they not been caught up in the bed curtains. As it was, the sabre sliced through Ernest's night-cap and blood flew up eight feet high on the wall. When he instinctively put out a hand to stop the blade he was cut between the thumb and forefinger. Altogether he had three wounds on his neck, one on his head, five on his right hand, one on his left arm, one on his left wrist, one on his leg, and one on his thigh. By the time Wathen arrived, the Prince of Wales and the Duke of Sussex had already seen their brother, and the room was crowded with servants, attendants and courtiers. Wathen immediately had the room cleared and that evening personally transferred Ernest to the residence of the Prince of Wales, Carlton House, getting him into a sedan chair with some considerable difficulty and walking alongside the chair all the way. He remained there with him for more than two months, sleeping in an adjacent room. Later Wathen was to testify that he had not attended the Duke in a professional capacity but merely as a friend.[12] However, in the aftermath of the attack Wathen was Ernest's doctor, nurse, counsellor, confidant and channel of communication with the royal household. For the first twenty-four hours the Duke was in great pain and in a very nervous state. If Wathen accidentally touched the bedclothes he cried out in fear and pain; nor could he bear the sound of Wathen's pen scratching, so all letters and reports had to be written in a separate room.

That Wathen was determined to do all he could to help and comfort his friend is beyond doubt. At the same time, he clearly relished being at the centre of a crisis and intimately involved with the royal family. His letters, written twice daily – at least – in the week following the attack, are ostensibly bulletins conveying the latest developments in the Duke's recuperation, and they serve their purpose more than adequately. Wathen's additional observations are, however, enormously revealing about himself and at times they combine obsequiousness and self-importance with almost comic effect, despite the gravity of the circumstances. Of course a greater degree of formality is to be expected from anyone writing two centuries ago, but the idiosyncrasies unconsciously displayed here are entirely personal to Wathen, – not least his habit of ending with an unsolicited account of his own well-being. Unsurprisingly, Wathen had little sleep whilst in attendance on the Duke. Nevertheless, always anxious to please and impress, he managed to compose frequent and often polished letters to keep the royal family informed from day to day. In one of the early bulletins Wathen addressed to Lieut. Col. Taylor for the King, he starts with a detailed description of the events of the night, and continues with an extravagant but eloquent tribute to the King, whose birthday (his 72nd) it happens to be:

"Carlton House, Monday morning, 4ᵗʰ June.

It is with the utmost satisfaction that I can send you for the information of their Majesties a very good report of the night; his Royal Highness has slept with little interruption since eleven o'clock last night till this moment and is still asleep. At the different periods of awaking he has complained much of the soreness and tenderness of the numerous and different wounds and bruises, but is <u>free</u> <u>from</u> <u>every</u> <u>febrile</u> <u>symptom</u>. Mr Home is to see him at twelve o'clock after which I will pay my duty to their Majesties with a further account.

I cannot forebear on the opening of this <u>happy</u> day to beg you humbly to present to his Majesty the most warm and dutiful congratulations of a loyal and grateful heart. May all the various blessings <u>he</u> has diffused over this land be returned tenfold into his own bosom & every other blessing of a good & kind Providence be continually showered on <u>him</u> and <u>his</u> both here and hereafter." [13]

The Duke made a steady recovery: he had a strong constitution, and was fortunate to have no infection in his wounds and no fever. Wathen considered that the "great quantity of blood lost from the division of the small artery in the head"[14] had been quite providential – bloodletting being thought of as a desirable treatment at the time. Wathen's role was to be a sympathetic and vigilant presence at the bedside, and to administer every few hours copious doses of laudanum to encourage sleep and dull the pain. After reporting on the Duke on Friday 8ᵗʰ June he ended his bulletin: "Excuse my scrawl for I can scarsely [sic] keep my eyes open. This will be the tenth night and I have had but one night's sleep."[15] A slight exaggeration on Wathen's part – it was actually the eighth night. The following morning he added: "I have been to bed for four hours during which I was only disturbed twice, and feel quite refreshed," but that evening he made a point of apologising: "I should have written by the 3 o'clock coach but was so completely worn out that on leaving Carlton House at eleven this morning… I went to bed and slept till 4, too late for the coach." By Sunday the Duke was feeling far more comfortable – and so was Wathen, "I have also slept the greater part of the night in his room & am quite renovated this morning."[16]

Over several weeks of this crisis, Wathen had ample opportunity to become better acquainted with the Prince of Wales who showed great sympathy, consideration and affection for Ernest throughout his brother's recuperation and convalescence in the apartments made available for him at Carlton House. Other members of the royal family visited the patient there, including his mother, Queen Charlotte. She was clearly not in the habit of being entertained by her eldest son and took advantage of the visit to inspect the Prince's latest extravagant improvements. Although she admired "many fine things", a comment to her daughter Princess Mary proved prophetic: "the house is not near finished & if it goes on in the manner it has done, it never will, for there is constant building up and pulling down". [17] The Prince incurred massive debts through his unrestrained spending on the luxurious house and its lavish furnishings but he was never satisfied, and it was eventually demolished in 1827. The grand portico and entrance columns were rescued, however, and still grace the National Gallery.

In 1811 the King's surgeon David Dundas[18] was commissioned to write a report weighing up the arguments for and against an operation to extract the King's cataracts. It was decided not to go ahead. The death of his youngest daughter, Princess Amelia, in November 1810, had been the trigger for King George to experience further immense mental distress and illness. The remainder of his life was spent in darkness and confusion, not recognising his closest family members. He was blind, deaf and suffered from dementia until his death in 1820, so this time a period of Regency, enthusiastically welcomed by the Prince of Wales, was inevitable.

Whilst a good deal of evidence still exists relating to Wathen's treatment of the King and the Duke of Cumberland, accounts of his dealings with less illustrious patients are rather scarce. There are, however, a few revealing anecdotes, and, fortuitously, a detailed first-hand account of a consultation for a minor ailment recorded by one of the leading diarists of the time. A letter on the subject appeared in *The European Magazine and London Review* of October 1808. The author had written to the Editor in order to reassure the aged about the speed and efficacy of the "beautiful operation of extracting the cataract… The operation is simple, attended with the slightest pain, that of a mere puncture; and it does not last more than three minutes. On his return from India, blind with cataracts, and shaken in every nerve by the hostile climate, having resolved to undergo this operation, he [Mr Draper] wanted a firm mind. At the mere touch of the hand, the agitated and terrified man fainted. It was during the swoon that the operation was performed; and when he recovered he saw once more the world which he seemed for ever to have quitted…… It is a mere act of humanity due to some who are afflicted by this melancholy disorder, to give them every cheerful hope, and to shew the ease with which they may promise themselves a perfect recovery; and it is a mere act of justice to inform the afflicted, that the operator, in both these cases, was Mr Wathen Phipps, whose zealous humanity excites the gratitude of his opulent patients, not less than of those who receive gratuitously from his hand a gift which would be worthy of Heaven itself to bestow on man!" [19]

A further anecdote, from a different source, underlines Wathen's good-heartedness and charitable impulses: "When Sir Wathen Waller, then Mr Phipps, was a very young man, and though but in the commencement of his practice, known as the most skilful and successful occulist [sic] of the day, two respectable ladies from

Dorsetshire came up to London for the purpose of having an operation performed, the fee for which was an hundred pounds, and which Sir Wathen accomplished with success. Some time after the ladies had returned into the country, Sir Wathen happened to be in company with a gentleman who came from their neighbourhood, and this naturally caused him to make enquiries respecting his patients. He had always considered them rich, but this gentleman corrected his mistake. As he was about to return into Dorsetshire, Sir Wathen begged him to take charge of a letter for the ladies in question, and with a liberality which reflected the highest honour on his heart, he returned the whole fee. The amiable manners of the ladies had particularly interested him during their stay in the metropolis, and he was gratified at having it in his power to prevent them suffering from some of the expenses attendant on seeking relief from a painful and distressing affliction." [20]

For a more objective account of what it was like to visit the Cork Street surgery of Wathen Phipps we can look to the Royal Academician Joseph Farington, who kept a daily diary from 1793 to 1821 – far longer than Samuel Pepys. His work caused quite a stir when first published in the 1920s, but in the opinion of an early reviewer, the author was "devoid of humour and lacked the malice which a diarist should feel".[21] The American critic Grant Overton nevertheless conceded: "as a conscientious accumulator of facts I can think of no-one who is his equal. Amid riches and grandeur, intriguery and wars and revolutions, surrounded by a glittery society in which one knew not which to worship, genius or scintillance, Joseph Farington scrupulously set down all the diseases of people he knew, all the dishes served at a dinner, how much everything cost and the money that everyone made, inherited, bequeathed or borrowed." [22]

Farington's depiction of the minutiae of daily life in the later Georgian era may well appeal to historians more than to literary critics: as primary source material for that era its value is inestimable. It so happens that amongst all the visits and incidents recorded he mentions an eye problem in 1807 which led him to become, briefly, a patient of Wathen Phipps, consulting him three times in one week. Unfortunately he makes no comment on his experience and no assessment of the treatment or the practitioner. However, he did return twice after the first visit, so presumably he felt he was not wasting his time or his money. As Farington was renowned for his accuracy, it seems likely that Watkin for Wathen is an error in transcription of the manuscript.

"September 19th, at ½ past 1, called upon Mr Watkin Phipps, oculist, in Cork Street, Burlington Gardens, who examined my eyes and told me that my complaint was seated in the eye lids, which from being overexerted had lost their tone, and did not properly supply moisture for their functions. He recommended me to apply a large sponge, steeped in water as hot as I could bear it to my eyelids for the space of 6 or 7 minutes 4 or 5 times a day, and to call on him again on Monday next, when he sh[oul]d better be able to determine what to do. I dined alone. His hours for receiving patients from ½ past 1 till 4 every day except Sundays. I gave him one guinea.

September 21st, Watkin Phipps I went to, who applied a sharp stimulus to my eyes. Directed an ointment to be touched to the edges and corners of my eyes for a minute the last thing at night, and then to be wiped off with a soft handkerchief. The bathing of the eyes to be continued as often as I please. He s[ai]d he sh[oul]d soon put my eyes to right.

September 25th, Watkin Phipps I went to. He gave me a caustic waxy preparation inserted in a quill and shewed me how it was to be applied. The size of a pin's head to be taken on the point of a small camel hair pencil, and dissolved by passing it through the flame of a candle or a fire, and then drawing the point of the pencil upon the lid of the eye, between the eye lash and the eye, of the upper and lower lid of each eye. The eye not to be touched, though no injury w[oul]d ensue from it. He directed me to continue the use of the warm water bath, and the eye water, but recommended the caustic application to be applied every morning rather than at night, as it would be better seen how to do it."[23]

Among the papers in the Waller Collection is an intriguing little note, unsigned and undated. Its author, clearly quite at home at Court (perhaps Lady Howe, a friend of the Duke of Cumberland and one of Wathen's patients?),[24] is keen to tell Wathen how well Sir Henry Halford, the foremost physician of the day, has spoken of him. There are a few clues regarding the note's date. Both men changed their surnames – Henry Halford was Vaughan until 1809, and Wathen Phipps was Waller from 1814. Both also became baronets at about the time they changed names. So it cannot have been written before 1809 or after 1814. In view of the King's interest in hearing about Wathen's skill as an "operator" (surgeon), it probably dates from 1809 or 1810, when George III still retained hopes that an operation might restore his sight. Interestingly, Halford, like Canning before him, had – at least initially – seen something of the "coxcomb" in Wathen. The note reads: "Now Phipps attend to me for I neither flatter nor lie. Sir Henry Halford p[r] chance named you to the King as having met you. He enquired much about you. He then said 'I look upon him as the first man in his profession, the first operator living, but I respect his private character. He is disinterested, kind-hearted, honourable and true, in friendship perfect and his conduct to me has been perfect. At first he has the appearance of coxcomicalness [sic] – this goes off and he is not in the least so, but all that he ought to be.' I am going, but stopp'd to lose no time in writing down S[r] Henry's words." [25]

Notes

1. Aspinall, A (ed), *The Later Correspondence of George III*, Vol IV, 1968, footnote to Letter 3132.

2. Lt-Col Taylor was appointed private secretary to King George III on 18th July 1805.

3. Younge, Charles Duke, *The Life and administration of Robert Banks Jenkinson, second Earl of Liverpool* (known as Lord Hawkesbury in 1805, succeeding his father as Lord Liverpool in 1808), 1868, p 197.

4. Aspinall, A, op.cit, Letter 3130, p 350.

5. Hardy, Thomas, *The Dynasts* ("the longest English drama in existence" in 3 parts, 19 Acts and 131 scenes), Act IV Sc I, pub London 1908.

6. Aspinall, A, op.cit. Vol IV, footnote to Letter 3130, p 351.

7. WCRO: 4436/1 Commonplace book of Jonathan Wathen Phipps, p 267.

8. West Sussex Record Office: Goodwood/351.

9. Wardroper, John: *Wicked Ernest*, pub Shelfmark Books, London, 2002.

10. Willis, G M: *Ernest Augustus, Duke of Cumberland and King of Hanover*, A. Barker, London 1954.

11. Bird, Anthony: *The damnable Duke of Cumberland*, Barrie & Rockliff, London 1966.

12. The information in this paragraph is from Jonathan Wathen Waller's Evidence at *The Trial of Josiah Phillips for a Libel on the Duke of Cumberland*, pub J. Hatchard & Son, London, 1833, pp 64-66, and from the Account of the Coroner's inquest in the same publication, p 116.

13. Aspinall, A (ed), *The Later Correspondence of George III*, Vol V, p 609.

14. Aspinall, A (ed), *The Correspondence of the Prince of Wales*, 1770-1812, Vol VII, p 41.

15. Aspinall, A (ed), *The Later Correspondence of George III*, Vol V, p 612.

16. Aspinall, A (ed), *The Correspondence of the Prince of Wales*, 1770-1812, Vol VII, p 40.

17. Ibid, quoted by John Wardroper in *Wicked Ernest*, Shelfmark books, London 2002, p 58.

18. Sergeant-surgeon to the royal household, formerly Apothecary; report of 11 June 1811.

19. Anecdotes with letter dated 18 Oct 1808, from D.J. *The European Magazine and London Review*, Vol. 54, July – December 1808, p 255.

20. Cliffe, Leigh: *Anecdotal remembrances of distinguished literary and political characters*, pp 129-130, 1830.

21. Holliday, Robert Cortes, reviewing the first volume of the recently published diary in *The Bookman* 1923. Quoted by Grant Overton, see below.

22. Overton, Grant: *American Nights Entertainment*, New York, 1923 pp 140-141. He also commented: "No literary discovery in years has made half the sensation of the finding of the Farington Diary, and quite rightly for what could be compared to the disclosure of a contemporary account in which Boswell, Burke, Goldsmith, Horace Walpole, The Thrales, Garrick, Mrs Siddons, Nelson, Howe, Mirabeau, Marat, Napoleon, Hoppner, Turner, Pitt, Warren Hastings, Lady Hamilton and Robert Burns were intimately noted?

and yet Farington, ruler of the Royal Academy although a most indifferent artist, came into touch with all these personages and was apparently never for one moment carried off his feet."

23. *Farington Diary*, Vol IV, 1807, pub Hutchinson, London, 1924. The 8 volumes were published from 1922 to 1928.
24. The note may have been from the Baroness Howe, who became Wathen's second wife.
25. WRCO: CR 0341/218.

HOWE FAMILY TREE
(simplified, showing royal connections)

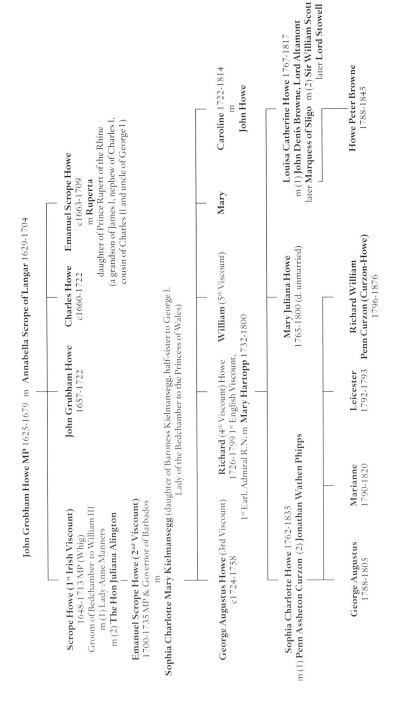

John Grobham Howe MP 1625-1679 m Annabella Scrope of Langar 1629-1704

Scrope Howe (1ˢᵗ Irish Viscount)
1648-1713 MP (Whig)
Groom of Bedchamber to William III
m (1) **Lady Anne Manners**
m (2) **The Hon Juliana Alington**
|
Emanuel Scrope Howe (2ⁿᵈ Viscount)
1700-1735 MP & Governor of Barbados
m
Sophia Charlotte Mary Kielmansegg (daughter of Baroness Kielmansegg, half-sister to George I.
Lady of the Bedchamber to the Princess of Wales)

John Grubham Howe
1657-1722

Charles Howe
c1660-1722

Emanuel Scrope Howe
c1663-1709
m **Ruperta**
daughter of Prince Rupert of the Rhine
(a grandson of James I, nephew of Charles I,
cousin of Charles II and uncle of George I)

George Augustus Howe (3rd Viscount)
c1724-1758

Richard (4ᵗʰ Viscount) Howe
1726-1799 1ˢᵗ English Viscount,
1ˢᵗ Earl. Admiral R.N. m **Mary Hartopp** 1732-1800

William (5ᵗʰ Viscount)

Mary

Caroline 1722-1814
m
John Howe

Louisa Catherine Howe 1767-1817
m (1) **John Denis Browne, Lord Altamont**
later **Marquess of Sligo** m (2) **Sir William Scott**
later **Lord Stowell**

Howe Peter Browne
1788-1845

Sophia Charlotte Howe 1762-1835
m (1) **Penn Assheton Curzon** (2) **Jonathan Wathen Phipps**

Mary Juliana Howe
1765-1800 (d. unmarried)

George Augustus
1788-1805

Marianne
1790-1820

Leicester
1792-1793

Richard William
Penn Curzon (Curzon-Howe)
1796-1876

Chapter 4

A change of name and status

"The hand of majesty metempsychosized the Aesculapius of eyes into the observed of all observers, at a moment's warning. He knelt down plain Phipps, and he rose Sir Wathen Waller, equal to superintend the ocular economy of the Great Mogul."
Anonymous article *"Titles"*, published in *The Polar Star*, London 1830

Despite his prosperity, social advancement and high-flying career, Wathen's life was not without problems and grief. In the first decade of the new century the network of family relationships which had provided him with affection and support all his life was completely unravelled. After losing his first two children and another infant son before he was thirty, Wathen had to cope with a rapid succession of further bereavements: the death of his grandmother Anne Wathen in 1800; of her brother, his great-uncle James Waller (who left him a substantial legacy) in 1802; of his mother Mary Smith and his aunt and mother-in-law Elizabeth Maria Slack in 1804; of his step-grandfather and mentor Jonathan Wathen in 1808; and of his uncle and father-in-law Thomas Slack in 1810. Worst of all, his wife (and cousin) Elizabeth died in January 1809 at the age of only 35, leaving him with four very young children. Georgiana was 8, Anna nearly 6, Thomas Wathen 3½, and the baby, Ernest Adolphus, just one year old.

We might immediately assume that maintaining a buoyant, and extrovert persona whilst beset by wave upon wave of private grief must have been enormously stressful for Wathen. Success in his career relied in large measure on raising the morale of his patients with an optimistic and reassuring "bedside" manner, so he may have been obliged to draw upon all his reserves of resilience and determination to appear confident, capable and professional in public during these difficult times. However, there is another possibility: he may not have been as overwhelmed by grief as we – in the twenty-first century – might expect. We should remember that Wathen's concept of death and its consequences was radically different from our own. From his earliest years he had been taught to rejoice when a friend or relation was "called to a better place". Some sadness might be inevitable, but prolonged mourning was considered inappropriate and self-indulgent. To those whose faith in an afterlife was unshakeable, the certain knowledge that salvation awaited the believer was cause for gladness rather than distress. What is more, Wathen's uncompromising upbringing had left him with certain obligations and expectations of himself. He had resolved to repay his debt of gratitude to his grandmother and step-grandfather by continuing to advance in his profession and in society.

We know little about Wathen's first wife Elizabeth – the broadest outlines only: her birth, marriage, offspring and death – but nothing of her personality or interests. Presumably it was she who supervised the sittings for a charming portrait of her two little daughters which has survived from their childhood days. It was commissioned in 1804 from no less a person than Queen Charlotte's favourite painter, Sir William Beechey, and shows Georgiana and Anna admiring a bubble which the older child has blown from a clay pipe.[1] At first sight the portrait seems to be simply a romanticised depiction of childhood, but since bubbles in paintings have traditionally symbolised the brevity and transience of life, there is a less sentimental, but wholly relevant message to be found in it. The choice of composition is somewhat puzzling, however, as these children were the only two of the first five to survive, and their parents scarcely needed a reminder of the fragility of life. We do not know how the children were cared for after Elizabeth's death, but there was money enough from Wathen's earnings and legacies to provide an abundance of nursemaids, tutors and governesses, and it is likely that Elizabeth's sister Charlotte Slack, destined to be the "maiden aunt" of the family, supervised the nursery. Her letters to Thomas when he was a young diplomat abroad demonstrate her affection for her nephew.[2] In their adult lives Elizabeth and Wathen's children maintained contacts with the Slack aunts and their surviving uncle, Joseph Albin Slack, who were also their father's cousins. During their childhood their only other uncle, Thomas Cartwright Slack, had died in devastating circumstances – a terrible house fire at his home in 1815, when he re-entered the burning building to look for his seven-year-old daughter.[3]

Wathen's second marriage, in 1812, was truly a life-changing event. When choosing a new wife, he clearly did not have foremost in his mind the need to find a mother-figure for his children. A less likely person would be hard to imagine. His choice fell upon (Sophia) Charlotte, Baroness Howe, who had consulted him as a patient, no doubt on the recommendation of the Duke of Cumberland, and had successfully undergone couching on one of her eyes. She was a widow with something of a reputation for haughtiness. A peeress in her own right, she possessed Howe family estates in Langar, Nottinghamshire, plus a substantial fortune in lands, properties and assets held on behalf of her son and heir Richard Penn Curzon, principally at Gopsal in Leicestershire and Penn in Berkshire. Lady Howe had been made welcome at Court for decades as a favoured friend of the royal family. An eye-witness relates a charming anecdote describing an informal visit she paid to George III and Queen Charlotte shortly after her the death of her first husband, Penn Assheton Curzon. "The Baroness Howe …. took her little boy then in petticoats to see the King and Queen, who always shewed particular regard to the family of Howe. The King took the child on his knee trying to amuse him in various ways, till at length, perhaps by being unused to that stillness which was imposed by the Royal presence, he fell asleep. The Baroness immediately prepared to remove the child; but the King would not allow it, and held him on his lap and in his arms for nearly three hours until the nap was finished."[4]

Lady Howe regularly attended Queen Charlotte's most formal and prestigious receptions – her Drawing Rooms – and under the new regime begun in 1811, the Regency, she was invited to all manner of lavish balls and parties hosted by the Prince Regent. A satirical print by George Cruikshank, published in 1812, the year of Lady Howe's marriage to Wathen, portrays the Baroness centre-stage among a large group of aristocrats, politicians and royalty at a Concert of "Ancient Music" – one of the highlights in the social and cultural calendar of the rich and influential at the time. She is escorted by the Duke of Cumberland and wears a fashionably high-waisted white Empire-line gown (reminiscent of Elizabeth Bennet's attire in every screen adaptation of *Pride and Prejudice*) with an ostrich feather headdress. In the crowded scene Lady Howe is second in prominence to just one other woman, the Regent's current mistress Lady Hertford, and her role in the ensemble is crucial. A question she addresses to the Prince (in a speech bubble), pinpoints the satirist's principal target, the blatant fickleness the Regent has displayed since coming to power, deserting his longstanding political friends the Whigs to favour the established Tory government. Lady Howe: "Well: since you have got rid of your Old Friends Howe do you like your New Ones?" The Prince: "Not at all. D—N them! Not at all!!!!" – hence the picture's title *Princely predilections, or Ancient music and modern discord*.[5] All but one of the figures caricatured have been identified by the British Museum's experts; the exception is a stout gentleman in a green jacket sitting on the right. Could this be Wathen? The likeness to his only known portrait is undeniable.[6]

On 1st October 1812, precisely six months after the Cruikshank print appeared, Mr Phipps and Lady Howe were married at St James's Church, Piccadilly. The bride was given away by HRH Prince Ernest, the Duke of Cumberland, one of the highest ranking peers in the land, who had been instrumental in bringing the unlikely couple together. Wathen's skill as an oculist had proved of inestimable value in his own case, and of course Ernest was keen to show his gratitude by introducing a potential new patient to his friend. There had probably been no intention of matchmaking; the difference of status ruled out any such thoughts. Yet, in an era when every man knew his place, Wathen, by marrying the Baroness, had pulled off a feat of dazzling chutzpah, almost unparalleled in the chronicles of social mobility. From time to time a woman of beguiling beauty (such as Nelson's mistress Emma, Lady Hamilton) had succeeded in "marrying up", but for a man such a thing was virtually impossible. What is more Charlotte had a highly visible public profile as the eldest daughter of

Admiral (Richard) Lord Howe, one of the country's most illustrious naval heroes, whose barony at his death, though not his earldom, had descended to her as his heiress. And not only was the Baroness a member of the nobility – she was recognised by the royal family as a not-too-distant cousin. The Admiral's maternal grandmother, the Hanoverian baroness Sophia Kielmansegg, was a half-sister of George I (the daughter of his father's mistress) and was described in letters patent issued by the king when granting her an Irish and an English peerage as "*consanguineam nostram*" – of our common blood. So the Admiral's mother, Lady Howe's grandmother, was George I's niece and a cousin of George II.

Few families could rival the Howes as insiders at Court over several generations. The Admiral's grandfather, Scrope Howe, was a Groom of the Bedchamber to William III; his father's sister Mary Howe was Lady-in-Waiting to George II's wife Caroline (when Princess of Wales and then Queen); his own sister, another Caroline, the Honourable Mrs Howe (who had married a John Howe), was a great favourite of George III and always treated as one of the family. At the age of ninety she attended her niece's marriage to Wathen Phipps, and along with the Duke of Cumberland signed the register as a witness. The Baroness's sister Lady Mary Howe, the Admiral's second daughter, was for five years Lady-in-Waiting to "the Princesses", George III's daughters. Lady Mary had been a bridesmaid to the Princess Royal, and it was she who wrote a graphic account of the reception in Portsmouth of Admiral Howe by George III, Queen Charlotte, Prince Ernest and five of the Princesses, on his triumphant return from his famous victory over the French, known as the "Glorious First" (of June, 1794).[7] The Queen gave Lady Mary a splendidly good-humoured and glowing 'character' or testimonial when she left her employ, and could find but one fault to mention – her habit of too frequently beating the monarch at backgammon. Tragically Lady Mary died in the very week she was to be married to Lord Morton, a fellow courtier, who was Lord Chamberlain to Queen Charlotte 1792-1818. The *Gentleman's Magazine* had actually already published the union as taking place on 2 March 1800 in its Marriages column, and had to retract the error in its next issue. The Duchess of Württemberg (the former Princess Royal) wrote to her father George III that on hearing of Lady Mary's death, "my spirits were very much shook".[8] Both the King and the Prince of Wales sent personal letters of condolence to her mother.

With such a family background, the Baroness was not just a vaguely recognised acquaintance of the royal family; she knew every one of them personally and there was genuine closeness and affection between them. In January 1805 the King had been adamant that Lady Howe should become governess to his granddaughter Princess Charlotte, the only legitimate child of the Prince of Wales, thereby second in line to the throne.[9] On the advice of his friends, courtiers Lord and Lady Harcourt, he had earlier recommended a Miss Leonora Dee as governess/companion to

Princess Sophia Matilda of Gloucester – an arrangement so successful that it was to last for forty years.[10] The Prince of Wales was not on speaking terms with his father, blaming him for the disastrous arranged marriage he had been obliged to contract with the King's niece Princess Caroline of Brunswick, Charlotte's mother. He was not prepared to accept a governess of his father's choice and expressed his views via the Lord Chancellor, Lord Eldon, who was playing the unenviable role of mediator between the sovereign and the heir to the throne. In the event no approach was made to the Baroness; her elder surviving son, sixteen-year-old George Augustus Curzon had died while the matter was under discussion, and all agreed it was not the moment to burden a bereaved mother with such a heavy responsibility.

Like Wathen, Lady Howe had suffered the sadness of numerous deaths in her family. At her second marriage, she had two surviving children, Richard Penn Curzon, aged 16, and Marianne Curzon, aged 22. Apart from George Augustus there had been another son, Leicester Curzon, who had lived only three months in 1793. The death of her husband Penn Assheton Curzon aged 40 had left her a widow in 1797. Soon afterwards she had lost her parents and sister all in the space of a year: her adored father the Admiral in 1799, followed by her sister Lady Mary and her mother the Countess Howe in 1800.[11] The Baroness had only one other close family member, her younger sister, Louisa Catherine, whose husband Lord Altamont had inherited the title Marquess of Sligo. The Marchioness was widowed in 1809 and a year after the Phipps-Howe marriage, she became the second wife of the judge Sir William Scott (later Lord Stowell), brother of Lord Eldon, the Lord Chancellor. Lord Cranley couldn't resist the opportunity for a verse!

On the marriages of Lady Howe and Lady Sligo

To Hymen, says Sligo
My sister and I go
We've tried the blind god both already;
Master Phipps she has got,
So I'll try Billy Scott
And to Hymen we'll always prove steady.

If we don't agree
Phipps will make us all see,
How to live in affection and ease;
And when tired of our lot,
Little big-bellied Scott
Will divorce us whenever we please.[12]

The Phipps-Howe marriage caused not a few raised eyebrows in society. Observations such as the poem above probably circulated in private at the time, but were not made public until some years later. The following scathing comments were published in 1830 by "a courtier" – said to be John Mitford – by way of introduction to some witty and satirical verses written by Princess Caroline, the estranged wife of the Prince of Wales and formerly a friend of Lady Howe:[13] "…It was that night that I first saw the verses about Lady Howe, who married Phipps the oculist to the great sorrow of her family, the gentleman being thirty and she sixty years of age (he was 43, she was 50):

JEU D'ESPRIT
On the Marriage of Viscountess Howe with Phipps, the oculist

Yes; I long for the lips
Of that dear Mr Phipps
The great oculist, to whom I must bow
To my utter surprise
He has charm'd both my EYES
Would to heaven he had not known Howe

But now 'tis too late
He has settled my fate
Of all others 'tis him I adore;
So by him I'll be kiss'd
For I cannot resist
He shall couch me and then I'll see more."

According to Mitford, the falling-out between the Princess and the Baroness was caused by a waspish comment made by Lady Howe, who "had the impudence to say: 'if Billy Austin [a child adopted by Caroline] was not the son of the Princess, he might have been; for no woman ever strove harder to increase and multiply without a husband.'" This anecdotal snippet, impossible to verify, nevertheless has a ring of truth about it, and is completely in the idiom of the period, when personal invective often passed for wit. It is possible to eavesdrop further on the gossip of the times thanks to a letter of 7 November 1812 from Lord Sheffield to his brother-in-law Frederick North, which has survived.[14] This time the Baroness is the target, as Lord Sheffield comments: "The Public is much gratified by the mésalliance of Baroness Howe, with her oculist Mr Phipps, because she had always exhibited abundance of disdain, contempt & superiority over others, and there withall was not agreable [sic]. She married the eldest son of Lord Curzon whom you probably recollect, and it is said that Lord Curzon with whom I dined at the Archbishop of Canterbury's last summer (he then in high preservation in his 84th year) intends to move the proper Court to take the children from her. Phipps is a widower, and his children are not to be admitted into the house."

The house referred to may possibly be Lord Curzon's house; if not, the last part of Lord Sheffield's comment is surely exaggerated, but Lady Howe's former father-in-law certainly suspected that her new husband had designs on her properties and money. In his eyes Wathen was an upstart and not to be trusted. In the name of his surviving grandson, Richard Penn Curzon, Lord Curzon brought an action against Lady Howe and Jonathan Wathen Phipps in the Court of Chancery on 9 October 1812, just days after their marriage took place. Up to this point his former daughter-in-law had been left to deal with her family's finances unhindered,[15] having been granted administration of her late husband's estates and assets some fifteen years earlier. Lord Curzon asked the Court to oblige Lady Howe to account for all the income and expenditure from her first husband's estate and also to appoint a "proper person" as guardian for Richard and someone to receive the rents etc., which in the meantime should be paid into the Court. (As Lady Howe's daughter Marianne Curzon was no longer a minor she was not involved in the case.) The task of preparing very detailed accounts for the Court must have been expensive and time-consuming, as well as humiliating for the Baroness, but she retained custody of her son Richard, who was a reluctant and nominal participant in the whole affair. The proceedings seem to have petered out after a few years as Lord Curzon became increasingly infirm. He died aged 90 in 1820.

For a couple as status-conscious as Mr Phipps and Lady Howe, the discrepancy between their stations in life and indeed their titles must have been all too apparent. It is perhaps to Lady Howe's credit that she was willing to marry beneath her, but the attraction of a successful and personable younger man may have been too much to forego. Nonetheless, not much time was wasted before Wathen's status was elevated. Both he and his wife had for several years been frequent guests at Carlton House, where the Prince of Wales held court in immense splendour after assuming his father's powers as Prince Regent in 1811. Given the closeness of his friendship with the virtual monarch, it would not have been difficult for Wathen to obtain permission to change his surname by royal sign-manual. In any case such a change was not unusual at the period. In 1814 Wathen adopted the name Waller, "from grateful and affectionate regard to the memory of his maternal Grandmother, Anne Allen (formerly Anne Waller and later Anne Wathen) and of his maternal great Uncle James Waller",[16] and was granted a coat of arms based on some traditional Waller heraldry. Subsequently the Prince Regent bestowed on him a baronetcy, the Letters Patent being granted in 1815.[17] So Wathen Phipps became Sir Wathen

Waller – a much grander-sounding name, and conveniently alliterative. He clearly felt that the Wallers had a more illustrious pedigree than the Phipps family, and later in life he spent a great deal of time and effort researching his forebears and re-inventing himself as a Waller. It mattered little that he had made his name and reputation as an oculist when plain Mr Phipps; earning a living was no longer a priority. Though nominally still oculist to George III until the king's death in 1820, Sir Wathen delegated his professional work to his assistant Henry Alexander.

Whatever Sir Wathen's children may have thought of their father's second marriage, they were obliged to make the best of the new situation, and to accept the roles of step-sons/daughters/siblings that were thrust upon them. Lady Howe was seven years older than her second husband, and her children were considerably older than his. At the first Christmas after the marriage in 1812, there were six "children" in the household, ranging in age from Marianne Curzon, aged 22, to Ernest Phipps, aged 5. We have no information as to how they got on, but the Phipps children probably felt rather gauche and intimidated in the presence of the sophisticated Curzons. They were certainly wary of their formidable stepmother, and had an uneasy relationship with her. The subsequent change of surname to Waller may have affected them even more profoundly. The whole Phipps family had assumed a new identity – no doubt to the bemusement of the two youngest children in particular, the boys. Georgiana, the oldest child, may perhaps have had an inkling that her father (now to be known as "Sir Wathen Waller of Braywick Lodge in the county of Berkshire"[18]) had become the object of ridicule in certain quarters. Adverse comments ranged from the simple but cutting: "[Lady Howe] took for her second husband the court oculist, Dr Phipps, who was made a baronet and on his promotion emerged from his plebeian chrysalis as Sir Wathen Waller",[19] to the elaborate and sarcastic: "Our old Acquaintance, Phipps, the oculist, – what the deuce was he till the steel transformation had made his renown? The hand of majesty metempsychosized the Aesculapius of eyes into the observed of all observers, at a moment's warning. He knelt down plain Phipps, and he rose Sir Wathen Waller, equal to superintend the ocular economy of the Great Mogul."[20]

Only one family letter survives in the Waller collection from the early years of the marriage: a rather sad little note sent by Sir Wathen's elder son Thomas Wathen Waller, also habitually known as Wathen, to his father from his prep-school. (To prevent confusion over the two Wathens, the name Thomas is used in this narrative to denote the son.) Thomas boarded at a school located close to Richmond Green[21], run by a succession of clergymen named Delafosse[22], who handed control as headmaster from father to son over three generations. Thomas was there in 1815, about the time that Daniel Charles Delafosse (later personal Chaplain to the Duke of Cumberland) took over from his father Robert Mark Delafosse. Thomas's note is in the familiar mould of the pupil's letter home – a standard weekly exercise in schools of the time, used for handwriting and spelling practice as well as for keeping in touch with the family. Thomas wrote carefully in his "best" copperplate handwriting, pencil lines having first been scored across the page. It is not a particularly impressive effort for a nine-year-old, and he seems to have been a rather unenthusiastic pupil. On a positive note, however, he is keen to get home to his father and stepmother, whom he calls Mamma, and obviously was allowed in the house despite what was alleged by gossips like Lord Sheffield. "Richmond 20th [March 1815] Dear Father, Horace [Walpole][23] thinking it right that I should let you know when the holidays begin, it is next Thursday, but please let me come on Wednesday early. I hope you and Mamma and the rest are well and that you have got your servants comfortably about you. I remain your affectionate Son, W.Waller."

In view of the connection between Ernest, Duke of Cumberland, and the Delafosse family it is likely that Wathen chose the Richmond Green school for his son on the Duke's recommendation. Writing to Charles Daniel Delafosse many years later, the Duke (now King of Hanover) reminisces about visiting the school: "I used to ride over on Sundays after church and partake of excellent plum puddings prepared by your worthy helpmate for the young folk brought up under your care." In another letter he sends a message for Mrs Delafosse: "Tell her from me that I remember her excellent Sunday plum puddings, and this being Sunday I should have no dislike to have a slice now."[24] A later pupil, the soldier and explorer Sir Richard Burton, had a less rosy view of the establishment, likening it to Dotheboys Hall.[25]

Since the Duke of Cumberland had been a close friend of both Wathen and Lady Howe individually before their marriage, it was to be expected that he would feature prominently in the couple's joint social circle. However, in April 1813, unforeseen events caused Ernest to take up residence on the continent once again. Misjudging the appropriate balance between private and public interests, he overstepped the boundaries of acceptable royal involvement in politics, and his departure became unavoidable. The crisis came in during a clash with the Commons over his alleged manipulation of votes in the Weymouth constituency. Such behaviour on the part of a peer was an inflammatory constitutional matter. At the time few people understood why the Dorset constituency mattered to Ernest, but he had been appointed trustee and guardian of the previous MP's heirs, and had acted (too zealously, but in good faith) to protect their interests.[26] Realising that he had become an embarrassment to the government, the Duke decided to leave England to join the fight against Napoleon in Hanover. He had never been popular in his home country and was vilified cruelly in the press, particularly in scurrilous cartoons. Rumours abounded about an incestuous relationship with his sister Sophia, as well as sustained speculation that he had killed his servant Sellis. In the circumstances a period of self-imposed exile seemed desirable and the resumption of active service would be an honourable course of action. Ernest would be thwarted in his military ambition but his self-imposed exile was to have unexpected and life-changing consequences.

Anticipating a lengthy absence, Ernest sold his sixteen horses, and disposed of his choicest wines at auction. His journey to the continent was much hampered by stormy weather, but eventually he arrived at the court of his uncle (Queen Charlotte's brother), the Grand Duke of Mecklenburg-Strelitz. There on 20th May 1813,[27] he met his pretty and charming cousin Frederica – who at the time was married to her second husband, Prince Frederick of Solms-Braunfels, though they were separated and she was seeking a divorce. Ernest was immediately attracted to Frederica. More than twenty years later he recalled the moment he set eyes on her as the most beautiful and happiest of his life.[28] When Solms conveniently died in April 1814, no divorce was needed: Frederica was free to accept Ernest's courtship and proposal of marriage. Queen Charlotte wrote to congratulate her son on his choice of her niece as his bride and enthusiastically welcomed the forthcoming marriage.[23] Then, inexplicably, she changed her mind. Ernest returned home to marry in 1815, but his mother refused to attend the wedding, or ever to receive the new Duchess. It was required of the Princesses, her daughters, to act in like manner. What happened to cause the Queen's sudden and implacable change of heart may be a secret to be discovered some day in the Royal Archives – or perhaps the evidence has been destroyed. In spite of the humiliation and social isolation caused by the Queen, Ernest was reluctant to escape to the continent once again, so for the first few years of the marriage the couple made their home in Kew, where he had always been held in respect. Frederica's agreeable personality and perfect manners endeared her to the public, and when in 1817 she became dangerously ill giving birth to a stillborn daughter there was widespread sympathy for her.

Another birth in the same year was to have more significant repercussions: the Regent's daughter, Princess Charlotte, George III's only legitimate grandchild, died aged 21 in November after giving birth to a stillborn son. The future of the monarchy was suddenly thrown into disarray. All hopes for the succession had rested on Charlotte, and with her marriage to Prince Leopold of Saxe-Coburg-Saalfeld and her subsequent pregnancy all seemed to be well. Now, with no possibility of the Prince Regent fathering a second heir, nor of his brother the Duke of York becoming a father after 27 years of marriage, the remaining royal Dukes all felt duty-bound to produce some legitimate offspring. Ernest's brothers, William, Duke of Clarence, Edward, Duke of Kent, and Adolphus, Duke of Cambridge, hastily sought suitable non-Catholic princesses, and, in an unseemly rush, the three of them married in the summer of 1818 at their mother's residence, Kew Palace. The four Dukes then applied to Parliament for increased allowances in recognition of their married state; these were reluctantly granted for all but Ernest, whose request had been turned down previously in 1815. He was not surprised when it was refused again. In the circumstances Ernest felt he could not remain in England with his wife, and established his household in Berlin, where he and Frederica lived happily, and, as he frequently observed, far more cheaply than in England. Ironically his mother, Queen Charlotte, who had caused the couple so much humiliation, died a few months later. Meanwhile efforts were made to provide a new generation of royal children. William was heir to the throne after his brothers George, the Prince Regent, and Frederick of York, but his wife Adelaide, Duchess of Clarence, suffered a miscarriage and two infant deaths. Fortunately, both Edward and Ernest, the next two in line, had births to announce in May 1819: Princess (Alexandrina) Victoria of Kent on the 24th, and Prince George of Cumberland just three days later. The birth of the Princess Victoria was particularly timely; her father the Duke of Kent died on 23rd January 1820, her grandfather George III six days later.

Notes

1. Roberts, W, *Sir William Beechey, RA*, Duckworth, 1907, p 108 and p 218.
2. WCRO: CR 0341/328/1-3.
3. Lewisham Local Studies and Archives: A90/7/56.
4. Craig, W M, *Memoir of Her Majesty Sophia Charlotte of Mecklenburg-Strelitz, Queen of Great Britain*, Caxton Press, London, 1818, p 77.
5. British Museum Satires, 11864; published in 'The Scourge' iii, 259, 1 April 1812.
6. National Portrait Gallery, D38014.
7. Letter from Lady Mary Howe to her sister Louisa Catherine, then Lady Altamont, begun 2 July 1794 and completed 4 July 1794, quoted in Sir John Barrow's *Life of Richard, Earl Howe, Admiral of the Fleet*, John Murray, 1838.
8. Aspinall, A (ed), *Later Correspondence of King George III*, Vol 1, Letter 2134, p 336, Duchess of Württemberg to the King.
9. Aspinall, A (ed), *Letters of the Prince of Wales*, Vol 5, pp 176-7, Letters 2001, 2002, 2005, January 17-25 1805.
10. Bodleian Library, University of Oxford: Additional Papers of Harcourt Family, D.Shelfmark MS.Eng.3880 (fols 86-118). Leonora Dee, daughter of the Vice-Consul at Belem, Portugal, had come to England with her sister, (Deborah) Charlotte Johnstone, in 1782. Charlotte had married Commodore George Johnstone in Lisbon that year. In 1790 she married her second husband, Captain Charles Edmund Nugent RN. Charlotte Nugent's significance in this narrative will become apparent later on.
11. Gainsborough's 1764 portrait of The Countess Howe, the Baroness's mother, is one of his best known and most highly regarded works.
12. Written by Viscount Cranley, son of the Earl of Onslow, and published in *The poetical note book and epigrammatic museum*, ed G Wentworth, 1824 [Hymen was the Greek god of marriage]. Wathen was perhaps quite amused by these verses as he included them in his Commonplace Book.

13. *Royal Intrigues and Amours of Many Illustrious Persons related to the Court of St J[ames]'s*, by a distinguished Courtier [John Mitford], London 1830, pp 85-6.

14. East Sussex Record Office: AMS 5440/426/3. Lord Sheffield's second wife was Lady Anne North, daughter of the former Prime Minister, Lord North.

15. TNA: C13/151/36.

16. WCRO: CR 0341/238 Grant of royal licence to Jonathan Wathen Phipps to assume the name and arms of Waller, 26 Feb 1814.

17. WCRO: CR 0341/10 Letters patent creating Jonathan Wathen Waller a baronet, 30 May 1815.

18. Braywick Lodge, formerly the property of Thomas Slack, Wathen's father-in-law.

19. Thorne, James: *Handbook to the environs of London*, 1876, Vol 2.

20. Anonymous article *"Titles"* in *The Polar Star*, London 1830, p 265.

21. In Richmond, Surrey.

22. Godsall, J R, *The tangled web*, Troubador 2008, p 13. The School was established in 1764 by Charles Delafosse, father of Robert Mark and grandfather of Daniel Charles.

23. WCRO: CR 0341/327/1. There were several Horace and Robert Walpoles. The Horace in question here was probably the sixth son of Robert Walpole, Ambassador to Portugal 1771-1800, who was a nephew of the Prime Minister of that name and first cousin to Horace Walpole of Strawberry Hill. This young Horace was born 27 August 1799 and entered Corpus Christi College, Cambridge, in the Lent term 1817, so he may well have been a prefect or a tutor at the school in 1815. The Walpole and Delafosse families were close, and the eldest son of Daniel Charles Delafosse was named Charles Walpole Delafosse.

24. Cornwall RO: X.673/16-23. Extracts of letters from the King of Hanover to the Revd D.C. Delafosse.

25. Godsall, J R, op.cit. p 13.

26. The Duke was a Trustee of the Will of Sir John Lowther Johnstone, former MP of Weymouth who had inherited considerable properties in Weymouth. The Johnstone family or their associates had represented the constituency for decades. The Duke was involved in this matter on account of a relationship that he managed to keep virtually secret during his life time (see Appendix).

27. The date, 20 May 1813, was to prove significant to the Duke in quite another context, though he was unaware of it at the time.

28. Willis, G M, *Ernest Augustus, Duke of Cumberland, King of Hanover*, London 1954, p 104: Letter from Duke of Cumberland to his wife, dated 20 May 1836, 23 years after they first met. "That moment is as alive in my memory as if it were yesterday. I see you at the head of the staircase, *you*, the old grandmamma and the ladies, and then there was a serenade from the musicians in the flower-gardens under my windows. What a superb night, and one caught the scent of the flowers…. I can say with the greatest truth that that was the most beautiful and happiest moment of my life".

Chapter 5

Pope's Villa, Twickenham

"Walked with Mrs D[amer] to Sir Wathen Waller's to see the wonderful collection of old Sèvres china at his house in Twickenham, to which he has added I know not how many rooms, all filled with china, the finest I have ever seen, even in France; he had also a quantity of valuable French furniture of all sorts."

Mary Berry

Braywick Lodge in Berkshire came into Wathen's possession from the estate of his late father-in-law, Thomas Slack (by inheritance or purchase). He never lived there and owned it only briefly, but the baronetcy was to retain the name and association as long as it survived. After his marriage, Wathen's principal residence and country seat became Lady Howe's home near the Thames at Twickenham, conveniently situated between the royal palace at Kew and Windsor Castle, and not too far from "Town" and the Court at St James's Palace. Twickenham was rapidly coming into fashion (and within a few years was mentioned by Jane Austen in *Emma* and *Mansfield Park* as a desirable rural location). Nearby Richmond and Petersham had long been popular among the wealthy and influential. The Baroness's mansion was built between 1807 and 1810, with pointed arch windows in imitation of the nearby neo-gothic castle, Strawberry Hill. She named it – apparently without irony – "Pope's Villa", although she had demolished the fine Palladian villa which had been owned by the poet Alexander Pope. Her "vandalism" caused outrage in the locality.[1] JMW Turner, a Twickenham neighbour, expressed his dismay by painting a riverside scene showing Pope's Villa in process of demolition.[2] John Bew, having mentioned Lady Howe's residence as one of the sights of Twickenham (in 1820), went on: "nearly adjacent …. was the villa of Pope, which the Baroness – on whose uncongenial spirit the softer graces of Poesy never shed their sweetly-attempering influence – needlessly levelled with the ground some years ago".[3] The Baroness clearly appreciated the agreeable riverside location, described by a visitor as "the happiest spot imaginable", but she could not tolerate tourists turning up to honour the dead poet; some even made cuttings from the famous willow tree he was said to have planted himself. She did, however, spare the underground grotto which linked the two parts of Pope's garden, and it remains *in situ* to this day.

Lady Howe had settled in Twickenham in a rented property soon after her first husband's death, and was immediately welcomed as a friend and neighbour into the circle of another widow, the sculptress Mrs Damer (the Honourable Anne Seymour Damer) to whom the writer Horace Walpole had bequeathed – for her lifetime – his extravagantly decorated mansion at Strawberry Hill. In his heyday Walpole had greatly enjoyed entertaining the literary, artistic and social élite with Anne, his young kinswoman (daughter of his first cousin General Conway), acting as his hostess, along with the Misses Berry, Mary and Agnes, well-educated and well-travelled young women to whom he took a great liking, providing them with a cottage named Little Strawberry Hill. They discussed the Arts and the philosophical preoccupations of the times as befitted the Age of Enlightenment, with a good measure of gossip thrown in, especially on Walpole's part. After the death of their benefactor, Mary Berry and her sister continued to hold *salons,* similar to those of her much admired "blue-stocking" friend Madame de Staël; the conversation centred mainly on the latest literary publications, current events and other intellectual topics and pursuits. On November 12th 1799 Mary noted in her journal that Lady Howe, a new neighbour, often visited them in the evenings at Little Strawberry Hill. A few days earlier the Baroness had attended a Drawing Room held by Queen Charlotte and had been struck by all the poor officers home from active duty who "looked very thin and weather-beaten, and none of them much liked talking of their adventures…never was there such deadly fighting……"[4]

When they met up in the summer of 1802, Mrs Damer and the Misses Berry had a great deal to tell the Baroness. Anne Damer had been taken by surprise by a letter of invitation from her old acquaintance Josephine, now the wife of Napoleon Bonaparte, the First Consul. She had first met Josephine more than twenty years earlier, soon after her marriage to Alexandre Beauharnais (who was guillotined during the Reign of Terror in 1794). Fortunately the Peace negotiations taking place at Amiens afforded a brief period of respite in the long-term conflict with the French, so with her two companions – inveterate travellers – Anne set off for Paris, eager to meet Bonaparte, whom she greatly admired.[5] Napoleon knew her to be a friend and supporter of the Whig statesman, Charles Fox, the "Man of the People", with whom he hoped to make contact, and asked her to sculpt a bust of Fox for him, to her great delight. She also hoped to sculpt Napoleon himself, though the opportunity never presented itself. (She did, however, sculpt another of her heroes, Lord Nelson, on his return from the Battle of the Nile.) Many years later she delivered the completed bust of Fox to Napoleon and received from him a "souvenir" gift, "a box in gold, enamelled, of an oval form, which has on the top, outside, a portrait of the Emperor Napoleon, within a circlet of twenty-seven brilliants." Mrs Damer bequeathed the box to the British Museum, and there it remains. Her "much valued friend", Sir Wathen Waller, named in her Will as her sole Executor and Trustee,[6] was responsible for carrying out her wishes.

Although Anne Damer and Mary Berry were generally like-minded and were both fervent Whigs, Mary did not share her friend's hero-worship of Napoleon. She rejoiced when his fortunes finally waned in 1815: "You little thought that your friend at Paris would be in England before yourself, and that your bust may return to that country it never ought to have left, without going out of the possession of the person to whom you gave it. Before I close this letter to-morrow, we shall probably have heard of his arrival in an English port… The state of France appears almost as wretched as ever. They have got rid of Bonaparte, it is true; but when will they get rid of the moral degradation which his reign fixed on them?" [7]

Mary Berry became Horace Walpole's literary executrix, and (under her father's name) edited several volumes of his writings. Mrs Damer retained some of his correspondence, however, including letters exchanged with Horace Mann. Walpole had requested that after his death these should be given to Sir Horace Mann the younger, but Anne Damer ignored his wishes and handed them to Wathen. The whereabouts of most of them is unknown, a few were sold and some may have been destroyed. A collection of more than a hundred letters to Walpole from the poet Thomas Gray, a friend since Eton days, was passed down in the Waller family and eventually sold in the twentieth century at a leading London auction house. [8]

Soon after settling in Twickenham, Lady Howe became acquainted with Louis-Philippe, Duc d'Orléans, an exiled member of the French royal family who arrived in England in 1800 having lost his money and estates in the Revolution. He spent the next seven years living frugally in Twickenham with his two younger brothers. They had fled France in 1793 and had travelled to Switzerland, Scandinavia, America and Canada before settling in England and renting a cottage. Their father, the former Duke of Orleans, also known as Citizen Philippe Égalité, had been an unlikely supporter of the revolution despite his royal blood and his residence at the *Palais Royal*. He had even voted in favour of the execution of his cousin Louis XVI, but was himself guillotined in 1793. In later life, Louis-Philippe remembered his period of "poverty" in Twickenham as a happy time, until it was marred by the illness and death of his brother, the Duc de Montpensier, on 18th May 1807. Although a Catholic, the young Duke was afforded a dignified and ceremonious burial in Westminster Abbey, attended not only by French émigré aristocrats, but also the Dukes of Sussex and York, and the Prince of Wales. [9] When his second brother's health began to fail in 1808, Louis-Philippe decided to move him to Malta's milder climate, but failed to prevent his decline and death soon after they arrived in Valetta. From there he moved to Palermo, where in 1809 he married Maria Amalia, third surviving daughter of King Ferdinand of Naples and Sicily and Queen Maria Carolina (a sister of Marie-Antoinette). The Duke and Duchess of Orleans raised their family peacefully in Sicily until Napoleon's abdication and exile to Elba in 1814 prompted a return to France, where Louis-Philippe managed to recover some of his fortune and properties. He had barely had time to establish the family on French soil, however, when Napoleon escaped and re-asserted his authority as Emperor. Once again Louis-Philippe sought refuge in "dear old Twick", this time living as his rank and status demanded in a substantial mansion which came to be known as Orleans House. Sir Wathen, now married to his Baroness, had in the meantime joined Twickenham society and was soon on visiting terms with the royal neighbour. The second, more comfortable, period of exile for Louis-Philippe was to last only two years: by April 1817 he felt confident enough to install his young family in their Neuilly estate in Paris, and on 16th June he wrote to Wathen and Lady Howe apologising for not receiving them there during their recent visit, on account of the Duchess's confinement. (Princess Clementine, their sixth child, was born at Neuilly on 3rd June.) He hoped they would be returning within a month, when, he assured them, he would receive them and have their company at dinner.[10]

By virtue of their acceptance as members of the Prince Regent's Carlton House set, Wathen and Lady Howe had numerous opportunities to admire the lavish furnishings of the royal palace. They were undoubtedly influenced by what they saw and – consciously or unconsciously – began to emulate the Prince's taste. They took great pleasure in furnishing the Twickenham mansion, Pope's Villa, to the highest standards, making frequent buying trips to France, where the most fashionable and most sought after items were to be found. (Some notion of the huge quantities of fine furniture and ornaments they acquired can be gained from a series of sale catalogues eventually drawn up to dispose of their possessions after their deaths.) We know that they did make a second trip to Paris in 1817, because Princess Sophia, the fifth daughter of George III, wrote to Wathen in November that year requesting him to take with him a French clock to be repaired for her as there was something wrong with its striking mechanism.[11] No doubt they were received at Neuilly, as was another Twickenham friend, Mary Berry, who, with her customary attention to detail, described the experience in her journal: "Wednesday 10th [July 1822]. Dined at Neuilly with the Duc d'Orléans…. A dinner of thirty covers. The silver service was magnificent – quite new, consequently not in such good taste as the old. The épergne and decorations all in ormolu; vases &c., ornamented with flowers – superb, but in too many small pieces and small figures; the dessert service, silver gilt and glass. The large baskets were very handsome, and of exquisite workmanship. The dining-room, a gallery well ventilated, and very pleasant. On returning to the drawing-room, we found all the children there (except the two little ones), to the number six – three sons and three daughters; one cannot see a finer family, not one which appears better brought up, nor more at ease with their parents……. It was very fine weather; and as the drawing-room opened into the garden, everyone went out, and the Duc d'Orléans proposed a walk… We passed by the little bridges to the small islands on the Seine, and I have not seen in France a garden and grounds so well planned, so well laid out, nor so well kept up, as at Neuilly. It would be a very charming villa in any country: and though built as a pavilion, which makes it very pretty outside, in the interior it contains rooms so high and large as to look like a palace……".[12]

Despite decades of political hostility to France since the Revolution, and intermittent wars, certain aspects of French culture remained much admired in England. French furniture and Sèvres porcelain were considered of the best quality and the most refined taste, and Sir Wathen and his wife had the means to acquire them. They again spent some time in Paris in the summer of 1820, taking up residence in the Hôtel de l'Empire, rue d'Artois,[13] for the purpose of buying furniture and china for Pope's Villa, including some former possessions of the late Empress Josephine.[14] The Prince Regent had finally become King, his poor blind, deaf and "mad" father, having outlasted his consort, Queen Charlotte, by two years. At the age of 42, Princess Sophia, freed from her role of dutiful daughter, was at last able to envisage a household of her own and excitedly took the opportunity to commission Wathen to buy numerous articles on her behalf: "It is wholly out of my power to say how very very sensible I am of all your kindness & anxiety to procure what may suit me – You are so exact in your accounts & the <u>portrait</u> you give of the Pier Tables so <u>very very</u> tempting that I must say, <u>buy</u> <u>them</u> & <u>keep</u> them snug for me – I have read the calculations & I think you may extend your purchases to <u>£350</u> altogether which if I am correct will give you after paying the Tables at 83 each £34 more to spend in whatever your fancy may please, for as I said before, I can see your taste is excellent & I had rather have less & that little really good – I am rejoiced to find dear Lady Howe continues to enjoy herself & that her health is good – Do pray give her many many loves from me." [15] Buying by proxy entailed much clarification of instructions, and a flurry of letters was exchanged that summer between Paris and London. "I like the idea of the candelabras & vases for the pier tables & all I beg is you will get them handsome & should you not consider the candelabras you have already purchased as sufficiently fine for the tables, I rely on your getting others and the vases <u>paid</u>, therefore if you want more money or should you meet with any thing well worth my purchase only let me know & I will answer at once; it w^d be a sin by your report of the pier tables not to have the whole <u>perfect</u>." [16]

Wathen's pocket-sized notebook for his "Purchases in Paris" survives in the Waller Collection;[17] in it he listed meticulously the items and their prices, and – in the case of commissions – for whom they had been bought. For Princess Sophia there were forty-seven expensive items. Wathen also bought vases for his daughter's mother-in-law Mrs Jarrett, for Princess Elizabeth, and for his stepson Lord Howe and his wife. On the last page of his notebook he recorded a payment of 3,600 francs for several panes of stained glass from "*St Chapel*" (no less a place than *la Sainte Chapelle*, on l'Ile de la Cité in Paris, the only part of the 13th century royal palace still standing). The chapel had suffered some vandalism during the French revolution, and Sir Wathen may have known better than to ask how the vendor had come by such priceless works of art. He was aware, however, that the opportunity to acquire such glass would never occur again, and so took advantage of his good fortune without hesitation. It would make a splendid gift for one of his royal friends.[18]

Despite her apparent willingness to send more money, Princess Sophia was unable to repay Wathen immediately. She had little previous experience of managing money, and had apparently splashed out excessively once granted her freedom, even adding luxurious perfume to the already extensive shopping list. Although her brother the King had raised her allowance, Sophia had fallen victim to some smooth-talking fraudsters and was obliged to postpone repayment more than once, to her evident embarrassment, as is shown in this extract from a letter dated 12 December 1821: "I really feel ashamed at the delay of payment between us; but the calls have been so great that should you allow me to trespass a little further & ask you to let me name April as the fixed period for refunding the sum you laid out for me, you will greatly & essentially oblige me. I am happy to hear good accounts of dear Lady Howe from my sister Mary [Duchess of Gloucester] but very sorry to learn of your having suffered so much from your old complaint – I hope it is eased by this time & I beg you will believe how ready I am at all times to oblige you if in my power, being very truly, your sincere friend Sophy." [19] She finally paid off her debt in April 1822. The "old complaint" mentioned here, she elsewhere calls "tic douloureux" (trigeminal neuralgia), an extremely painful nerve disorder intermittently causing a spasmodic stabbing sensation to one side of the face. Wathen suffered from it for the rest of his life, depending on ever-larger doses of laudanum to ease the pain.

Pope's Villa was not far from Bushy House, home of the Duke of Clarence (later William IV) who lived there first with his mistress Mrs Jordan and their brood of ten children, and subsequently with his wife Adelaide from their marriage in 1818 until his accession in 1830. Since they were all on visiting terms, the Villa had to be quite literally fit for a King. The former Mr Phipps prided himself on providing lavish entertainment from time to time for the royal family and more frequently for the nobility and society of the area. There were dinners, receptions and balls, opportunities to dress in all their finery and show off their exquisite furniture, china and objets d'art. There were also open evenings, when anyone could join in the celebrations.

Mary Berry was thoroughly impressed: "Saturday 14th [August 1824]. Walked with Mrs D[amer] to Sir Wathen Waller's to see the wonderful collection of old

Sèvres china at his house in Twickenham, to which he has added I know not how many rooms, all filled with china, the finest I have ever seen, even in France; he had also a quantity of valuable French furniture of all sorts."[20]

From time to time an item from Pope's Villa still crops up at a leading auction house or an exhibition, providing a rare glimpse of the exceptionally fine quality of the Waller-Howe possessions. A sumptuous cabinet with thirty-four Sèvres porcelain plaques is currently in the collection of the Metropolitan Museum of Art in New York. In 2007, a pair of flamboyant gilt-bronze candlesticks commissioned by Sir Wathen from Pierre Philippe Thomire of Paris, formerly Napoleon's *ciseleur-fondeur-doreur,* were sold at Sotheby's. No doubt they graced the dining table on every grand occasion at Pope's Villa. They are decorated with a Waller coat of arms flanked by two knights, a banner engraved "Azincourt" and the motto "haec fructus virtutis". Along with his baronetcy, Sir Wathen had been granted a coat of arms and had devised it to emphasize his presumed descent from Sir Richard Waller, one of Henry V's "band of brothers". According to legend and family tradition, Sir Richard had accepted the surrender of Charles, Duke of Orleans at the Battle of Agincourt in 1415 and held him captive for twenty-five years at his moated manor house at Groombridge, in the parish of Speldhurst, Kent. Anxious to lay claim to a distinguished pedigree, Sir Wathen applied himself to some serious genealogical research, apparently tracing the family back through twenty-four generations as far as Alured de Waler of Newark (of Norman descent), who is mentioned in the Domesday Book.[21] Wishful thinking may have fuelled Sir Wathen's research, but his diligence is not in doubt: much of his correspondence on the subject survives. The resultant family tree was formally copied on to a vast sheet of gilt-edged paper, and illustrated with the relevant coats of arms. Sir Wathen then erected a memorial tablet in St Mary's Church, Speldhurst, proudly setting out the Waller pedigree and commemorating his ancestors. The candlesticks emblazoned with heraldic devices similarly celebrate this family history.

There is no doubt that Wathen and his wife were for a time the stars of Twickenham society, respected, admired, and fawned upon. As "patrons" their names appeared on the Richmond Theatre playbills. They were local celebrities – fashionable and very well-connected. Yet Wathen could sometimes appear a caricature of the kind of person he aimed to be – possibly because he was not born to a life of such opulence and strove too hard to match his acquaintances in the social circles now open to him. Taking care to distance himself from the incident, one guest, Grantley Fitzhardinge Berkeley, describes an occasion in which the Waller-Howe hospitality was cruelly abused: "Our host of those days at Pope's Villa was most hospitable but he always marred his wealth and lavish profusion by some excessively pompous vulgarity that set his guests rather mischievously against him;

and hence the most reprehensible trick played by two friends of mine, now no more, the perpetration of which was unknown to me at the time – of opening a lot of sandwiches on the refreshment table at one of his balls, and sticking the several and greasy contents of them between the valuable and illuminated leaves of a very handsomely-bound book, to its utter destruction. I never either sanctioned or indulged in such practical and ruinous jokes as these; and had I felt personally offended at anything my host had said to me, as one of his guests collectively or individually, I should simply have abstained from going to Pope's Villa again." [22]

Lord Byron might seem a rather unlikely dinner guest to be found at the table of Lady Howe and her husband, but a charming anecdote from a Victorian memoir places him at Pope's Villa accompanied by his good friends the poet Samuel Rogers, and the Irish song-writer and playwright Thomas Moore.[23] Some thirty years after the event, Rogers described a conversation between the three of them while dining at Pope's Villa. It clearly made an impression on him at the time. The topic under discussion was fame. As they exchanged views, singing was heard in the distance, and soon a boat full of people floated past. They were singing "Love's young dream". Byron put a hand on his friend's shoulder, saying: "There, that is fame." (The song was one of Moore's ballads, and the title phrase lives on a couple of centuries later, though its author is largely forgotten.)

It might cynically be supposed that Wathen had married the Baroness purely as a means of enriching himself and securing social advancement. However, a short poem he addressed to her at New Year in 1827, suggests that it was genuinely a love match:

> *"To Her who surely ought to know*
> *All that in my Heart doth glow,*
> *To Her who many a Year hath been*
> *Bone of my Bone, Skin of my Skin;*
> *This little New Year's Gift I send,*
> *To Her my Love, my Wife, my Friend,*
> *Till Years shall cease & Seasons end."*
> JWW. [24]

Lady Howe gave Pope's Villa to Wathen early in their marriage, but he later claimed he had never liked the house, and he sold it as soon as he could after his wife's death in 1835.[25] By then the estate had expanded to cover 147 acres – with extensive gardens, orchards, outbuildings and a farm. Part of the land was divided into lots for building, being "most desirably situate and admirably adapted for the erection of villas." Rural Twickenham was thus reinvented as suburbia.[26]

Notes

1. Cobbett, R S, *Memorials of Twickenham*, Smith, Elder & Co 1872, p 288:
    [Lady Howe] *razed the house to the ground and blotted out utterly every memorial of the poet. For this act she has been roundly abused by every writer on the subject; and it is impossible to excuse so bold an act of vandalism. "It might have been hoped, nay, might have been expected, that Pope's house and gardens would have been purchased and held sacred by some kindred character, and that the vaticination which follows would have been fulfilled:*
    > *Grateful posterity, from age to age,*
    > *With pious hand the ruin shall repair,*
    > *Some good old man, to each enquiring sage,*
    > *Pointing the place, shall cry: the bard lived there."*
    Here Cobbett quotes from *Lady Howe's Villa* in Cooke's *Thames Scenery*.
    Berry, Mary: *Journal*, 21 November 1807: *"we went into Pope's back garden, and saw the devastation going on upon his 'quincunx' by its new possessor, Baroness Howe."*

2. J.M.W. Turner's *"View of Pope's Villa during its dilapidation"* (1808) was sold at Sotheby's for £5.4 million in July 2008, and exported to the US when no British gallery offered a similar sum to retain the picture in the UK. Turner also drafted a verse, which (perhaps wisely) he left unfinished:
    > *"O lost to honour and the sense of shame*
    > *Can Britain so forget Pope's well earned fame*
    > *To desolation doom the poet's fane*
    > *The pride of Twickenham's bower and silver Thame."*
    Wilton, Andrew: *Painting and Poetry: Turner's verse book and his work of 1804-1812* Tate Gallery, 1990.

3. Bew, Jon, *The Ambulator*, 1820, p 320.

4. Berry, Mary, *Extracts of the journals & correspondence of Miss Berry, 1783-1852,* ed. Lady Theresa Lewis, Vol 2, p 103.

5. Thomson, Mrs M T, & Wharton, Philip, *The Queens of Society*, 1860, pp 394-5.

6. WCRO: CR 0341/237. Wathen knew Mrs Damer by 1805 (seven years before his marriage to Lady Howe) when she gave him a ring, said to date from the reign of Edward IV, as a birthday present.

7. Berry, Mary, op.cit. Vol 3, pp 63-4n.

8. Waller Sales were held at Sotheby's 5/6 December 1921, and at Christie's 15 December 1947.

9. *Biographical Memoirs of Louis-Philippe the first, King of the French, with a Sketch of the Revolutions of 1830 and 1848*, Cradock, London 1848. Louis-Philippe commissioned a monument for his brother with the following inscription: *"The most illustrious and Serene Prince Anthony Philip, Duke of Montpensier, descended from the Kings of France, second son of the Duke of Orleans, from his earliest youth bred to arms, and even in chains unsubdued, of an erect mind in adversity, and in prosperity not elated; a constant patron of*

the liberal arts, polite, pleasant and courteous to all, nor ever wanting in the duties of a brother, neighbour, friend, or the love of his country. After experiencing the vicissitudes of fortune, he was received with great hospitality by the English nation, and at length rests in this asylum for kings. Born July 3, 1775. Died May 18, 1807, aged thirty-one. Louis-Philip Duke of Orleans erects this monument in memory of the best of brothers." (From *A historical description of Westminster Abbey, its monuments and curiosities*, Newman 1827.)

10. WCRO: CR0341/212, Louis-Philippe to JWW, 16 June 1817.
11. WCRO: CR0341/157, Princess Sophia to JWW, 25 November 1817.
12. Berry, Mary, op.cit. Vol 3, pp 317-318.
13. Wellcome MS 7826/21.
14. *A Guide to the Knowledge of Pottery, Porcelain and other objects of virtue*, p 45 catalogue of sale of items from the collection of Ralph Bernal beginning 5 March 1856. "*Lot 599. A magnificent centre vase and cover: Gros bleu with upright handles, of foliage, a festoon of leaves raised, gilt, encircling the vase and falling over the handles, the lower part fluted with pendant lines of leaves; in the centre is a most exquisite painting of a peasant and two girls gathering cherries, a donkey with panniers filled with cherries at their side, a group of flowers on the reverse – on square plinth……. From the collection of Sir Wathen Waller who most probably purchased it at the Empress Josephine's sale in Paris after her death.*" See also Marryat, Joseph: *A history of pottery & porcelain, medieval and modern*, pub John Murray, 1868. "*At the sale of the late Colonel Hugh Baillie in March 1857, a pair of magnificent turquoise vases and covers, with white and gold flutings and handles, formerly the property of Madame de Pompadour, purchased at Sir Wathen Waller's sale, fetched 410 guineas.*"
15. WCRO: CR 0341/178, Princess Sophia to JWW, undated.
16. WCRO: CR 0341/160, Princess Sophia to JWW, 28 July 1820.
17. WCRO: CR0341/264.
18. Sir Wathen presented the stained glass to William IV who gave it to Lord Howe. It was used in the refurbishment of the East window of Twycross Church on Lord Howe's Gopsal Estate in Leicestershire.
19. WCRO: CR 0341/162, Princess Sophia to JWW, 12 December 1821.
20. Berry, Mary, op.cit. Vol 3, p 354.
21. Sir Wathen's version of the Waller Pedigree is along these lines: "*The ancient family of Waller derives from Alured de Waller, of Newark, in the county of Nottingham, who d. in 1183, (see Domesday Book), and from whom lineally descended David de Waller, master of the rolls to King Edward III for thirty years. This David d. issueless; but from his only brother, Henry Waller, sprang John Waller, of Groombridge, in the county of Kent, who m. the daughter and heiress of Landsdall, esq. of Lansdall, in Sussex, and was father of Richard Waller, a gallant participator in the glories of Agincourt, who, in honor of having made prisoner the Duke of Orleans in that memorable conflict, obtained, from Henry V the*

addition to his crest, of a shield of the arms of the duke, pendent from the sinister side of a walnut tree, which his descendants have ever since borne. The French prince having been brought to England, was confined at Mr. Waller's seat, at Groombridge. The grandson and direct successor of this gentleman, John Waller, esq. of Groombridge, m. Anne, daughter of William Whetenhall, esq., and dying in 1517 left two sons, William, his successor [and] John, ancestors of the Wallers of Beaconsfield, in the county of Bucks; of which family was Edmund Waller, the poet." (Burke, John, *A General and Heraldic Dictionary of the Peerage and Baronetage of the British Empire*, pub. H. Colburn and R. Bentley, 1832, v. 2, p 581-582.)

22. Berkley, G F, *My Life and Recollections*, Hurst & Blackett, 1865, Vol 1 p 194.

23. Richmond Local Studies Collection, extract from Ross, Janet, "Early days recalled" 1891, re-telling an anecdote related to her parents by Rogers in 1848.

24. WCRO: CR 0341/257.

25. Pope's Villa was advertised for sale in *The Times* of 27th January 1840, and shortly afterwards the building materials from the house, including 400,000 bricks and eleven tons of lead. The outside wings were taken down and the central portion divided into two houses.

26. Richmond Local Studies Collection: Leaflet advertising the sale of lots on Pope's Villa Estate on 29 August 1843.

Chapter 6

Children and step-children; royal friends at home and abroad

"my regard & friendship for you are the same as ever……."

Ernest, Duke of Cumberland

From 1832 onwards, we can almost feel that we know Wathen's younger daughter Anna, so informative and vivid are her fortnightly letters describing her daily life to her absent brother Thomas (see Chapters 10 – 14). Always candid, Anna has frequent changes of mood: she is philosophical, frivolous, anxious and delighted by turns. Her words bring to life for the twenty-first century reader one woman's first-hand experience of a bygone era. Although the correspondence is one-sided, much can be gathered about Thomas's movements, his work, friends, thoughts and preoccupations. Ernest Waller also wrote to his brother from time to time with news of his own, and a contrasting perspective on events. But in the interval before the stream of letters begins, Wathen and Charlotte's children and step-children grew up together at Pope's Villa – at least in school holidays – on the fringes of the royal circle which absorbed so much of their parents' time and attention. In this unusual setting, where Court and private life continually overlapped, they gradually began to make their way in the world, and establish independent lives of their own. All but one, that is: Marianne Curzon died at Pope's Villa in 1820.

Little is known about Marianne, except that she had an interest in art and poetry, and particularly enjoyed drawing and painting, often signing her work with her nickname "Mink". Among the few items surviving to shed some light on her personality is a batch of satirical sketches, mainly caricatures of her mother's sister, Aunt Louisa (the Dowager Marchioness of Sligo), and her cousin, Howe Peter Browne, second Marquess of Sligo. Both are depicted as enormously fat[1] (presumably a humorous exaggeration, as Louisa had been a glamorous society beauty in her day). Marianne was probably rather delicate, as she wrote her Will at the tender age of 23, eighteen months after her mother's second marriage. In it she left numerous specific bequests, including £100 each to Wathen Phipps and his four children, and the same sum to Louisa.[2] However, she was to outlive her aunt, whom she accompanied to Holland in October 1817 on a shopping trip. They intended to choose furnishings for Howe Peter's splendid mansion in Ireland. Louisa's second husband, Sir William Scott, had been spending a few months in Switzerland, and she planned to meet him in Amsterdam on his way home. However, the meeting never took place; in November she was taken ill, and died a few days later before Sir William could reach her. Her niece "administered all possible consolation and assistance on this trying occasion",[3] to no avail. Marianne lived on for three more years, dying at Pope's Villa at the age of 29, just a month before her brother Richard was married. Within weeks a third death in the family was announced: Viscount Curzon died in Lower Brook Street, Westminster, aged 90. By coincidence, Richard, the Baroness's only remaining child, inherited the Curzon viscountcy on 21 March 1820, just two days after marrying Lady Harriet Georgiana Brudenell, second daughter of the 6th Lord Cardigan (and sister of the officer in later life notorious for ordering the Charge of the Light Brigade in the Crimean War). After taking the additional name Howe by royal licence in the following year, Richard was briefly known as Lord Curzon-Howe, until the Baroness prevailed upon the new King, George IV, to re-create her father's earldom for her son; thereafter he bore the title Earl Howe. He served as a Lord of the Bedchamber to the king in the last year of his reign.

Meanwhile Wathen's sons, Thomas and Ernest, progressed to Harrow School, following in the footsteps of Lady Howe's firstborn son, George Augustus, who had been enrolled in the same intake as Lord Byron. The Waller boys subsequently went up to Oxford. The *Alumni Oxoniensis* lists the matriculation dates at Brasenose College, Oxford, of Thomas Wathen Waller, 23 October 1822, and Ernest Adolphus Waller, 4 June 1825. Thomas left Oxford without a degree, but his brother duly graduated (BA 1829, MA 1832) and was ordained as an Anglican clergyman (deacon 1830, priest 1832), and took an unpaid curacy in Pett, Sussex, from December 1830 to 1832.[4] We know nothing of the education of their sisters Georgiana and Anna, which may have been at home or at school, but it was evidently thorough. They were well read, and highly literate in French as well as English. Serious-minded by disposition, they digested heavy theological tomes, and kept abreast of the politics and economics of the day. In her teens Anna wrote poems, some of which survive, but her favourite pastime was music; she was a talented pianist and an avid concert-goer. The girls acquired all the feminine accomplishments and social graces of their class, making them presentable in any company, and at ease dining with dukes. In true Jane Austenish fashion they could dance, sing and converse wittily at receptions and balls in grand country houses.

In 1823, at the age of twenty, Anna Waller married John Jarrett, an old Etonian who had inherited from his father, Herbert Newton Jarrett, substantial sugar plantations in Jamaica – complete with slaves, overseers and managers. John received his income as an absentee landlord, and never set foot in the West Indies.

The family was well connected, John's paternal grandfather, also John Jarrett, having been a friend of the Prince of Wales and of George III, whom he visited in Weymouth on his yacht, *Liberty*.[5] Anna had accepted John's proposal of marriage on the specific condition that she would not have to live with her widowed mother-in-law, Anne Jarrett, who had inherited from her father James Stephens the Manor at Camerton in Somerset with several farms and coalfields. Anna had evidently lived quite long enough with a dominant older woman, and was keen to take charge of her own household. The marriage took place at St George's, Hanover Square, with Anna's uncle the Reverend Thomas White officiating.[6] The young couple set up home in stately rented accommodation in Hampshire, first at Marelands House, Bentley, near Farnham, and later at Hale House in the New Forest, moving to Camerton only after the death of John's mother. There John lived the life of a country gentleman with hunting, shooting and fishing as his principal pursuits, though he served the local community as a conscientious and fair-minded magistrate, and as Deputy Lieutenant of Somerset.

Wathen's elder daughter, Georgiana, would later marry a widowed clergyman, the Reverend Sainsbury Langford Sainsbury, Vicar of Froyle, near Bentley, in Hampshire, very probably a friend of the Jarretts from their time at Marelands. The marriage took place at Hale,[7] home of her sister Anna. Unfortunately, no letters from Georgiana survive (apart from a few lines added to one of her sister's letters to Thomas), so all that is known about her is related at second-hand. In the twenty-eight years of his first marriage Sainsbury had had no children, but Georgiana produced five in rapid succession and so had little time for letter-writing.

Sir Wathen may have been less than pleased that his elder son failed to graduate, though the poor health Thomas suffered in early life, mentioned by Anna in a letter of 1835,[8] may have been partly to blame. In the same letter Anna refers to the fact that her elder brother did not get on well with Lady Howe, and that this had led him to accept a diplomatic post abroad – thus starting him on a career path which was not always to his liking. The most obvious option, the military, was probably discounted on health grounds. Thomas's first posting was to The Hague, an arrangement his father had negotiated with his good friend King George IV, as indicated by William, Duke of Clarence (later King William IV): "I am glad your eldest son is appointed to Sir Charles Bagot and I trust you found the King well and in good humour."[9] At that time patronage was taken for granted as a means of advancement, and Wathen's friends in high places willingly came to his aid to find a suitable occupation for his son. The Duke of Clarence took the trouble to write to Thomas on Boxing Day, enclosing a couple of letters of recommendation to take with him.[10] In all, Thomas's service as a diplomat took him to five different countries in more than twenty years. The letters he received from his family, with the royal letters addressed to his father, form the kernel of the Waller Collection.

Sir Wathen Waller and Lady Howe were very much part of the royal "set" in the 1820s, their lives revolving around visits and invitations given and received: soirées, receptions and balls, hosted by them or their aristocratic and royal friends. Bushy House, William's home, was within easy reach of Pope's Villa, and he and the Duchess (plus the now adult FitzClarences, William's illegitimate children) were frequent guests. Several of the royal letters from this period are from the Duke of Clarence, making or accepting invitations, altering arrangements, apologising for absence. The following extracts from four of his letters give a flavour of the easy relationship between the neighbours.[11]

"10 January 1823
I send this by a servant to make my excuses to you and the dear and excellent Lady Howe for my non appearance last night at your Arabian Villa. The Dutchess [sic] literally kept me at home but desires me to assure you and her favourite Lady Howe if she is unable on the twenty third to go herself she will insist on my making personally her excuses that evening ……. Lord Erroll [husband of William's daughter Elizabeth FitzClarence] went to bed ill with a heavy cold early in the evening which prevented my daughters having the advantage of assisting at the elegant entertainment of last night."

"I have this instant received yours of last night and hasten to assure you that 20th April is equally convenient to us and Princess Augusta will certainly be of the party."

"Lady Erroll will have with her at Hampton Court during the Easter week the Ladies Paget and she is very desirous of being permitted to bring her young friends to your ball on 20th April. I will therefore thank you to give my daughter leave to bring them with her to your fête.
26 March 1827"

"I cannot permit this day to pass over without desiring you to say everything that is kind and proper to the Baroness Howe as the daughter of the Earl who commanded the King's Fleet this day <u>Thirty</u> <u>Seven</u> years ago [the naval victory over the French known as the "Glorious First of June"]. I could not spend the day at Twickenham and therefore being Sunday I attended Divine Service at the Royal Hospital of Greenwich with those who had the honour and happiness of serving with Earl Howe on that memorable day. Once more remember me most kindly and particularly to my fair Cousin and ever believe me,
Dear good Sir
Yours truly
William 1st June 1828"

Twice in the surviving letters William refers to Lady Howe as his cousin, thus acknowledging the family relationship between the Howes and the House of Hanover. It was Lady Howe's annual custom to host, with her husband, a lavish party to celebrate the anniversary of her father's famous victory. Members of the royal family were always invited. During his time as oculist to the Royal Family, which officially came to an end with the death of George III in 1820, Sir Wathen came to regard as his particular friends not only William, Duke of Clarence, but also George (when Prince of Wales, Prince Regent, and eventually King) and Ernest, Duke of Cumberland. His relationship with the three brothers, initially dependent on patronage, had developed rapidly into genuine affection and concern for their well-being. Hints in the royal letters suggest that Wathen was closer to each of them individually than they were to each other. As William put it: "at least in you my brother [George IV] had a real and sincere friend with truth."[12] There were times during William's reign when Ernest passed messages and letters to the king via Wathen, who spent far more time at Windsor Castle than he did.

As shown in Chapter 2, the first of these friendships was with Ernest, before he became Duke of Cumberland. It had been forged and deepened through Wathen's attentive care in times of injury and distress for the Duke (in 1796 and 1810), and was by no means dependent on the social whirl or on invitations to receptions at Court. When Ernest lived for many years on the continent, his friendship with Wathen survived the long separation. The earliest of his letters in the Waller Collection dates from 1826,[13] thirty years after he returned from the Flanders war to consult Wathen (then Mr Phipps) about his wounded eye. Ernest habitually started his letters to his friend with the words: "Dear Phippy". Writing from Berlin in April 1826 to resume their interrupted correspondence, he repeats the affectionate nickname at the end before adding his signature. It appears that some letters have been lost in transit. "I was quite surprised to hear the other day that you had complained I had quite forgotten you, & that I had never answered any letter you had written, & I can give you my sacred word of honour, that I have never seen a line of your handwriting since I saw you last in England in 1823[14] and so far from my thinking I had given you any cause to think I had forgotten you, I imagined that you had forgotten me…. no letter of yours has ever reached me, I hope you will believe me when I say that my regard & friendship for you are the same as ever…".[15]

Ernest mentions his anxiety about his brother the King's health, complains about the dreadful winter weather, and concludes by asking about Wathen's chronic ailment (trigeminal neuralgia), and whether he is yet a grandfather - assuming not unnaturally that Anna might have had a baby in the three years since her marriage. Worries about the health of various members of the royal family form a major part of Ernest's next few letters, along with occasional homesickness, his lack of a useful role, and irritation at the inadequacy of his income compared with the more generous allowances granted to his brothers. Like Wathen, he took his protestant faith very seriously, and he accepted the ups and downs of life as manifestations of God's purpose for him. "The mention of dear <u>Kew</u> <u>Green</u> always makes me feel <u>low</u>, for there is no spot in the world for which I have such a tender as that…… I do not deny to you that sometimes a melancholy overcomes me, when I think that I might perhaps have been of some use to my brother either at home or on the Continent and that this separation from him and from my family gives me moments of spleen. Yet on the other hand I cannot feel sufficiently grateful to Providence for having made my life so happy by giving me the best of wives and blessing us with a very fine healthy son, so that it would be an act of deep ingratitude on my part was I to murmur at His Will and Dictates."[16]

Ernest's happiness with Frederica and the love and pride they lavish on their son George are recurrent themes in the Duke's letters. He is more than satisfied too with the tutor he has appointed, who, apart from educating the young Prince, would soon become his invaluable advisor and personal assistant: "I have now living with me a young man of your acquaintance the Revd Mr Jelf as Tutor to my son – the more I see of him, the more I like him & he is a very great acquisition to me personally & our little chick; he was very intimate at Archdeacon Cambridge's from whose house he used to attend your balls at Twickenham of which he speaks with great delight." [17]

Contented as he was with his family in Berlin, Ernest was always kept up to date with affairs at home. In January 1827 there occurred another shift in the line of succession: Ernest's brother Frederick, Duke of York, died after a long illness, and William, Duke of Clarence, became heir to the throne, with his young niece Victoria following in second place, and Ernest himself next in line – nearer to the throne than he had ever expected to be. What is more, as far as the throne of Hanover was concerned, he had become next heir after William, since the succession in that territory was handed down only through a male line. So there was a very real possibility that he would one day become King of Hanover.

Ernest was much taller, leaner and more active than his brothers, taking exercise on horseback for hours every day. His only real problem was that his one remaining "good" eye had developed a cataract, and something would have to be done about it. In June 1827 the Duke wrote to Wathen in the best of spirits, delightedly informing him of the outcome of the operation performed by Baron von Graefe, the leading European ophthalmologist of the day. It had been a spectacular success, and naturally he assumed that his friend, though no longer practising as an oculist, would take a professional interest: "Dear Phippy, I think you will be pleased to receive a few lines from me to prove to you how perfectly I have recovered my sight for which I must sufficiently acknowledge my thanks to the Almighty. So perfect is the cure that I can now see at a distance I never remember to have seen before; in short I am long sighted instead of being short sighted. I use no spy glass now, only when I read and write, I use preserving glasses…… All the profession are unanimous in their opinion that they never remember so perfect or wonderful a cure. I thought this account would interest you, & therefore have dwellt [sic] so much upon it." [18] In his next letter he continues to express delight at his improved sight – he has been riding ten to twelve hours daily with no ill effect and can play billiards; he is also thinking of taking up shooting.

No letters from the Duke of Cumberland to Sir Wathen survive from 1828; perhaps none were needed, as he came to England in April of that year with Prince George and Mr Jelf, and was able to meet Wathen in person. He took the opportunity to re-acquaint George IV with his godson, now aged nine, and to take, rather belatedly, his oath of allegiance to the King. His intention was to resume his seat in the Lords, and become active in politics, as debates on several issues close to his heart were anticipated. Initially he expected to support his good friend the Duke of Wellington, a national hero since his victory at Waterloo and recently appointed Prime Minister of a Tory administration. In the event, to Ernest's great dismay, Wellington spoke in favour of a Bill[19] which granted concessions to Dissenters. As a matter of principle Ernest was opposed to anything likely to weaken the authority of the Established Church, fearing that concessions to Catholics would be next; he therefore felt obliged to vote against him. Ernest did not dislike or avoid people who were Catholic (his brother George's secret wife, the Catholic Mrs Fitzherbert, remained a friend even after "Prinny" broke with her). However, the protestant House of Hanover to which he belonged and whose rights he upheld had succeeded the Stuarts in the wake of tumultuous times and religious wars – culminating in the Jacobite rebellions. For Ernest, an anti-Catholic stance was a constitutional matter, and he was determined not to allow any Catholic to gain a foothold on power again if he could prevent it. It had long been understood that support for the Established (Anglican) Church was a cornerstone of Toryism, but before he returned to Berlin in the summer of 1828 Ernest felt it necessary to hold a long discussion on the subject of Catholic Emancipation with the Duke of Wellington, who assured him that he would never consent to it.[20] As a result Ernest felt able to rejoin his wife, who had not been well, leaving a proxy vote for most matters, but resolving to return to England if the subject of emancipation was broached.

The Duke of Cumberland was right to be wary that the Tories were weakening over the matter of Catholic Emancipation. Early in 1829 it was clear that Wellington had been less than honest: he had changed his stance completely, and – with the aim of wrong-footing the Whigs and appeasing the Irish – he had decided to introduce a Bill granting emancipation. Sir Robert Peel took the Bill through the Commons, and it was up to Wellington to steer it through the Lords.

When Lord Eldon, a loyal friend and the former Lord Chancellor, [21] advised Ernest that his presence was needed, he set off from Berlin at once, despite the wintry conditions. He opposed the measure as vehemently as he could, arguing against his brothers the Dukes of Clarence and Sussex amongst others, but his efforts came to nothing. Although he emerged as the leader of the ultra-Tories, the party was split and Wellington's larger faction prevailed. Ernest realised that to fight the next battle, parliamentary reform, he would have to make himself available on a more permanent basis. He therefore brought his wife and child back from the continent and set up home once again in Kew.

A letter from Princess Sophia, written in November 1829, emphasizes the overlap between Sir Wathen's family life and his role as confidant of the royals. The Princess, like several other members of her family, had been suffering long-term problems with her eyes, and here describes in detail her symptoms and her fears, desperately seeking reassurance from her former oculist. However, she starts her letter by relating to Wathen a conversation she has had with the wife of the British Ambassador to France, knowing how delighted he will be to hear Lady Stuart de Rothesay's complimentary remarks about his son Thomas: "I am sure my dear Sir Wathen will take in good part the receiving [of] a few lines from one who has so many years experienced his friendship and kindness, that she naturally takes a lively interest in the welfare of his children; & having seen Lady Stuart de Rothesay who unasked named your son as being a very valuable addition to the Embassy, from his excellent conduct, his discreet manner of proceeding in his business which has induced Lord Stuart to employ him very much of late, during which time he has increased the good name he bore already, & added to these essentials in the profession he has chosen for himself, she finds him a very great acquisition in their sociable circle, all this together I considered as so naturally stated, as doing common justice to your son, that I could not refrain from giving you the comfort of hearing it: & as Lady Stuart was not aware of the interest I took in [Thomas] Wathen's welfare, it was not detailed with any view of complimentary idle talk. I sincerely wish you joy, for how natural that a parent should feel proud on having such a character of his son – & I assure you it does not afford me a trifling gratification being the bearer of such welcome tidings…".

This long-winded preamble to the real point of the letter reveals the rather wittering, hesitant style characteristic of Princess Sophia. Her tiny handwriting is instantly recognisable, and even at its best is barely legible; in subsequent letters it deteriorated rapidly as her sight went from bad to worse. She goes on: "I know you will kindly expect I should mention my eyes. The very cold air I certainly find attacks the bad eye & unless very cautious (which I now am) of keeping my veil down & the handkerchief up to the eye as I get into the carriage, I suffer from an aching pain which I conclude is the effect of the bleak air striking on the eye – one day last week, the sun was out & I thought the appearance so inviting, that I went a short time into the garden – that afternoon I was very uneasy, & from that time, I have carefully avoided feeling the air but by degrees, according to the above precautions. I sometimes have misgivings, about the left, though I cannot decidedly say I see less well with it; but I have been very nervous lately which I trust may partly be the cause of these fears; you know that while I hope I do not allow myself to make complaint, or to presume to murmur at the Decrees of Providence, still the sight is so precious a gift, it is natural I should feel alive to the most trifling occurrence, that leads me to think of the possibility & probability of my becoming so complete a dependant on others as I must be if Alas! I was completely blind. May Heaven in its Mercy avert such a calamity!!!" [22]

The Princess's fears were not without foundation, but in 1830 it was George IV's state of health which above all preoccupied Wathen.

Notes

1. National Library of Ireland: Westport Estate Papers, PD 4267 TX/1.
2. The National Archives: PROB 11/1626: Will of the Hon. Marianne Curzon.
3. *The Annual Biography and Obituary of 1817.*
4. Clergy of the Church of England database.
5. Kerr, William James, in *The Genealogical Tree of the Family of Jarrett of Orange Valley, Jamaica, and Camerton Court, Co. Somerset,* tells of the occasion when "Mr Jarrett entertained at dinner, in Portland Place [his London home], the Prince Regent" [when Prince of Wales]. The repast was apparently "of such a sumptuous character that His Royal Highness remarked across the table to the Chancellor of the Exchequer, who was also present, 'Don't you think you might raise the sugar duties a little?' " [Orange Free Valley website].
6. 15 July 1823 at St George's, Hanover Square. The Revd Thomas White had married Anna's aunt, Harriet Slack, at Bray, 13 September 1802. Harriet was Wathen's cousin as well as his sister-in-law.
7. 6 July 1830, at Hale House near Salisbury.
8. WCRO: CR 0341/327/96, AJ to TWW, 29 May 1835.
9. WCRO: CR 0341/17, Duke of Clarence to JWW, 10 December 1826.
10. WCRO: CR 0341/18, Duke of Clarence to JWW, 26 December 1826.
11. WCRO: CR 0341/13; CR 0341/23; CR 0341/19; CR 0341/20, Duke of Clarence to JWW.
12. WCRO: CR 0341/17, Duke of Clarence to JWW, 10 December 1826.
13. WCRO: CR0341/58, Duke of Cumberland to JWW, 3 April 1826.
14. The Duke had paid a brief visit to England in July/August 1823. According to GM Willis op. cit. p 166, it was to make sure that his apartment at St James's Palace was not allocated to anyone else in the course of the refurbishment and reorganisation of

the building. He was determined to keep a pied à terre in London. He was impressed by the changes in London since he left, and found Regent Street "the merriest thoroughfare in Europe".

15. WCRO: CR 0341/58, Duke of Cumberland to JWW, 3 April 1826.
16. WCRO: CR 0341/60, Duke of Cumberland to JWW, 7 July 1826.
17. WCRO: CR 0341/61, Duke of Cumberland to JWW, 13 November 1826.
18. WCRO: CR0341/62, Duke of Cumberland to JWW, 11 June 1827.
19. The repeal of the Test and Corporation Acts for Dissenters.
20. Willis, G M, op.cit. p 171.
21. Lord Eldon was the father of Anna Jarrett's closest friend, Lady Elizabeth Repton (née Scott), who was also a great favourite of the Duke of Cumberland.
22. WCRO: 0341/166, Princess Sophia to JWW, 18 November [1829].

Chapter 7

The death of King George IV

"There was never an individual less regretted by his fellow-creatures than this deceased king. What eye has wept for him? What heart has heaved one throb of unmercenary sorrow?… If he ever had a friend… a devoted friend in any rank of life – we protest that the name of him or her never reached us…"

The Times 16th July 1830

"Thus terminated a Friendship of about 35 years, which notwithstanding the wide difference of our Rank in life had existed with unvaried kindness and affection on the part of his Majesty and with the warmest Devotion on mine."

Extract from a Manuscript book of Sir Jonathan Wathen Waller

After nine years as Prince Regent, George eventually became King on the death of his father in January 1820. He was 57 and well past his prime. Decades of self-indulgence had taken their inevitable toll on him physically. Nevertheless he had spent his whole life in anticipation and expectation of succeeding to the throne, and was determined to begin his reign with a flourish. He relished all that was theatrical: processions, costumes, uniforms, marching bands, putting on a show. During the Regency the country had been able to celebrate lavishly Napoleon's defeat not once, but twice (in 1814 *and also* in 1815), because the Emperor had returned from exile in Elba, resuming power until the decisive battle at Waterloo. Of course the jubilant Prince had led the victory celebrations on both occasions. Now a monarch in his own right at last, George IV was determined that his Coronation would outshine any enthronement ever seen before: it would be unquestionably grander and more extravagant than the imperial ceremony devised by Napoleon in 1804 – even if it took eighteen months to plan. The costumes would be in Tudor style in homage to the most memorable of England's past dynasties. His own robes were naturally the most ostentatious and costly, in red velvet with a train 27 feet long, trimmed with ermine and embroidered with gold stars. In the event the King's attire alone cost £24,000, and the Coronation Procession, Banquet and Hyde Park Fête, complete with Chinese lanterns, elephants, fireworks and balloon ascents, exceeded in magnificence all festivities previously held in the kingdom. George's subjects could not fail to be impressed, at least for a while. They had almost forgotten what it was like to have a highly visible king, and George was well aware that royal public relations required him to be seen by as many people as possible, with an immense entourage of courtiers and lackeys – the very embodiment of majesty and authority. He followed the London ceremonies with elaborately staged visits to his subjects in Ireland, Hanover and Scotland, everywhere receiving the utmost acclaim. The Scottish tour was masterminded by Sir Walter Scott, whose work George greatly admired. Predictably the king ordered an array of costumes worthy of a troupe of travelling actors, including full highland dress, with a tartan kilt – worn with pink tights instead of the traditional bare legs – and knee-high socks. The visit had become a pageant, a theatrical extravaganza, but the Scots felt acknowledged and appreciated rather than neglected, and they delighted the King with the warmth of their welcome.

Popular in some quarters George IV may have been, but he also attracted an abundance of negative comment. The diarist Charles Greville's description of him (posthumously published) is utterly damning: "he is a spoiled, selfish, odious beast, and has no idea of doing anything but what is agreeable to himself, or of there being any duties attached to the office he holds… he only wishes to be powerful in order to exercise the most puerile caprices, gratify ridiculous resentments, indulge vulgar prejudices and amass or squander money: not one great object connected with national glory or prosperity ever enters his brain." [1] Few critics of the king were quite so harsh, but many considered him little more than a national joke – an embarrassment – and this stereotype has persisted. Posterity has shown him no mercy: obsessively concerned with his own image, he was destined to be remembered most readily via a handful of iconic caricatures. It was his misfortune to have lived in the heyday of the satirical print, and to have been an irresistible target for savage but brilliant cartoonists, who continually lampooned his extravagance and particularly his obesity, so ironically at odds with his inordinate love of clothes and fashion. Having rebelled against his father's frugality in his teens, George ran up enormous debts in his twenties, spending immense sums not only at the gambling tables (like his friend the Duchess of Devonshire) and the races, but on his wardrobe and the homes he bedecked with extraordinarily sumptuous furnishings. As his brother William remarked, he had "damned expensive tastes in knickknackery".

In his teens and twenties George had been a golden youth – handsome, glamorous, party-loving and rich – the ultimate super-celebrity. But, sadly lacking self-restraint, he squandered not only his money but his good looks as well, calling to mind Henry VIII (and Elvis Presley in more recent times). As early as 1792 (when Prince of Wales and only thirty years old) he had been depicted by James Gillray as "*A Voluptuary under the Horrors of digestion*", with his bloated stomach bursting out of his waistcoat and breeches, the epitome of gluttony. Nearly three decades later the same huge stomach dominated George Cruikshank's portrait of the Prince Regent in military attire, adorned with a multiplicity of medals and emblems and a wide hat, à la Bonaparte, from which three bedraggled peacock feathers protrude in lieu of three white ostrich plumes. The Scottish painter Sir David Wilkie, who painted him in highland dress towards the end of his life, found the sittings "a most difficult and melancholy business", as the King was only fit to be seen from a distance, like an actor on a stage. He might then just pass muster, "dressed up in robes and hung about with ribbons, but to see him at close quarters was parfaitly frightful… It took three hours to dress him, to lace up all the bulgings and excrescencies… he looked like a great sausage stuffed into the covering." [2] With a child's uninhibited candour, his niece Princess Victoria also found "Uncle King" just too disgusting, as his face was covered in greasepaint.

By the latter years of his reign, George's great desire to be seen had evaporated, and he craved seclusion. He remained out of sight at Windsor as much as possible, crippled with the agony of gout, which often confined him to his bed. Security procedures were devised to enable him to be driven around Windsor Park and to Frogmore without being observed, when he was well enough, sometimes accompanied by his brother Ernest and his young nephew Prince George of Cumberland. He felt old and ill; cataracts in both eyes had left him almost blind. In the spring of 1830 the king was suffering, as ever, from frequent attacks of gout; in addition he had hardening of the arteries, gallstones and dropsy. As his life drew slowly and painfully to an end he was in a pitiful condition. Few redeeming features made this existence bearable but one was the attentive care of Wathen Waller, who later wrote to his son Thomas that his priorities had been altered by spending three months in the chamber of a dying monarch.[3] George's death affected Wathen profoundly and was one of the most momentous events his life. All published accounts agree that he was present in the king's final hours. They differ, however, about his role at Windsor Castle, variously describing him as the King's page or the King's physician. Wathen was neither. He was there in no official capacity at all, but simply offering such comfort as he could as a *friend*. He it was who held the king's hand as he died. Although no letters from George IV survive in the Waller Collection, it is obvious that there was a genuine, close and durable bond between the two men, dating from 1796 when Wathen first attended Prince Ernest at his brother's residence, and reinforced during a further two-month stay at Carlton House in 1810, in the wake of the Sellis attack. All the same, it was the unlikeliest of friendships: the self-indulgent monarch would appear to have embodied all the vices and faults which Wathen, with his strict non-conformist upbringing, most despised – unbounded profligacy, promiscuity, gluttony, selfishness and so on. Perhaps the aura of royalty led Wathen to apply different moral standards once he entered Court circles, or possibly – as seems to have been the case – George IV was thoroughly likeable at close quarters, and despite his image and reputation was capable of affectionate and loyal friendship. The two men did have at least one thing in common. Both knew what it was to endure pain on a daily basis, and both were heavily dependent upon the favourite opiate of their times, laudanum.

Wathen remained a constant presence at the king's side throughout his long decline. Power, status and wealth were of no further use to the monarch who faced the agony of his dying days with no wife, no child, not even a sibling or friend whose company he craved – apart from Wathen. At a stage in life when affection and kindness is all that matters, it was to Wathen that George turned. There is no doubt about the sincerity of Wathen's attachment to the King and his emotional reaction to his death. He produced several handwritten accounts detailing the events leading up to it, mainly for members of the royal family or as formal records, but he allowed his feelings to show more openly when relating the sad events to his son. In his formal report to George's successor, Wathen refers to himself in the third person, concentrating on the sovereign's physical condition and the circumstances of his final hours with no detail spared.[4] The King's physician, Sir Henry Halford, who had been on duty since seven in the morning, was dismissed shortly before midnight, and George – no longer able to lie at all comfortably in a bed – settled into his habitual sleeping position, in a specially adapted armchair (a gift from his brother the Duke of Sussex), leaning on a table, his head on one hand, with Wathen's hand in the other. Like this he managed to sleep for a couple of hours, woke long enough to take his medicine, and then slept for a further hour "when he desired the bell to be rung for the pages as he required the night table. The King had a purgative motion & for some moments after seemed unwilling to move, but returned to his armchair & ordered the windows to be thrown open as had been his custom for some time both during the night & the day. His Majesty then expressed himself a little faint & desired some sal volatile & water. This he several times endeavoured to drink but could not, & Sir H. Halford was immediately called. His Majesty then pressed the hand of Sir Wathen Waller, which still remained in his, more strongly than usual, & looking him full in the face distinctly exclaimed: 'My Boy this is Death!!' & immediately closed his eyes & reclined back in his chair…. [He] expired just as the clock struck the ¼ after 3, June 26th. "

Writing privately to his son Thomas, in Paris at the time, Wathen was able to express his heartfelt grief: "27 June 1830. Long before the arrival of this, My Dear Boy, which cannot go from hence till next Tuesday evening, you will have learned by telegraphic dispatch my great & irretrievable loss. My beloved friend & monarch expired in my arms at ¼ past 3 o'clock on the morning of yesterday." [5] There was, of course, immediate business to attend to; the matter of the new King's accession took precedence over all other considerations, and once more, Wathen's position was centre stage. "About an hour after [the King's death], I left the Castle as I had promised the Duke of Clarence, now William the 4th, to do, & took Halford officially to announce the event & was the first person that kissed his hand. He received me with more than his usual kindness & I remained with him two hours & then came on here [Pope's Villa]." Although Windsor, Bushy Park and Twickenham are relatively close to each other, a car journey between the three locations is scarcely a matter of minutes even today. For a sixty-year-old man, the journey by horse-drawn carriage after a sleepless night and in a state of distress was a considerable undertaking, quite a feat of stamina. Yet after a brief pause, during which he composed his reports and wrote to his son, Wathen was ready to resume his self-imposed duties: "I am now going to him [the new King] at Bushy [6] & shall add to this on my return. I am truly brokenhearted & have lost one of the most affectionate friends man ever possessed & one whose memory will ever be attended with a bitter tear. It is true that in William the 4th I believe I shall possess as kind a sovereign & as firm a friend but at my age I can ill spare a <u>friend</u> whose eye ever beamed with pleasure on me for nearly 40 long years…. I can ill bear it…"

Exhausted and distressed, Wathen had some difficulty in composing himself when describing George's dying moments to the late King's siblings, but he had resolved to see them all (except Adolphus, Duke of Cambridge, who was in Hanover, and Elizabeth, Landgravine of Hesse-Homburg) to give them his personal account of events. To Thomas he reported the latest news:

"I have been all morning at Bushy and am sadly overcome with my interviews with Princess Augusta & the Duchess of Gloucester [Princess Mary] who are both there. I find my nerves are more shook than I imagined. This I did not feel whilst I was obliged to exert myself. A little quiet will however soon restore me. The King insisted on my remaining with him during the first Service performed before their Majesties. It was read & well read by Augustus FitzClarence [William's youngest son, a clergyman] & when it was ended the Queen presented me with the Prayer book she had used & requested I would hereafter use it for her sake. In the first leaf I found written as follows: 'This Prayer Book which I have long used as Duchess of Clarence & also this first Sunday after becoming Queen of England, I offer to Sir Wathen Waller as a token of the high regard I feel for him & of the sincere gratitude I feel for all his attention and true friendship shewn to our most beloved late King George the 4th during his life and last lamentable long illness, with the wish that Sir Wathen Waller will use it in future for my sake.
Adelaide, Bushy House, June 27 1830.'
This was all done with so much kindness & friendship that it quite overcame me & the King said that he & I infected each other & therefore he would not let me dine there today but commanded me tomorrow…"

One can well imagine the elderly king and his middle-aged confidant – immaculately groomed and dressed in court finery as the occasion demanded – intermittently dissolving into uncontrollable sobs. By the following day Wathen was more composed and able to tell Thomas of the call he made to commiserate with his old friend Ernest Duke of Cumberland in Kew. It must have been a great disappointment to find only the Duchess at home. Of the three remaining interviews, planned for Tuesday in Kensington, the one with Princess Sophia, whom he knew so well, would be the most emotional. As for the widow of the Duke of Kent and the Duke of Sussex, they were acquaintances and occasional guests rather than intimate friends. "Monday night. ½ past 11 o'clock. I am just returned home from dining with the King who is quite well……. I paid my duty at Kew this morning & was well catechized by the Duchess of Cumberland, the Duke was not at home. Tomorrow I am to see the Duchess of Kent & Duke of Sussex & Princess Sophia & then my task is over."

In addition to the Queen's prayer book, Wathen treasured other gifts from members of the royal family: in gratitude for his devotion to King George IV, Princess Mary, Duchess of Gloucester, had a favourite portrait of her brother copied for him[7]. The King himself had presented Wathen with a diamond seal ring bearing the three feathers emblem and coronet of the Prince of Wales – a ring that had been commissioned by King James I for his eldest son, Henry.[8] A less valuable but more personal memento was a sheet of paper[9] showing the first five impressions (of varying strength) from a stamp bearing the King's signature ("George R"). The stamp was made for the King when his hands had become excruciatingly painful, and Wathen had helped him to try it out when it was newly acquired. Such an item could only have been handled by the sovereign's most trustworthy courtiers.

George IV had died in the early hours of 26th June 1830 and "the breath was scarcely out of his body", according to Greville, "before the press burst forth in full cry against him and raked up all his vices, follies and misdeeds, which were numerous and glaring enough…."[10] The Times obituary published on 28th June was particularly scathing, attacking the late King's "most reckless, unceasing and unbounded prodigality …. indifference to the feelings of others…. the tawdry childishness of Carlton House and the mountebank Pavilion, or cluster of pagodas at Brighton." As for his profligate lifestyle, it was "little higher than that of animal indulgence."[11] A fairer assessment might have mentioned that within two years of coming to the throne, King George had put his Private Secretary, Sir William Knighton, in charge of his financial affairs as Keeper of the Privy Purse – with the principal task of clearing his debts. Like Wathen, Knighton had earned the king's trust and friendship, and he worked tirelessly in his service. In three years he was able to report that the debts were cleared; it would take Queen Victoria far longer to clear the debts of her father, the Duke of Kent. George was particularly grateful that he was thereafter able to make small gestures of generosity to charitable causes, having frequently been inhibited about doing so by the burden of his debts. Knighton was co-executor with the Duke of Wellington of the late king's Will. Their tasks included examining all his papers and, at their discretion, destroying them. Knighton had shared the vigils with Wathen in the final months, sitting up with the dying king on alternate nights. He, more than anyone, knew how exhausting the experience had been, and he was well placed to appreciate Wathen's invaluable assistance and devotion. On 1st July he wrote from Windsor Castle: "from the combination of anxiety, fatigue, and wretchedness, under the late circumstances, it is no wonder that one should feel the effects most severely. I can say that your benevolent affection and attention to the late beloved King, I shall ever have before my eyes…. The moment the sacred remains are removed for the purposes of State, I shall go – since everything connected with private duty will then be at an end!" [12]

Not content with an excoriating obituary, the Editor of *The Times* returned to the attack the day after the King's funeral, claiming that "There was never an individual less regretted by his fellow-creatures than this deceased King. What eye has wept for him? What heart has heaved one throb of unmercenary sorrow?…If he ever had a friend… a devoted friend in any rank of life – we protest that the name of him or her never reached us…" [13] Had this man never heard of Wathen Waller whose view could not have differed more completely? He described himself as "broken-hearted", having suffered "a great and irretrievable loss". Specifically mentioning their widely differing ranks in life, Wathen lamented the loss of a friendship which had existed for thirty-five years: "with unvaried kindness and affection on the part of his Majesty and with the warmest Devotion on mine." [14] But it was the Duke of Wellington, in a carefully crafted eulogy, who most skilfully managed to sum up the mass of contradictions that was George IV: "a most extraordinary compound of talent, wit, buffoonery, obstinacy and good feeling – in short a medley of the most opposite qualities, with a great preponderance of good." [15]

For several months Wathen had lived at Windsor Castle, with scant time to devote to his family. Now he moved seamlessly from the role of unofficial personal assistant to King George IV to performing the same function for the new king. Fortunately his children were all well able to fend for themselves, and his wife, through her son, Earl Howe (Lord of the Bedchamber to George IV), could feel vicariously involved in the momentous royal affairs. But the timing of the late King's death was far from convenient for the Waller family. Wathen's daughter Georgiana was to be married within days, and a daughter's wedding was not an occasion to neglect, whatever the circumstances. In the midst of all the grieving and funeral planning, Wathen's presence was required in Hampshire to give away his elder daughter, who was to marry the Reverend Sainsbury Langford Sainsbury at Hale, home of her sister Anna and brother-in-law, John Jarrett.[16] The planned journey was hastily re-scheduled: after performing his fatherly duty as expected, Wathen would return to Town in time to support the new king and pay his respects to his "beloved monarch and friend." He concluded his letter to Thomas, written two days after his harrowing experience at the late King's side: "…… I am much better today & feel sure a little quiet will make me quite well. Instead of Monday I shall go Saturday to Hale & return here on Wednesday, as the King does not like me to be absent from him at present." [17]

Notes

1. Quoted by Smith, E A, *George IV*, Yale University Press 1999, p 268.
2. Smith, E A op.cit., p 269, quoting Wilkie's remarks made to J G Lockhart, biographer of Sir Walter Scott, and author of a biographical monograph on Wilkie.
3. WCRO: 0341/207, JWW to TWW, 4 July 1830.
4. WCRO: CR 0341/204, Copy of the Paper given to H. M. King William 4th.
5. WCRO: CR 0341/206, 27 June 1830, JWW to TWW.
6. King George IV had died at Windsor Castle and Wathen had to take the news to the new King, William IV, formerly Duke of Clarence, at his home at Bushy House, near Hampton Court.
7. WCRO: CR 0341/134, Duchess of Gloucester to JWW, 1 December (no year).
    [I] "am delighted that you have received the picture and that it is as like as I have been anxious it should be to my dear brother, and I can not tell you the gratification it is to me that you are pleased and like the copy and that it has been in my power to present you with what I know you will value and love so much."
8. WCRO: CR 0341/236.
9. WCRO: CR 0341/210.
10. Greville, Charles, *Journal*, Vol 2, pp 1, 2.
11. *The Times*, 28 June 1830.
12. WCRO 0341/221, Sir William Knighton to JWW, 1 July 1830.
13. *The Times*, 16 July 1830.
14. From Sir Jonathan Wathen Waller's Manuscript book (sold at Auction at Strides of Chichester, June 1996).
15. The Duke of Wellington, quoted by Hibbert, Christopher: *George IV, Regent & King, 1811-1830*, Penguin 1976, p 310.
16. The church at Hale is in the grounds of Hale House.
17. WCRO: CR 0341/206, 27 June 1830, JWW to TWW.

Chapter 8

King William's reign begins; riots and reform; Prince George of Cumberland's accident

"ponder my presumptuous attachment, that dares to breathe this opinion in your royal ear."
Jonathan Wathen Waller

Within weeks of William IV's accession to the throne Wathen became extremely anxious about the sovereign's mental health. He was able to observe the King at close quarters, and found him in a constant state of agitation and excitability. Keenly aware that the position he occupied as an insider at Court was an immense privilege, Wathen felt a duty of responsibility towards the monarch. Given the King's behaviour, it would do no good to stand idly by, muttering to himself that someone ought to calm William down: some action on his part was called for – though it would not be easy. In mid-July 1830 Wathen drafted and re-drafted the most delicate and important letter of his whole life, involving a considerable risk to his own position as a favoured friend and courtier. Still hesitating, he asked Princess Sophia to read it and give an opinion. She approved, agreed it was necessary, but advised him to pick carefully the right moment to send it. On 28th July he took the dangerous step of sending the letter (which is quoted in full in the Prologue), advising the King to moderate his inappropriate behaviour. It ends: "Forgive then Sire, & ponder my presumptuous attachment, that dares to breathe this opinion in your royal ear; & having thus discharged, what I considered an imperious duty, I will only add, that whilst my heart continues to vibrate, it will still glow with the strongest attachment & loyalty towards your royal person, & to its last pulsation I remain your Majesty's most faithful & devoted servant & subject, JW Waller."[1] Clearly Wathen feared that his good intentions might be misinterpreted, but he desperately hoped that his motivation would be seen to be honourable and the criticism and advice well meant. Fortunately, the King understood and appreciated what Wathen was trying to do. What is more, he took to heart the warning, attempting to control his informality and occasional buffoonery by slowing down and going about his business with a more dignified and regal demeanour.

On 27th July, while Wathen was busy polishing his highly sensitive letter, riots and rebellion broke out in France, and lasted for three days. Once again barricades appeared in the streets, followed by looting and arson. The Bourbon line of the French royal family had been re-instated after the Napoleonic era and the elderly King Louis XVIII, brother of Louis XVI, had reigned from 1814 to 1824, apart from Napoleon's 100 days in 1815. He was succeeded by a younger brother, Charles X, who was deposed in what came to be known as the "July Revolution" of 1830. In his place, Wathen's old friend Louis-Philippe, Duke of Orleans, became King of France, or rather "King of the French" – a significant nuance. With notable revolutionary and royalist credentials, Louis-Philippe, the Citizen King, was the first French sovereign to come to the throne not on the hereditary principle, but by parliamentary proclamation. He was to be a constitutional monarch: he adopted the flag of the Revolution, the *Tricolore*, and dressed in bourgeois attire, eschewing pomp and ceremony. For him there was no ostentatious and extravagant Coronation at Reims as had hitherto been demanded by tradition.

The news of the July Revolution would have taken a few days to reach Wathen in London, so it is unlikely that the timing of his letter to the King was affected by the situation in France. However, it cannot have been long before events in Paris were the talk of the Court, and the apprehension that revolutionary thinking would spread across the Channel was never far away. There were disturbances in English towns and cities from time to time, and pressure was mounting for changes to be made in the voting system. Earl Grey, leader of the Whig opposition to Wellington's Tory government, had already spoken in favour of parliamentary reform in June 1830; Wellington, on the other hand, insisted that the existing system of representation was as near perfect as possible.[2] It is difficult to understand how he was able to maintain this stance when there existed "rotten boroughs" – constituencies in the shires with a mere handful of easily bought voters returning two MPs – while towns such as Manchester, which had expanded enormously through industrialisation, had no representation at all. Yet the Tories, including the Duke of Cumberland and his great friend Lord Eldon, were implacably opposed to change, fearing anarchy and revolution. Unsurprisingly, the memory of the guillotine lingered amongst the aristocracy. When Wellington's government was defeated on a vote of confidence, he resigned, and Grey's opportunity to seek reform had arrived.

For the moment, however, Court life continued much as usual. Baroness Howe's son, Earl Howe, was appointed Lord Chamberlain to Queen Adelaide, and the routine of elaborate receptions (King's Levées and Queen's Drawing Rooms) went on as tradition and protocol demanded. The King let it be known that he did not want a Coronation, as the last one (for George IV) had been a hugely expensive and flamboyant affair. He was persuaded by his brother Ernest amongst others that a Coronation was essential, if only for its religious elements, so a compromise was reached and a pared-down version planned for 8th September 1831. In June of that year Sir Wathen and the Baroness held their traditional "fête" or party at Pope's Villa – the annual celebration of Admiral Howe's famous victory of "The Glorious First of June" – at which Wathen habitually appeared wearing his illustrious father-in-law's medals. For the first time, Wathen was able to receive his friend William as a reigning monarch, and with him, every member of the royal family living in England (except the young Princess Victoria of Kent). He proudly kept a copy of his VIP guest list, and it survives in the Waller Collection.[3] A contemporary press report provides some additional detail: "The dinner was served in the great gallery and the library; in the former were three tables of twenty-four covers, and in the other four tables of one hundred and fifty covers. The party did not break up till nearly ten o'clock."[4]

The Reform Bill was first proposed in the House of Commons in March 1831 and its passage was a long-drawn out and complicated procedure which has been minutely dissected in numerous tomes dedicated to the subject. So determined were the Dukes of Cumberland and Wellington to halt the Bill's passage through the Lords – once it had been passed in the House of Commons in September 1831 – that they put aside their differences, and managed to resume their friendship. "It appears to me," wrote Cumberland, "that, in times such as these, it is necessary for every well-wisher to his country, who is attached to the Monarchy and the Court, to meet and resist the Revolutionary Bill now pending in Parliament; which, if carried out, must, according to my humble opinion, annihilate all our institutions both in Church and State."[5] In October the Upper House debated the Bill for a whole week, with several all-night sessions. Lord Eldon (then aged 80) and his fellow die-hard Tories were in attendance throughout the proceedings and they all made heart-felt speeches. Their efforts were rewarded with a majority of 41 against the Bill.

Riots and serious disturbances which had been simmering during the long debate broke out in London and numerous towns and cities:[6] the worst were in Bristol, where public buildings and houses were set on fire and twelve people died. Thirty-one of the rioters were sentenced to death.[7] The extent of the violence and destruction has been played down in most accounts of the period, the English preferring to believe that political reform was achieved peacefully, and that episodes of mob rule were far more characteristic of the continent. However, in addition to the urban incidents of arson and looting, some prominent Tory peers were individually targeted; several received threatening letters,[8] and from time to time rioters besieged their homes. The windows of Apsley House, the Duke of Wellington's residence, were broken,[9] and the Duke of Cumberland was dragged from his horse in Hyde Park. In late October Lord Eldon took advantage of a brief parliamentary recess to visit his country estate at Encombe, Dorset, and was fortunate that a planned attack on his property was thwarted. It was said that the mob from nearby Poole was frustrated by a Tory sympathiser who bored holes in the canoes they intended to use for a ferry crossing.[10] When a new Reform Bill (a slightly amended version of the old one) was put forward, it was again passed in the Commons. Subsequently Grey let it be known that the King was prepared to create dozens of Whig peers to ensure its acceptance by the Lords and the threat was enough for the Upper House Tories to admit defeat. The Representation of the People Act (otherwise known as the Great Reform Act) became law in 1832, but it did not go far enough to silence all protest.

Whenever the Duke of Cumberland took an active part in politics, the slurs, whispering campaigns and attacks on him in the press increased both in number and in viciousness, in the hope of deterring him from the course of action he had set himself. They tended to have the opposite effect as far as the Duke was concerned, but were nevertheless distressing, especially to Frederica, the Duchess. She was appalled at the way the English allowed political motivation to overrule all other considerations, and explained to a friend: "The party-spirit so demoralises them that it tears the most sacred bonds. I know of brothers or sisters who did not speak together during the time of the Reform Bill and let sad events in the families of brothers or sisters pass by without any feeling or sympathy simply because one was for and the other against the Bill. When such things can take place inside families, you can imagine the spirit of persecution towards other persons, of which so much is directed against the Duke."[11] From 1829 to 1832, the attacks reached unparalleled proportions. The old slanders were repeated: that he had killed his servant Sellis, and had had an incestuous relationship (and an illegitimate child, known as Tommy Garth) with his sister Sophia. To these were added alleged new sins: an assault on Lady Lyndhurst, and an affair with Lady Graves[12] which caused her husband's suicide. *The Times* made frequent attacks on the Duke, in which it was joined by a scurrilous publication called *The Age*, and the newly created pamphlet *Figaro in London*; this last specialised in scandalous political cartoons and epigrams, cruelly and relentlessly lampooning the Duke, whose reputation has never recovered. Lytton Strachey, though born about thirty years after Ernest died, had no qualms about thoroughly damning him in a powerful verbal sketch: "the Duke of Cumberland was probably the most unpopular man in England. Hideously ugly, with a distorted eye, he was bad-tempered and vindictive in private, a violent reactionary in politics, and was suspected of murdering his valet and of having carried on an amorous intrigue of an extremely scandalous kind." [13] Mud does indeed stick.

Worse was to come. 1832 brought the Cumberlands the most distressful period of their lives. With his accustomed loyalty and eagerness to please, Phippy was of course on hand to support and assist his friend. The Duke had been ill for most of January and February, but he continued to attend the House of Lords until the passage of the Reform Bill was inevitable. Then in March a pamphlet entitled *The Authentic Records of the Court of England during the Last Seventy Years* was published by one Josiah Phillips, author unknown. Its name was misleading, since its purpose was to attack the Duke in as wounding a fashion as possible. The tone was set from the beginning by generalised insults: "We will now recur to a Prince, whose very name has proved a stain upon the Kingdom in which he was born. Sensibility and virtue were strangers to his breast, while cruelty and the baser passions had perfect control over his imagination and actions. His countenance was indeed an index to his mind; as it is scarcely possible that more horrible features could be associated in one human being."[14] As if this were not enough, the anonymous author went on to assert that twenty-two years earlier, Sellis, the Duke's valet, had discovered that the Duke and another servant, Neale, were accomplices in "the grossest and most unnatural immorality", and that the Duke had subsequently ordered Neale to silence Sellis by murdering him.

This time the Duke decided that such stories had hovered around him for long enough, and that a prosecution for libel might put an end to the defamatory accusations. Inevitably, however, the whole Sellis affair had to be raked over and aired again and again during the long-drawn-out and stressful legal process. A preliminary hearing took place in April-May 1832 and the trial proper began in May of the following year. Wathen appeared for the prosecution to give evidence about the gravity of Ernest's wounds, almost over-egging his testimony in his desire to be of help.[15] The pamphleteer had, however, made an elementary error: he had foolishly based much of his case on a hypothetical statement which a man named Jew (a former footman in the Duke's household) might have given, had he been called at the original inquest. It was alleged that he was deliberately not called at that time because his evidence would have condemned the Duke, and he was now in Belgium and so beyond the court's jurisdiction. In a masterly *coup de théâtre*, the prosecution, led by Sir Charles Wetherall,[16] produced the man – actually named Joseph Joux – who categorically denied all the invented testimony it was said he would have provided. The defendant was found guilty without the jury retiring,[17] and the torrent of libels ceased.

In the interval between the preliminary hearing and the trial, a far more personal and tragic incident occurred: an accident to Prince George of Cumberland who was by all accounts a delightful boy, handsome, charming, polite and intelligent[18] – the pride and joy of his parents. They hugely appreciated their good fortune in having had such an exemplary son comparatively late in life. It was far from impossible that he would one day become king: his cousin Victoria might die in childbirth like her cousin Charlotte, and after his father, Prince George was next in line. He was brought up with this in mind, and seemed ideally suited to the role, although he had lost the sight of his right eye – possibly through measles – earlier in childhood, causing his mother to remark: "<u>something</u> always disturbs human perfection." [19] Then on 12 September 1832 Ernest wrote to Wathen about a seemingly trivial mishap: "George, it appears, perfectly unknown to us, struck his eye yesterday afternoon with a piece of ivory, a bauble at the end of his purse." [20] Apparently he had gone out to the Green at Kew in front of his house to give a few pence to some poor people he had noticed there. Returning in high spirits, he was swinging his purse around his head when a carved acorn embellishing the purse hit his "good" eye. The Duke was most anxious that Wathen should advise him as soon as possible: "I should esteem it as a <u>great favour</u> if you <u>will come early & breakfast here</u> tomorrow morning <u>at ½ past nine</u> and see what ails him." It was soon apparent that George could see very little, and sometimes nothing at all. The oculist and the surgeon to the royal household, Henry Alexander and Sir Astley Cooper respectively, were summoned for their opinions on 15th September (along with Wathen, of course). They advised quietness, rest, avoidance of riding or any major physical exertion. Although distraught, the parents hoped against hope that George's intermittent sight would improve, with or without an operation.

Some months spent quietly by the sea were recommended for Prince George's health, and where better than Hastings? Some years earlier Wathen and the Baroness had a bought a town house there for the benefit of their health. Hastings was being promoted at the time as a resort with a perfect climate for invalids and convalescents, and the newly built Breeds Place, right on the sea front, was considered ideal for the Cumberlands. They decided to spend the winter 1832-3 there; Wathen would be on hand to offer advice, treatment and company. By his mere presence he managed to provide reassurance that all would be well, just as he had for George III in 1805. The Duke was less than happy to be away from Kew and St James's, and writing to the Duchess of Richmond in December commented: "[there is] nothing to communicate from this place…the dullest in all England." [21] Nevertheless, he was prepared to make any sacrifice for the sake of his son: "George has certainly improved both in Health and Vision since he has been here, the latter is gradual, but I trust a <u>sure</u> amendment. Sir Wathen Waller is perfectly satisfied at the manner it is going on." [22] The Duke managed to escape to London in January for a "cruel" dental operation, [23] and to remain there on political business for several weeks. He had set himself the task of uniting the various Tory factions to form "but one Conservative party", [24] and with patience and hard work, he made considerable progress towards this goal. When the Duke of Wellington persuaded him to stay an extra week Ernest wrote to Wathen as follows: "Dear Phippy Many thanks for yours received this day and for the excellent accounts you have given me of our dear little man, I trust & hope that <u>his</u> being able – as the Duchess writes me Wed – to have taken so much exercise <u>proves</u> how much his strength must have recovered and it appears the sight is equally gradually recovering. God grant I may find those so dear to my heart all well on <u>Saturday</u> when I propose returning to Hastings." [25]

Despite the optimism expressed by George's parents and by Wathen, there was no improvement in the Prince's sight. His aunt, Princess Augusta, the oldest of Ernest's remaining sisters, took a more realistic view of the situation, and had attempted as early as November 1832 to be of some practical help by proposing to Wathen the acquisition of a Braille (or similar) machine: "the anxiety I am under with respect to dear George naturally leads me to reflect upon any thing which may tend to his present comfort and future wellfare [sic]. It has therefore occurred to me that without its distressing him, he might be led to write with one of those machines invented for the blind. It must be an additional pass time now and if it should please God to spare us from the greatest of calamities, his becoming blind – it will be an advantage to him hereafter, at any time that he has a cold or inflammation. Should the worst occur, he has that resource. If you are of opinion that you could persuade him to try it without it hurting his feelings I would beg of you to get a machine and to give it him in my name sending me the bill directed to Brighton. I really think that with your kindness and cheerfullness [sic] you might persuade him at least to attempt writing a few lines. I beg you will allow me to take this opportunity of expressing though but very feebly, my sense of gratitude to you, for your unremitting attentions and tender feelings for that dear boy. I assure you all his family feel the same." [26]

Naturally enough George's parents sought the opinion of the leading ophthalmologist of the day, Baron von Graefe, whose operation on the Duke's eye six years earlier had been such a success. He was consulted in August 1833, and felt that an operation at some time in the future would be possible, but George would have to spend some time under his care in Berlin. The family set off at the beginning of October, calling on Ernest's sister Princess Elizabeth (Landgravine of Hesse-Homburg) en route. Her reaction on seeing George is recorded among her letters: "Never did I exert more not to show what I felt at our first meeting, for to see that lovely creature led about is not to be told. His good humour, his sweet way of expressing himself, his gratitude for every kindness is not to be expressed." [27]

The family waited patiently as years passed; at last in January 1840 von Graefe felt that the right moment had come to attempt an operation – more than seven years after the accident had happened. All that time they had retained the fervent hope that George's sight would be eventually be restored. Ernest, by now King of Hanover, kept Wathen informed of the latest news: "naturally we had to consult the patient's own feelings as to the time he wished to have it performed & George desires it may be done this Spring. God grant us His Divine Aid, and that we may at length see all our anxiety and alarm relieved !!! I feel most certain that this will

Sir Jonathan Wathen Waller, *a hand coloured lithograph by an unknown artist, c1834.*
Wathen is wearing the ribbon and star of a Knight Grand Cross of the Royal Guelphic Order.
© *National Portrait Gallery, London.*

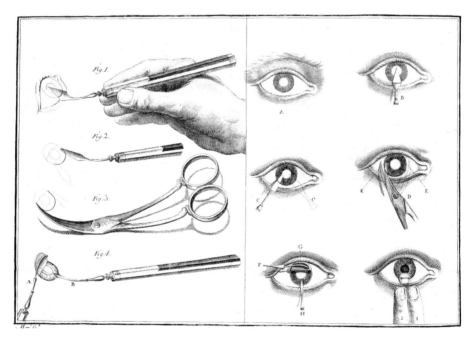

Ernest Duke of Cumberland (1771-1851), *by Sir William Beechey, painted after 1796 and no later than 1802, when the portrait was exhibited at the Royal Academy. The artist has taken care to disguise the Duke's injuries to his left arm and eye, sustained in battle at Tournai, Flanders, in 1794. Royal Collection Trust | © Her Majesty Queen Elizabeth II 2013.*

Note from Ernest Duke of Cumberland to Sir Jonathan Wathen Waller. *Dear Phippy, I did not know when I saw you last Friday that I was to be the Director [at an Ancient Music Concert] for the day after tomorrow or I should have invited you to dine with me at half past 5 o'clock which I now do per Epistolam. Yours sincerely Ernest. © Warwickshire County Record Office (CR 0341/64).*

Instruments for cataract operation, *by Johannes de Gorter. A print from 1780, when Jonathan Wathen and James Ware's surgical practice was in its heyday. © Wellcome Library, London.*

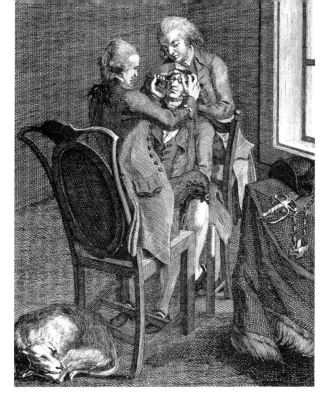

A surgeon performing an operation for cataract, by Gregorio Francisco de Queiroz after Silva, 1793. When this Portuguese engraving was published Jonathan Wathen Phipps had just entered into partnership with his oculist step-grandfather Jonathan Wathen. © Wellcome Library, London.

Georgiana, Duchess of Devonshire (1757-1806) by Thomas Gainsborough. The influential Duchess was one of Wathen's earliest patients. Reproduced by kind permission of Chatsworth Settlement Trustees. © Devonshire Collection, Chatsworth.

Georgiana and Anna Phipps, by Sir William Beechey, 1804. This portrait of Wathen's daughters was exhibited at the Royal Academy in 1807. Licensed for reproduction by Masterfile UK Ltd.

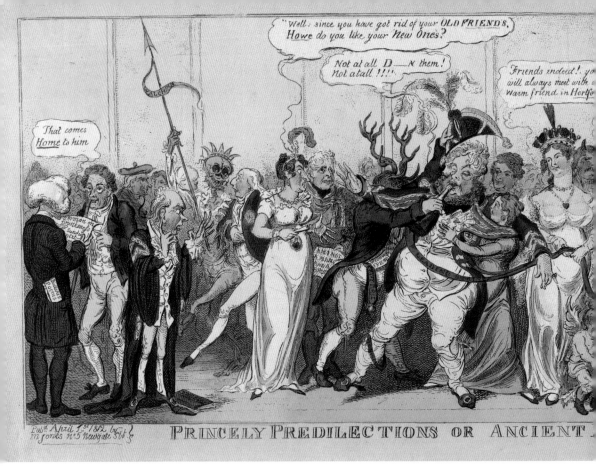

Sophia Charlotte, Baroness Howe of Langar, *by Thomas Lawrence (pastel on paper, probably as a preliminary to an oil portrait) c1822. Wathen's second wife shown about ten years after their marriage in 1812. Reproduced by kind permission of www.artwarefineart.com.*

Detail from the certificate of matriculation of the armorial ensigns and supporters to the coat of arms of Sir Jonathan Wathen Waller, 11 June 1816. *© Warwickshire County Record Office (CR0341/11).*

ND MODERN DISCORD.

G Cruikshank fecit

Pope's Villa in 1828 *by William Westall. Lady Howe destroyed Alexander Pope's riverside villa at Twickenham, and replaced it with this new villa in his cherished gardens.*

V

A snuff-box given to Mrs Damer by Napoleon on 1ˢᵗ May 1815. She bequeathed it to the British Museum in 1828 and Wathen, as Executor of her Will, was responsible for carrying out her wishes. © The Trustees of the British Museum.

A Voluptuary under the horrors of digestion, by James Gillray, 1792. Satirical print depicting the self-indulgence of the Prince of Wales, sometimes described as the "Prince of Whales". © The Trustees of the British Museum.

George IV in highland dress, by Sir David Wilkie, painted to celebrate the King's successful visit to Scotland in 1822. Royal Collection Trust | © Her Majesty Queen Elizabeth II 2013.

List of royal guests at a Dinner given by Sir W Waller & The Baroness Howe at Pope's Villa Twickenham on the 4ᵗʰ of June 1831 in Commemoration of the Glorious 1ˢᵗ of June. © Warwickshire County Record Office (CR 0341/240).

The terrace of Camerton Court, Somerset.

The west side of Camerton Court, with Orangery (by kind permission of Mr and Mrs Ken Biggs).

The first altar frontal used at St John the Baptist's Church, Peasedown St John, Somerset (by kind permission of Mr Hywel Carr). This frontal was made from Anna Jarrett's wedding dress and donated by her daughters Anna Mary and Emily to the church they founded.

*Detail from **Prince George of Cumberland, later King George of Hanover (1819-1878)** by Sir Thomas Lawrence, 1828. This portrait of his nephew aged nine was commissioned by George IV. Royal Collection Trust | © Her Majesty Queen Elizabeth II 2013.*

Ernest Augustus, Duke of Cumberland, King of Hanover (1771-1851), *miniature by Alexander Schäfer, 1846 (after a portrait by Egmont Koken, 1842). Royal Collection Trust | © Her Majesty Queen Elizabeth II 2013.*

Mrs George Bankes and her three elder children, Georgina, Maria and Edmund, *by William Ross, 1830. This miniature may have been commissioned by the Duke of Cumberland. © National Trust Images/Derrick Witty.*

gratify you much, and that you will give your fervent prayers on the occasion."[28] Ironically and tragically, von Graefe died suddenly a few days before the due date. An operation was attempted by a Dr Jaeger in September 1840, and – for once using an alternative nickname – Ernest gave Wathen a detailed report of the proceedings:

"Hannover Sept[r] 23[d] 1840
Dear Wathy
    I felt sure you would take a deep interest in learning how the operation had succeeded with the Prince Royal… Thank God up to this moment we have had no hitch of any sort, no inflammation to give a moment's anxiety, and I believe this is much owing to the preventing of any fresh Inflammation taking place by taking away a few ounces of blood within the first 24 hours, and not allowing this to shew itself…. we cannot be too cautious & prudent. Dr Jaeger assures me no later than this morning, that he is perfectly satisfied, he has examined the eye most minutely and says all adhesion has been removed, and from all the Prince Royal explains as to his feelings at present, & especially since the last two days, he should say that he believes that the absorption has already begun to take place; the feel of the eye is that it is not swelled, but much lighter in comparison, & the pupil is getting clearer, and is perfectly steady…. All this to one who is not an oculist sounds perfectly rational & satisfactory, and coming from such authority must give hopes. All now that can be done must be left to nature and his constitution which is thank God capital. We cannot be too gratefull [sic] to the Allmighty [sic] for his Divine Mercy in having heard our prayers, & I feel an inward conviction He will complete our hopes and restore him his sight."[29]

    Sadly, in spite of Ernest's hopes and prayers, the operation achieved nothing and George was to remain blind for the rest of his life.

Notes

1. WCRO: CR 0341/25, Copy of a letter from JWW to King William IV.
2. Cooke, George Wingrove, *The history of party: from the rise of the Whig and Tory factions,* J.Macrone 1837, Vol 3, p 583. Wellington's speech, November 1830: "I am thoroughly convinced that England possesses at this moment a legislature which answers all the good purposes of legislation; and this to a greater degree than any legislature ever has answered in any country of the world."
3. WCRO: CR 0341/240, List of royal guests at "The Glorious First" party, 1831.
4. The event was described in *The Royal Lady's magazine, and archives of the Court of St James's, 1831,* p 128.
5. Willis, G M, op.cit. p 210, quoting a letter from the Duke of Cumberland to the Duke of Buckingham, 8 April 1831.

6. They included Birmingham, Derby, Nottingham, Leicester, Yeovil, Sherborne, and Exeter, *www.learningcurve.gov.uk/politics/*.

7. Ibid.

8. Lord Eldon received letters signed IGNIS (i.e. fire).

9. Watkins, John, *The life and times of "England's patriot King", William IV*, 1831, p 729.

10. A slightly different version was recorded by Mary Frampton, the daughter of a prosperous landowner in Dorset, in her Journal on 5th November 1831. "This morning intelligence was received that a mob from Poole were intending to attack Lord Eldon's place at Encombe, and also Corfe Castle. Mr Bond's troop of Yeomanry were in consequence called out, and stationed on and about the bridge at Wareham, thus effectively guarding the only approach from Poole."

11. Willis, G M, op.cit. p 222, quoting a letter from the Duchess of Cumberland to Countess von Voss, 28 November 1832.

12. Both women were old friends of the Duke of Cumberland, and some flirtatious banter was apparently deliberately portrayed as something far more sinister. Lady Lyndhurst was the wife of the Lord Chancellor, and Lady Graves the sister of Ernest's old friend, the Marquess of Anglesey. Of the latter, Princess Lieven, the German wife of the Russian ambassador, wrote that the rumours of an affair with the Duke could not possibly be true, as Lady Graves was 50 years old, the mother of 13 children and wore spectacles. *Letters of Princess Lieven*, p 212. The scurrilous press had a field day with dozens of puns based on Lord and Lady Graves's name.

13. Strachey, Lytton: *Queen Victoria,* Harcourt Brace & Co., New York, 1921, p 5.

14. *The Trial of Josiah Phillips for a Libel on the Duke of Cumberland* (from the shorthand notes of Mr Gurney), J Hatchard & Son, London 1833, p 3.

15. Ibid, p 65, Wathen describing the Duke's wounds: "They were severe beyond all description, and the suffering of the Duke afterwards was such, as I have not ever seen equalled." Wathen was questioned by Mr Jelf, the lawyer brother of his son's tutor, who was one of the prosecution team. Although he would have had ample time to rehearse his evidence, Wathen embarked on a characteristically personal account and the presiding Judge had to interrupt him: "How long after you had heard of His Royal Highness being wounded, was it before you saw him ?—A very short time: the circumstance, I believe, was briefly this; I was awoke in the morning by my servant knocking at my door with a message from a person who was there, begging to know if I was going down to Wimbledon to breakfast with…… THE LORD CHIEF JUSTICE.— All this is not material."

16. Sir Charles Wetherall was a staunch Tory and a good friend of the Duke of Cumberland. He was a noted anti-reformer, whose processional entry into Bristol as Recorder for the Assizes in October 1831 had triggered the Bristol Riots.

17. Willis, G M, op.cit. p 429; Phillips broke bail and fled the country.

18. See Sir Thomas Lawrence's portrait of Prince George in 1828, in the Royal Collection, Buckingham Palace.

19. Willis, G M, op.cit. p 220, Duchess of Cumberland to the Grand Duke of Mecklenburg-Strelitz, 11 September 1830.
20. WCRO: CR 0341/65, Duke of Cumberland to JWW, 12 September 1832.
21. West Sussex Record Office: Goodwood/351, Duke of Cumberland to Duchess of Richmond, 17 December 1832.
22. Ibid.
23. Willis, G M, op.cit. p 224.
24. Ibid, quoting a letter to Lord Eldon of 1 January 1833.
25. WCRO: CR0341/68, Duke of Cumberland to JWW, 24 January 1833.
26. WCRO: CR 0341/130, Princess Augusta to JWW, November 1832.
27. Willis, G M, op.cit. p 231.
28. WCRO: CR0341/85, Duke of Cumberland to JWW, 23 January 1840.
29. WCRO: CR0341/86, Duke of Cumberland to JWW, 23 September 1840.

Chapter 9

A father's fears

"As Death finds us, <u>such</u> must we appear at the <u>final</u> Audit!! Either as the Disciples of the blessed Jesus & safe beneath his powerful Protection, or as the Followers of Mammon & consequently partakers of that eternal Punishment awarded to the Devil & his Angels."

Jonathan Wathen Waller

It is not surprising that Wathen kept the letters he received from members of the royal family and passed them on to his elder son; future generations might find them of interest and they might even acquire monetary value. Less predictable was the survival of family letters, but Thomas treasured those he received from his father and siblings while serving at various foreign Embassies. The family's need to keep in touch with each other has become a source of personal and social history for the 1830s and 1840s, and has enabled us to get to know the Wallers of this period in an unusually close way. Wathen, full of anxieties on his son's behalf, sends fatherly advice with his current news. Anna, who missed Thomas enormously, describes her daily life, thoughts and feelings in a positive vein for the most part, well aware that a lively letter had the power to raise her beloved brother's spirits.

While most of the family letters are endearingly parochial and domestic in focus, from time to time they touch on current events further afield. A brief outline of what was happening in the world at this time may therefore be useful, not least because Thomas had embarked on a diplomatic career, and his life had become bound up with British foreign policy. Huge political changes were afoot in the early 1830s, some of which re-drew the map of Europe and the Near East: France had a new King, Louis Philippe, and a new constitution in 1830; the Kingdom of the Netherlands was divided in 1831 and the new state of Belgium was created; Portugal was engaged in a civil war and Spain's sovereign in 1833 was a three-year-old princess; Greece's independence from the Ottoman Empire was finally recognised in 1832. In addition, Turkey was a battleground of opposing influences if not armies, with the potential to erupt into war. An Egyptian force advanced towards Constantinople from the south in 1831, and invaded Syria. By way of deterrent, Russia engaged in gun-boat diplomacy, massing troops in the Black Sea and the Bosphorus. Great Britain, much preoccupied by riots and Reform at home, preferred to save the expense of getting involved. In the event, the Egyptians retreated and the Russian warships could return home, but Turkey and Russia had formed an alliance,[1] and this threat to the balance of power was not at all to the liking of Palmerston, the British Foreign Secretary. He announced that if Turkey should be threatened with Russian intervention again, a combined English and French force would proceed to Constantinople to defend the Bosphorus.

Thomas began to save his private letters in April 1832, some six years after starting his diplomatic career. He was then 27, an unpaid attaché at the British Embassy in Paris, and his family was dispersed. Sir Wathen at 62 was busy at Court in his new role of Extra Groom in Waiting to William IV. At last he had been officially recognised as the King's friend, assistant and confidant. He also saw frequently the Duke of Cumberland, Princess Sophia, and Princess Mary, Duchess of Gloucester. Wathen's elder daughter, Georgiana, was 33; she had been married to the Reverend Sainsbury Langford Sainsbury, Vicar of Froyle in Hampshire, for two years. They had a baby boy, named after his father, and Georgiana was expecting a second child. Her sister Anna was 29 and still childless; she was living with her husband, John Jarrett, at their grand but rented country house, at Hale near Salisbury. They were trying to find a new tenant to relieve them of their obligations under the now tiresome rental agreement. John's mother had died in 1830, leaving him her estate at Camerton in Somerset, comprising a manor house, several farms, and some coal mines, but their landlord at Hale had refused to release them from their contract. From his father, John had earlier inherited five sugar plantations in Jamaica, and he would have been a very wealthy man, had he not been hampered by the millstone of his profligate grandfather's debts; money matters were never far from his mind. Ernest, the youngest of the Waller children, was 25, and somewhat in limbo in 1832 after completing his Oxford degree and theological studies. He was an ordained priest and had been an unpaid curate in Sussex, but now he needed a proper job, either as a curate (preferably not far from Camerton) or, if his father could pull the right strings, as a royal chaplain. In the meantime he was leading a rather idle life, visiting his father, his sisters and former school and university friends.

We have seen Wathen in his professional and public roles, and in his relationships with his royal friends over more than thirty years. Through his letters to his son Thomas we can glimpse far more of his character as a person and as a father. There was undoubtedly a strong bond of affection between the two, and each was desperately anxious to please the other. Yet Thomas sometimes found it difficult to live up to his father's expectations. Wathen's own upbringing had given him a conviction that the parental role was above all to instil religious faith and righteous behaviour in his children. It was the heaviest of all his responsibilities. He may have felt guilty that his son and his second wife, Lady Howe, did not get on well. There were no doubt many difficult or awkward moments in the household until Thomas took up a career abroad – thanks to his father's friends at Court. Unsurprisingly, Thomas had mixed feelings about his father's interference in his life. He needed his father's help, but he rather resented it. Wathen's well-meaning aspirations for his son and heir meant that the relationship between the two of them, though close, was from time to time fraught with tension.

Religion was never far from Wathen's mind, and after the death of George IV it preoccupied him more than ever. He was, of course, getting older and facing the prospect of his own death, so the absolute necessity of meriting salvation, thereby entering into the joy of eternal life in the presence of God, was of supreme importance to him. Given his literal belief in heaven and hell, a product of his strict Calvinistic upbringing, nothing could be more logical and understandable than this manner of thinking, but in our post-Darwinian era it is nevertheless hard for many of us to imagine. Wathen's mindset was unshakeable: he had no doubt that the Day of Judgment was inevitable, and greatly to be feared. On that day the righteous would be separated from the unrighteous and the judgment would last for eternity. Who would not tremble at such a thought, reinforced by preachers and hymn-writers such as John and Charles Wesley, known personally to Wathen and related by marriage to his uncle James Waller? What is more, as a child Wathen had absorbed the unwavering thinking of an earlier generation (in the person of Anne Wathen, his grandmother) – the generation of his parents having had little if any influence in his upbringing. Consequently he was even more dogmatic in his religious beliefs than many of his peers, and considered it his bounden duty as a father to pass them on to his children so that their eternal salvation would also be assured.

Georgiana (a vicar's wife) and Ernest (a parson) seem to have gained their father's approval by leading worthy, God-fearing lives. However, Thomas and even devout Anna worried from time to time about their lack of adequate faith, and the difficulty of living up to the religious ideals of their father. Whilst Anna seems to have confided only in her brother, Thomas openly acknowledged his doubts to his father, who responded with a torrent of admonitions and instructions. We have no detail about what happened, but in 1832 Thomas suffered a spiritual crisis, and felt obliged to confess it to his father. He was no longer sure what he believed, and his conscience was agonisingly troubled. From past experience he must have known that his father would inevitably lecture him about sin and divine retribution – for his own good, of course. It is surely no coincidence that Thomas began to retain letters from home at this particular point in his life. His confession provoked lengthy exhortations from his father, differing radically from his usual conversational style. No doubt they were read and re-read over and over again.

Wathen was wracked with anxiety. His response to his son's misgivings was to counsel repentance: "Remember Death is certain, whether it be <u>near</u> or <u>distant.</u>

We must <u>all</u> appear before the Judgment seat of Christ to answer for all the deeds done in the flesh."[2] The context makes clear that Wathen is not referring to sins "of the flesh" but rather to sins committed during a physical lifetime on earth; uppermost in his mind is the worst of all sins, lack of faith or as he calls it, "infidelity". For Wathen, although the afterlife was a certainty, the nature of the life to come was far from certain. The fate of those who were not granted salvation would be unspeakable; it was not something he wanted to dwell on, though the fear of it never left him. He had actively encouraged Thomas to work abroad, but in the spring of 1832 Wathen regrets this decision, and is horrified to think that he may have unwittingly placed his son in both moral and physical danger. Secure in his own firm faith, he had overlooked the fact that France was a hotbed of freethinking, where 'Enlightenment' ideas had been rife for decades. He should have anticipated the potential influences prevalent in a society which had bred atheists like Diderot and the 'Encyclopédistes', not to mention the deist Voltaire, who considered Christianity of marginal use – and only for the lower classes. What is more, the political situation in France was known to be unstable, and his son was an impressionable young man in a foreign city, lacking sophistication, and prey to all manner of potential vices and ills.

Once Wathen has put pen to paper he does not stop till he has covered eleven sides. He urges Thomas to leave Paris, where a cholera epidemic is raging – a sure sign of God's wrath towards unrepentant sinners and infidels. If necessary, Thomas must abandon his career in the diplomatic service. "The dreadful account of the state of Paris, from the ravages of this dire cholera, which have appeared in the public papers, both of Saturday & of this morning, alarm me greatly my dear boy, & render me most <u>anxious</u> about <u>you</u>. I … trust that you will procure leave of absence, & come home, or, if the danger be as <u>great</u> as represented <u>here</u>, & you <u>cannot</u> obtain <u>leave</u>, that you will at once <u>throw up</u> your profession, & endeavor to make yourself <u>happy</u> with <u>what</u> your father can do for <u>you</u>, for I can never think it your <u>duty</u> to run farther risk of your <u>life</u>, for a <u>Government</u> that has been so <u>unmindful</u> of your services." Both father and son had expected a swift rise for Thomas through the junior diplomatic ranks.

The eleven pages are mostly taken up with a passionate "sermon", continued in like manner in the next letter. The message is forceful and heartfelt. Ironically, the father, an eminently worldly man, accuses his conscience-burdened son of leading an empty and sinful life. "I can fully understand your feeling the <u>utter</u> void left at the <u>hour</u> of calamity, in <u>that</u> heart which has been devoted <u>solely</u> to a life of pleasure or to the pursuits & objects of <u>this</u> world. Solomon, the wisest of mankind … after having drained the cup of pleasure & sensuality to the very <u>last</u> drop … found it <u>only vanity</u> & <u>vexation of spirit</u>. In spite of <u>this</u> truth however, every man, in his different station seems <u>determined</u> to <u>renew</u> these experiments for <u>himself</u>, & happy is he, who by grace, discovers in time, the emptiness of the shadow, & turns to the only source of real & permanent peace; the service of his God & Saviour!!"[3]

For Wathen, brought up in the Evangelical movement, loss of faith is the ultimate sin. Appalled that his son has confessed to doubts in the matter of religion, he refuses to enter into any philosophical debate or to consider atheism or agnosticism as potentially valid viewpoints. For him there is only one path to salvation: "Believe & live". Any faith remaining must be reinforced systematically, through prayer, Bible study and observing the Sabbath. Wathen sets out the régime to be followed at great length, citing 'self-evident' lessons to be learned from recent and current epidemics, as well as historical plagues and disasters. His appraisal of disease as punishment is more than a little shocking to a twenty-first century reader, especially coming from a man with medical training and a career in surgery. Equally alien to our global perspective and notion of a multicultural society is his judgmental commentary on the sins of foreign nations; clearly tolerance and forgiveness scarcely feature in Christianity as Wathen understood it: "It is curious but it appears to me plain, that the present devastating pestilence, is the punishment of national infidelity, for nations must be punished in this world, individuals in the next. The cholera began I understand in Persia, an idolatrous kingdom where its ravages were terrific; from thence it has passed to the followers of Brama & Mahomet & thousands have fallen before it… It has now attacked Paris, the heart of Christian infidelity & there it again puts on its terrific form." Although the letter is littered with underlining – often double underlining – the handwriting is not rushed but controlled and well-spaced. Wathen is making his points emphatically, but not writing in anger. He continues: "Now cast an eye back to the page of history. The profligate Charles the 2nd brought with him from France at his Restoration, the infidel principle, & with it, the Plague followed, & amidst the ravages of pestilence & fire, England & London in particular was taught to remember the God of her fathers, & the Saviour of the World. I say more on this subject my Child, as I have every reason to think, that it is the rock surrounded as you are, on which you are most likely to be wrecked… Shun it my beloved Boy, more than pestilence or fire. They can only kill the body, but infidelity irretrievably destroys both Body & Soul to all Eternity."

These two letters from Wathen to his son are untypical of the subsequent correspondence in both tone and content. They must have been painful to read, but Thomas is left in no doubt as to his father's motivation in sending them: he is determined to bring his son to repentance and a life of faith and religious observance. Embarking on the second letter without waiting for a reply, Wathen continues in the same vein, well aware that he is playing the preacher: "I do not think my dear [Thomas] Wathen, that I should have written to you a second Sermon on these points, until I had learned how my former had been received, did not yours before me, say that 'you wished to collect around you every help in your power'." Wathen explains that he owes the strength of his own beliefs to his grandmother, whose portrait still serves to remind him of the precepts she instilled in him as a small child. Now charged with parental duties himself, he is perhaps only too aware that he has not always been an ideal role model, and may not have appeared to practise what he preached. "Do you not suppose the love I bear to my <u>dear Grandmother</u>, to whom under <u>God</u> I owe not only <u>every</u> comfort I enjoy in <u>this</u> life but <u>every</u> prospect I look forward to in <u>another</u>, does not become even stronger by viewing that picture at this instant before me! Yes; & her constant & last injunctions can <u>never</u> be forgotten. I may <u>often</u> have acted <u>contrary</u> to <u>them</u> & often lamented that <u>disobedience</u>, but whenever I look at that picture, <u>they</u> rush in my <u>memory</u>, & become more & more <u>urgent</u> in <u>my heart</u>, &, <u>you</u> well know, [they] are & ever will be a <u>principal</u> guide of my actions. Hers was a life of religion!! Hers was the death of a Saint!! <u>Her</u> injunctions ever those of her <u>God</u>, & enforced by parental anxiety & parental affection, & praise be God, they have not been <u>lost upon me</u>." Pausing after his lengthy and emotional diatribe, Wathen reverts briefly to his habitual epistolary style, resuming his everyday topics. So commonplace for him are dinners with the royal family that he observes without irony: "I have no news to send you. I dined yesterday at the Duke of Cumberland's to meet their Majesties. We were only 20 & just the King's own set & had a pleasant day." He concludes by expressing his paternal love for his 'wayward' son: "I long for tomorrow when I shall hear again from you. God bless & preserve thee my beloved Child, Your affectionate father, JW Waller."

Just as his grandmother's injunctions were not lost on Wathen in his youth, his were not lost on Thomas, who made strenuous efforts to seek his father's approval, and to regain his faith through the prescribed religious study and observance. In this he was helped by his sister Anna and by his clergyman uncle, Thomas White, both of whom recommended to him specific commentaries on the Bible and other religious treatises. To Wathen's evident delight, his harsh but well-intentioned words had the desired effect, as this birthday letter a couple of years later shows:

"Pope's Villa, Thursday, June 26th 1834.

On the anniversary of this day which gave birth to my much loved boy, I must seize its earliest moment to send him his father's <u>best</u> & warmest blessings & never did son better deserve it. May that God we both adore continue to you my dear child not only the temporal blessings which he has mercifully bestowed on you, but more especially those spiritual & best gifts of his grace & spirit, which I have lived (I praise him for it) to believe he has vouchsafed to <u>you</u>. May these more particularly be continued & increased to you, till they are perfected in your complete union with your Saviour, & admission into his eternal enjoyments in Heaven. The hope & prospect of <u>this</u> afford more comfort & real pleasure to <u>your Father</u>, than all the prosperity & splendour this earth could bestow upon you."[4]

Set side by side, this expression of a father's love and an eleven-page sermon preaching hell-fire and damnation could scarcely be more contrasting in content and epistolary style. Whilst there is no doubting the warmth of Wathen's feelings in the birthday letter, implicit in it is a huge sigh of relief. The lost sheep has been saved; salvation in the afterlife – eternal life in heaven – now awaits him. Gone is Wathen's declamatory style, and with it the fear (terror, even) and burden of guilt that weighed so heavily upon him when Thomas was wavering in his faith. He praises God that he has been spared to bring to fruition that most vital of parental obligations, the inculcation (in one's offspring) of belief in God and Jesus Christ the Saviour and Redeemer. Wathen can now contemplate his own death. Secure in the knowledge that he has not failed in his paternal role, he can face the "final audit" of the Day of Judgment, and is overcome with joy and gratitude. "At 65 which I am next October, the lease of human existence is nearly run out…… but when I reflect on the mercies I <u>have</u>, & still do enjoy, & call to mind my <u>utter</u> unworthiness of the <u>least</u> of them, I can only 'take the Cup of Salvation & praise the name of my God'.[5] Amidst the multitude of <u>these</u> mercies, are my <u>dear children</u>. Whilst I see & hear of fathers all around me bitterly complaining & lamenting over the conduct of their Sons, I have <u>only</u> cause for gratitude & praise. What can I render to my God for all his mercies?

> "My days of Praise shall ne'er be past
> Whilst Life & Thought & Being last
> Or Immortality endures."

These words are the refrain from a hymn by Isaac Watts based on Psalm 146.[6] As Wathen surely knew, they were the last words spoken by John Wesley in his final sermon, and sung by him a few days later on his death-bed. The favourite hymns and psalms of his grandmother's were never far from Wathen's mind.

Remembering that he was writing a birthday letter, Wathen turns to more mundane and trivial topics (including the weather), in another radical change of tone: "The Queen leaves England on the 7th of July. They remain in Town till the 4th. I think I never experienced so overcoming a heat as that of the rooms at St. James's on Friday evening last at the Queen's last Ball. I got away as early as I could. Since that, the weather has been cooler, indeed only agreeably warm. The crops of hay are very light & gooseberries & strawberries are scarce… Some of my grape houses have failed but others are abundantly productive so that on the whole I am very well off. I hear the draining has done miracles on the farm."

Though we learn little from this letter about the recipient, it illustrates perfectly the paradoxical nature and thinking of its writer. How characteristic of Phippy to juxtapose in one letter the life ever after and the efficiency of drains.

Notes

1. Hunkar Iskelesi Treaty 1833.
2. WCRO: CR 0341/ 327/2a-d, JWW to TWW, 22 April 1832.
3. WCRO: CR 0341/327/4a & 4b, JWW to TWW, undated but probably May 1832.
4. WCRO: CR 0341/327/9, JWW to TWW, 26 June 1834.
5. A line from Psalm 116.
6. Wathen's father Joshua Phipps bequeathed to his mother-in-law Anne Wathen (Wathen's grandmother) six volumes of the works of Isaac Watts – see Chapter 1.

Chapter 10

A new posting for Thomas; a new house for Anna

Thomas did leave Paris in 1832. He spent some weeks in England, partly at Hastings, where his father was looking after Prince George of Cumberland after the accident to his eye, and early in December he set off for the continent again – initially to Italy. He was to meet up with Lord Ponsonby, recently nominated Ambassador to Constantinople, and travel to Turkey with him as "paid attaché". Ponsonby, however, seemed to be in no hurry to leave Naples, where he had been Envoy for only a few months, so Thomas had time for some sightseeing in Italy. Although Russia, France and Egypt were on the brink of conflict over Turkey, Ponsonby – either intentionally or through force of circumstances – managed to delay his arrival in Constantinople till May 1833. He took up residence in the British Summer Palace at Therapia on the Bosphorus, as the Embassy building in the Pera district of Constantinople had been destroyed by fire in 1831.

Anna was close in age to Thomas, and from their earliest childhood they had shared confidences readily. To show him how much she loved and missed him she resolved to write to him at least once a fortnight. Reading the letters in sequence is almost like reading chapters in a novel, or watching episodes in a family saga. Dramatic events and minor incidents in the lives of the Wallers are recounted as they happen. The letters are conversational in tone but elegant in phrasing. Much of their charm lies in Anna's own words, her own "voice". Her first letter, written in London in December 1832, indicates that Thomas's new posting (his first *paid* diplomatic post) is a promotion. She does her best to sound positive, although she regrets the far-flung destination. After all, behind the scenes Wathen is busy trying to engineer a posting for Thomas closer to home, so she is looking forward to his prompt return: "…till then I will view the bright side of the picture. I will rejoice at your having gained a step in your profession, at the opportunity afforded you of seeing a part of the world you so anxiously desired to see; at the prospect you hold out of the probability of your passing the winter in Italy, which I am sure will be a source of great gratification to you, and above all will I cherish the <u>dear</u> <u>dear</u> hope that our separation will not be very long, but that after a time my Father's exertions (which he declares shall be <u>unremitting</u>) will get you removed to a nearer Embassy, and that again you may be comparatively <u>within reach</u>."[1] She is determined to keep her letter light in tone: "I need scarcely add that poor old Driver [Thomas's dog] shall be loved and cherished for your sake. He shall want neither care nor attention. He was delighted to see John, and has attached himself to him as before. This said dear husband sends you his kind love, his best and warmest wishes for your happiness, and the assurance of his willingness to make your old dog as welcome and as comfortable as he can. He goes down with us to Froyle tomorrow <u>inside</u> the carriage, and shall lie at my feet, to keep them warm. I think dear Ernest will be quite sorry to part with him. He loads him with caresses, and seems so very fond of him." While hoping to hear of a suitable curacy, Ernest was resigned for the present to leading a peripatetic existence: "[he] starts for Hastings tomorrow; after spending a week or 10 days with my Father, he will go to Froyle for a short time, and then proceed to take up his abode with us, for the rest of the winter, I hope."

In the same letter, Anna tells her brother about the major building project she and John have decided upon. In spite of their money problems they were determined to maintain a standard of living worthy of their status in society, and planned to build an entirely new house in Camerton on a much grander scale than the existing manor house. Very much her father's daughter in matters of religion, Anna concludes with a lengthy and heartfelt prayer for her brother's safety and salvation:

> "may our prayers for each other, ascend together to the Throne of Grace, and draw down a blessing on our heads. Now my beloved brother, Adieu. Once more, <u>God bless thee</u> now & ever. My heart is on my pen, and I would fain find more words to express to thee how truly, how fondly, and how devotedly I am
>   Your most affec[tiona]te and faithfully attached Sister.
>   Anna Eliza Jarrett"

When she next writes to Thomas, shortly before Christmas, Anna is with her sister Georgiana at Froyle Parsonage for the baptism of the new baby. "The children are both quite well. The eldest grows a most engaging boy, and the youngest Miss <u>Anna Maria</u> (who is to be christened tomorrow) is a most <u>magnificent</u> <u>specimen</u>. I seldom saw a finer infant. We leave this [place] for Hale on Saturday the 22nd, and I hope the Reptons[2] will come to us on the 24th, to eat their Xmas dinner, but it must depend, I am sorry to say upon the improvement of their health."[3] Anna realises that Wathen is still fretting over Thomas, unsure whether he has done the right thing in obtaining for him the new posting. She, on the other hand, her insight reinforced by pragmatism, realises that dwelling on negative thoughts will do him no good : "Our dear Father wrote to GG the other day and touched upon the subject of your departure. He is still very low, but assures us he is striving to conquer it. His time just now is so fully occupied [looking after Prince George of Cumberland and his parents in Hastings], that I hope he will soon succeed. It is fortunate that he has not leisure to cherish his melancholy thoughts, but will necessarily be obliged to exert himself to throw them off. I wrote to him a few days since, and mentioned how my own feelings were strangely compounded of regrets and rejoicings, but I observed the <u>regrets</u> must be all for <u>ourselves</u>, the rejoicings all for <u>thee</u>."

Wathen's letter to Thomas from Hastings dated 27 January 1833 differs hugely in tone from the "sermons" sent to his son in Paris. Having calmed down and resumed a much gentler fatherly attitude, he is in his element dealing with practicalities and passing on snippets of news: "Your letter from Rome my dear boy of the 10 Jany arrived here last Friday, & most truely happy did it make me, from the knowledge of your safety, health & comfort. By it I learn you were to sail as yesterday,[4] I suppose from Naples, to Constantinople, & rejoiced shall I be to hear you are <u>safely</u> arrived at your <u>destination</u> …… I have written to Messrs Hoares & desired them to send a Letter of Credit for you as you requested to Mr Hunton of Constantinople for £500. You did not mention <u>any</u> sum, & <u>that</u> I thought was more than you could at any <u>one</u> time want. Now as to your books from Paris. I yesterday heard from Grundy that they are <u>safe at Pope's Villa…</u>. The Duke of Cumberland has been absent this week past on a visit to the Duke of Wellington but returns today to dinner. Prince George much the <u>same</u>. We often talk of you, & P. G. desires you will not <u>forget him</u>, & always, as well as the Duke & Duchess, sends <u>love</u>. We remain here till <u>Easter</u>. I had a letter from the King <u>today</u> with a good account of all at Brighton [Pavilion] & the Duchess of Gloucester [Princess Mary] is now so much better that she comes down for an hour <u>every</u> evening to the drawing room. We go on here much in the old routine & on the whole are tolerably comfortable… and now my beloved child accept again & ever the best blessing of your affectionate Father, JWW." [5]

Anna, still at Hale at the end of January, does her best to send Thomas news that he will want to hear – how they are pampering his dog, Driver, for example: "I sometimes ask old Driver whether he remembers his Master, but I fear he has quite forgotten his grief in his present happiness. He is so caressed, and taken such care of! He has a saucer of milk for his breakfast every morning, and John does not allow him to be fed down stairs, lest they should overfeed him through kindness. Every day therefore after dinner, <u>with</u> the bottle of Claret enters a pewter plate full of meat for Driver, which is given to John, who feeds the old dog with a <u>silver fork bit by bit</u>, lest he should eat too fast, and so not get the proper nourishment from his viands. He then comes to me for his dessert of Biscuit, and his water, and at night is put to bed on a down pillow on the sofa in John's dressing room, and carefully wrapped up in a horse rug. Heard you ever the like? 'Love Master love Dog' holds good here at any rate." They are at last packing to leave Hale, but first John is going to Camerton to close down a coal mine, which is losing £400 a year. Their main source of income comes from the sugar plantations in Jamaica, but John still has inherited debts to clear. In a hastily added postscript imbued with thoughtless self-interest, pious, good-hearted Anna comments: "They talk of emancipating the Negroes directly without any compensation. What will become of us?"[6]

In February Ernest mentions that his father is still busy lobbying the King on Thomas's behalf – and indeed also on his own (Ernest's) behalf, as the King is seeking a new Chaplain: "Of all that took place on my Father's late visit to Brighton of course he has sent you word, I think it looks well for you, and if I am to be any person's chaplain of course I had rather be his Majesty's: it is at least a feather in a man's cap, and as I am fourth on the list, I suppose I really stand some chance." He also shows some awareness of the recent political changes, though he is not impressed: "The reformed house of commons seems to be very noisy, and as yet they have done nothing but talk about the address. And the radicals although very noisy and good speakers I should say <u>would</u> be able to do nothing."[7]

Anna often worried about Georgiana's health, and in late February she is feeling rather guilty that she has not rushed to Froyle to look after her sister, who is suffering from rheumatic fever, especially as her brother-in-law, Sainsbury, is seriously depressed. Though she says nothing on the subject, she may well have been envious of Georgiana's ability to produce one child after another, while she, married far longer, has been unable to conceive. Perhaps she protests too much in her efforts to justify her behaviour: "I should have gone to her instantly, but hearing that however painful & tedious, her malady was not <u>dangerous</u>, and that her new maid was a most incomparable, and tender nurse, and knowing she had excellent medical advice, and a kind husband to watch over her, I felt that I ought to be contented to remain here, where just at the present moment I should ill be spared… … Sainsbury has promised that should the <u>slightest</u> change take place for the worse, he will send a man & horse to me, and I can be with her in a few hours. But of that I trust there is no fear. Ernest went to Froyle yesterday, in order to spend a few days with Sainsbury and cheer him up, as he wrote to say that he was <u>blueified</u> to the deepest tint."[8]

The Jarretts' plans were well under way for the proposed new house. As regards the expense, they were fortunate in two ways: one was that they had their "own stone" (that is, quarries on their own estate); and the second was that George Stanley Repton, the husband of Anna's oldest and dearest friend, Lady Elizabeth Repton, was a renowned and fashionable architect, and he had agreed to draw up the plans. "Our building is quite <u>decided</u> upon, and we are going to begin immediately. Mr Herbert [the builder] has sent in his estimate which is £6800 – I think it <u>most reasonable</u>. Mr Repton originally said £6000 and the old materials which were about £500 more. The estimate therefore only exceeds his original supposition by £300 – and we have added different things to the house of full that amount. It will be a most comfortable house, and as large as we could possibly desire. The plan has been shewn to many people, two of whom guessed the cost, one at £20,000, and one at £25,000. Of course having <u>our own stone</u>, and Mr Repton as our architect, makes an <u>immense</u> difference, or we could not build <u>such</u> a house, for anything <u>like</u> the sum. Mr Repton's kindness has been more than I can express. He has taken such indefatigable pains & trouble, not only to make it <u>comfortable</u>, but <u>economical</u> that I feel sure, we owe more to him, than even <u>we</u> are aware of. We have £5000 to sell out, and I trust that we shall save the rest out of our income, living quietly at Camerton, for we have quite given up the idea of going to Scotland, as too expensive at present. I trust also that <u>more than half</u> our debt to Mr Deffell,[9] will be wiped off on the 1st of May, which is no small comfort. I think I told you we had let the farm. The coal business is also in train, but we must make up our minds to the loss of about £400 per annum: However if we open a new pit that may partly make it up to us."

Thomas has still not reached Constantinople when Ernest writes to him on 14th March, describing how impersonal Hale House looks now that Anna and John are at last about to depart. He is also able to report that their new house is under way, but that his search for a curacy, albeit with Anna keeping an eye on opportunities, has so far come to nothing. "I am heartily tired of being without regular employment, and if I do not get something about Camerton before very long, I shall be much tempted to take any thing that offers, be it where it may."[10]

By May, Anna is feeling settled and happy at Camerton, no doubt influenced by her husband's enjoyment of being back in his childhood home, despite the old manor house leaving much to be desired. John is relishing living in his own property after nearly ten years of renting accommodation: "I wish you could see this place <u>now</u>. It is <u>quite lovely</u>, and I become every day more and more attached to it. My dear husband takes the greatest interest in the improvement of it, and is as happy and contented as possible. He is of course very busy, and confesses that there <u>is</u> a great difference in a man's feelings about his <u>own</u> or a <u>hired</u> place."[11] Anna is delighted to tell her brother that John laid the foundation stone of the new house on 12 May [1833]. There is further good news: their financial situation is improving, thanks to good crops in Jamaica, and their debts are almost paid. From Anna's perspective the plantations and mines are above all sources of problems and anxieties, especially for John. "The Coal business is not yet settled and I fear will not be so for some time." As for the miners: "They are troublesome, and wrong headed – these black gentlemen."

Thomas, of course, has preoccupations of his own: a lack of warmth and approachability on the part of Lord Ponsonby, the Ambassador with whom he must work, and his continuing anxiety about the inadequacy of his Christian faith.

Anna offers him plenty of advice on the latter problem: "You say that your religion is a conviction of the <u>head</u> and not of the <u>heart</u>…… Persevere my own brother, and your rewards will be <u>great</u>. <u>Great</u> even in <u>this</u> life, and <u>unspeakable</u> in another…… Earnestly strive to do your duty, pray to God to enable you to love and serve him more & more, and leave the rest to Him. May His choicest blessings rest upon thy precious head!"

Several times Ernest and Anna wrote joint letters to Thomas, but the first from Ernest on his own is from Pope's Villa, dated 16 May 1833. He is more inclined to comment on politics and current affairs than his sister, but he also talks of his search for a curacy, of books he is considering ordering for Thomas, of Anna's new house, and of Georgiana's fast-increasing family. Also he has noticed while staying at Twickenham that all is not sweetness and light between Sir Wathen and the Baroness. "Every thing here out-doors seems to be going on very well, the farm prospers, and shows that it is well taken care of, the garden looks well, and so far all goes on quietly, but with every thing around to produce happiness & peace, I cannot say that I see much symptoms of improvement indoors; with Lady Howe I am neither in the sunshine or in the frost, and am very well contented that things should remain as they are, if I could only see more happiness existing between her & my Father. Thank God he seems very well in health, and his face the week that I have been at home seems to give him very little pain."[12] As Ernest's visit was only a couple of weeks before the annual party to celebrate the "Glorious First of June", preparations for the event may have been causing stress and friction in the household.

On Anna and John's behalf Ernest took an interest in the current debate on abolishing slavery. "The proposal of Ministers about the West Indies appears to give universal dissatisfaction; on the one side it is complained of by the immediate emancipationists as not going near far enough & therefore they are dissatisfied; by the West India interest it is looked upon as going too far and as a point blank deprivation of property – how it will end remains to be seen, but it is thought the bill under these circumstances can never pass." As befits a priest, Ernest ends his letter with a blessing and some words of encouragement to his brother about his Christian faith and behaviour: "And now my own dearest Brother may God bless thee, and preserve and further in thee those sentiments with which you left us….. He will never leave us nor forsake us, neither shall our labours be in vain."

A couple of weeks later Anna is on a visit to London, thoroughly enjoying a change of scene and the bustle of the capital. Her sister Georgiana is also there, but seems far from well. Anna suspects GG is pregnant again. "Too quick," is her only comment.[13] She says nothing, even to her brother Thomas, about her own childless state after ten years of marriage, but is clearly less than delighted by her sister's third pregnancy in three years. Thomas is still feeling aggrieved about the unfriendliness of Lord Ponsonby, and Anna advises her brother to remain cheerful and bide his time. She has an important piece of news to convey, namely that Ernest has heard of a curacy in Warwickshire near Leamington, and has accepted it. The same topics are taken up again in mid-June: "GG and Sainsbury are …going to add to the size of their present nursery …. for fear there will be a new inhabitant in December. This is having no rest truly, and I am sorry for it, as GG is far from strong. Ernest has taken the Warwickshire Curacy…. Papa is furnishing his house for him, which I hear is <u>most diminutive</u>……. I am so entirely glad that he should be employed in the active duties of his profession, that all other considerations, even that of having him near me <u>here,</u> yield to the feeling. He is nervous about it, but when once embarked, I am confident he will go on well. Experience is what he wants, and that he must learn…… with his excellent moral & religious principles, and his sincere anxiety to do his duty, I have little fear with God's blessing for the result."[14]

Anna is able to report that her father and Lady Howe have held their "Glorious First of June" party as usual: "We went down to Pope's Villa to be present at the Royal dinner. It was a splendid sight, and went off very well indeed. Papa is tolerably well, but I think he looks <u>pale</u> and <u>worn</u>, and <u>aged</u> within these two years. His face has been very painful of late." Wathen's chronic trigeminal neuralgia was never to leave him for long, and to lessen the pain he took ever larger doses of laudanum as he got older. It probably caused the mood swings apparent in his letters – signs of depression, for instance, creeping into accounts of the grandest celebrations. Writing to Thomas from Windsor Castle in August 1833 Wathen describes Queen Adelaide's birthday celebrations: a Dinner (lasting from 4 to 8 pm) for 70, followed by an evening party for 300. Wathen had struggled to keep his composure at the Dinner: "my heart was the most melancholy of the group as my late <u>dear</u> Master [George IV] was never one moment absent from my thoughts." He feels that his own death cannot be far off, and has settled his affairs: "I have now lived long enough to see all my own dear children of age and able to manage for themselves and my life has also been spared to see the orphan girls of my poor sister under similar happy circumstances and thus by the blessing of God all the business I had to do in this world is brought to a close, and except preparation for a better, I have nothing more to do. I have outlived, except my family, almost all those who cared for me and indeed for whom I cared and society now has lost all its charms for me. The royal family and about half a dozen others are now all I wish to see, or associate with, and all that is called and I once thought pleasure has lost its charms and become insipid."[15]

The abolition of slavery continues to preoccupy Anna, though she tries hard to adopt a philosophical and suitably Christian attitude when contemplating the potential repercussions for her husband's sugar enterprise: "As for our West India concerns – <u>most</u> people say we are utterly ruined – some <u>few</u> that we shall do very well, and that the Bill will effect wonders. Who shall decide when doctors disagree? For my own part, I strive not to think about it, and to keep my mind calm & tranquil upon the subject, and to persuade my dear husband to do the same, not <u>only</u> I hope because it is a clear case that <u>fretting</u> can do us no good, but from the higher motive of dutiful submission to the will of God. If good befall us, may we with thankful hearts look up to Him, from whom all good gifts do come! If on the contrary, He permits affliction and troubles to overtake us, may He give us strength to support them patiently… I will continue (as I always have done through life) to <u>hope for the best</u>." [16] Anna's father was far more pessimistic, considering the Jarretts "in a pack of troubles with the coal mines at Camerton and the West Indian Estate… [they] seem to me to get nothing from either…. [and] are fleeced on every side." Anna's optimism was eventually vindicated when John Jarrett received substantial compensation – £14,200 – for freeing the 745 slaves he owned on his five Jamaican estates.[17]

When she next writes to Thomas Anna is irritated that at least one of his letters to her has gone astray: "I am the more vexed as I know this lost one would have told me so much that I want to know. <u>How</u>, and where you are settled, how you got on … after the unpleasant dilemma of your first landing…. But I will not take up any more paper with my grumblings about what I cannot help. I must <u>grin and bear it</u>."[18] Much to Anna's delight, Thomas has offered to send her a Turkish carpet for the new house, and she sends the dimensions of their spacious dining room – 27 feet 3 inches by 18 feet 2 inches. Seventeen months later, in November 1834, she is able to confirm that the carpet has reached them; it "fits very well, and looks extremely handsome."[19] From time to time Anna and others sent gifts to Thomas, and the letters are strewn with follow-up enquiries as to whether they have arrived, whether they are suitable, whether he likes them and so on. After some dithering about its size and shape, Anna sent him a locket (at his request) and, separately, a Venetian chain. She also sent books on theology, and some comic books for light relief. Lady Elizabeth Repton sent a dressing case (which went missing for some months en route), his father sent a watch, and the Duke of Cumberland a memorandum book. John had promised some hunting dogs, but he was uncertain at first whether to go ahead, not knowing how long Thomas would remain in Therapia.[20] From time to time Anna would send Thomas a food parcel, listing the contents so that he would know what to expect: "a large Jar of West India Green Sweetmeats (Limes & Citrons)… 3 small Pots of Strawberry – 1 of Quince – 1 Damson – 1 Apricot… a jar of West India Ginger, one of Jamaica Hot Pickles, some Brandy cherries, some Apricot Cheese, and some Damson Cheese, and some Apple Jelly." [21]

In return Anna expected to be regaled with descriptions of the exoticism of the Turks. She is sadly disappointed to hear how westernised they have become: "how unmercifully you destroy my romantic ideas of a Grand vizier, in a huge white turban covered with jewels, and robes weighed down with gold and precious stones!!! how cruel to talk of 'white trowsers' and 'wellington boots'! Can any thing in nature be more unpicturesque?"

Notes

1. WCRO: CR 0341/327/49, AJ to TWW, 12 December 1832.
2. The Reptons: Lady Elizabeth Repton, daughter of Lord Eldon, and her husband George Stanley Repton, architect and son of landscape gardener and architect, Humphrey Repton. Lady Elizabeth was a great friend of all the Wallers, and in particular, Anna. She was also a close friend of the Duke and Duchess of Cumberland. Before her marriage she had been considered a possible lady-in-waiting or companion for Princess Charlotte, the Regent's daughter, but despite Princess Mary's recommendation no formal appointment was made.
3. WCRO: CR 0341/327/50, AJ to TWW, 19 December 1832.
4. The departure was planned for January, but it was postponed.
5. WCRO: CR 0341/327/3, JWW to TWW, 27 January 1833.
6. WCRO: CR 0341/327/51, AJ to TWW 31 January 1833.
7. WCRO: CR 0341/327/52, EAW & AJ to TWW, 13 February 1833.
8. WCRO: CR 0341/327/53, AJ to TWW, 27 February 1833.
9. John Henry Deffell was John Jarrett's London agent, responsible for receiving and despatching goods, dealing with Customs & Excise payments etc.
10. WCRO: CR 0341/327/54, AJ & EAW to TWW, 14 March 1833.
11. WCRO: CR 0341/327/55, AJ to TWW, 13 May 1833.
12. WCRO: CR0341/327/25, EAW to TWW, 16 May 1833.
13. WCRO: CR0341/327/56, AJ to TWW, 4 June 1833.
14. WCRO: CR0341/327/57, AJ to TWW, 20 June 1833.
15. WCRO: CR0341/327/6a, JWW to TWW, 14 August 1833.
16. WCRO: CR 0341/327/8a, JWW to TWW, 8 May 1834.
17. Internet database: ucl.ac.uk/lbs – records of compensation given to slave-owners when slavery was abolished.
18. WCRO: CR0341/327/59, AJ to TWW, 17 July 1833.
19. WCRO: CR0341/327/90, AJ to TWW, 26 November 1834.
20. WCRO: CR0341/327/60, AJ to TWW, 7 August 1833.
21. WCRO: CR0341/327/89, AJ to TWW, 27 October 1834 & scattered other references.

Chapter 11

1833: A curacy in Warwickshire; a social whirl in Norfolk

"Ernest is at his Curacy... I have just sent him at his particular request, a little of my <u>experienced</u> advice as to Schools, Penny Clubs &c ... accompanied by a few of my <u>least murderous</u> medical recipes... He says he has already had many funerals!"

Anna Jarrett

"The Ball in St Andrew's Hall, was I think as beautiful a sight as could be seen of its kind... I am fairly come out of my shell and am launched on a sea of dissipation!"

Anna Jarrett

Although Ernest Waller had no particular desire to settle in Warwickshire, he was relieved to have at last found a curacy where he might begin his spiritual and pastoral work. He could not have known that his acceptance of an appointment to the parish of Bishop's Tachbrook near Leamington (thereby making the acquaintance of the Wise family) would have repercussions affecting the rest of his life, and also his brother's life.

On his arrival in the village in July 1833 he was obviously thrilled to have some real news to impart to Thomas. Enthused by the novelty of a previously unknown location, he launches into a detailed description, so that Thomas can conjure up the whole scene in his mind: "It is a straggling country village, between Warwick and Leamington; out of the main road to each place, very prettily situated on a hill, looking down over the cornfields and meadows, upon Warwick Church and castle. The greater part, indeed with the exception of a few cottages & a little land, the whole belongs to Lord Warwick. And the land is rented by about six different farmers. The cottages I cannot say are good, but they are decent and appear to be kept in tolerable order, most of them clean inside. The population is about six hundred, and amongst them no small proportion of what you may be allowed to call rough ones. Indeed, by what I hear the good parishioners are not in the very highest repute among the magistrates, and some of them have been known to be transported; however I hope nothing more of this kind will happen. The squire's house, Tachbrook Park, is rented by Mrs Nutcombe, the sister of Mr Wise of

Offchurch [the vicar], and she is a most delightful old lady indeed, but since the death of Mrs Wise, she lives almost entirely with him, and takes care of his children, so that we have nearly lost the benefit of her residence here, although she still takes a lively interest in all that goes on in the parish, & her purse is open on every occasion, & the great house is the resort of all those who are in distress." [1]

As for the church, "It is rather a handsome old building standing in the middle of the village … The interior is very neat & in good order, well pewed, and has two rather handsome monuments… I have no organ in the church and the charity children, that is to say the children of the national school & Sunday combined, sing the Psalms." There are two services every Sunday, so he is kept satisfyingly busy. The congregations are not as large as he would wish, however, and the behaviour of the parishioners leaves a good deal to be desired. He attributes some of the blame to "the workings of those horrid beer shops", but also to the nearness of Leamington, where there is plenty of well-paid work available, and the villagers "learn what it will take them some time, and cost them some trouble, to unlearn again. I am told it was not so before Leamington became the place it is now." This was a period of major house-building in Leamington, as spa towns had become the height of fashion.

The parsonage, though small, delights the new curate, as it will be the first home he can call his own. It is "a longish cottage made out of two or three… really pretty, although any thing but grand. Half tiled & half thatched, standing in the midst of a little garden, with a field of three acres at the back, with a walk on one side of it. The stable/coach house is detached and planted out." Ernest goes on to describe the whole layout of the house in minute detail, proud of his new status as a householder, albeit on a small scale. He concludes: "Of course the sloping ceilings of the upstair rooms proclaim clearly it is a cottage originally, but the place is really pretty, and not ungentlemanlike. The stipend is £77 in money, the house, field, orchard &c making, it is reckoned, about 100 a year, & with the 400 my Father allows me I think I shall do well," – well enough, evidently, to employ housekeeper, maid and manservant to look after him.

The one thing that slightly disconcerts Ernest is that none of "the good people about here" have called on him. He had expected that at least some of the local clergy and gentry would have done so. All the more welcome, therefore, to a young gentleman from a well-to-do background, were invitations from Lord Howe, his step-brother, to join shooting parties at Gopsal Hall, a manageable ride away in Leicestershire. Later, he was able to ride out with the Warwickshire hounds, and also to visit a university friend, Henry Barton, at his newly acquired property, Rangemore Hall ("good shooting, near the hounds") in Staffordshire.[2] The role of a country parson cannot have been easy for Ernest: there was the delicate matter of quite where on the social scale he should place himself. He would certainly expect to be considered a gentleman but, unlike his friend Barton, he had no property to his name, let alone a country estate, and so did not really fit in comfortably with the landed gentry. As an Oxford-educated man he might have considered himself something of an intellectual, but his scholarly background must have separated him quite markedly from the villagers who were his parishioners. He needed to empathise with them and not to appear patronizing, yet had very little experience of country life or of country folk. Fortunately, he had an excellent sense of humour and could laugh at himself. In a year or two he had really settled into his country parish. "We are beginning to look so green and so pretty, and I am turned botanist and muse most sagely over a hedge weed, with books before and microscopes by my side, finding out what a dandy lion's genteel name is, and to what class it may deign to belong." [3] His personification of a dandelion which might *deign* to be classified is a witty and memorable image. Doubtless Ernest was an amusing person to know. As time goes by he merges into his environment even more, and in a later self-portrait sees himself as "shabby genteel……. somewhat country bumpkinified." [4] He has devised an incentive scheme to encourage the village schoolchildren to learn. "Tickets are distributed to each child every week of the year and according to the number of good tickets they are rewarded. After lecturing some and praising others, I invited all the good to come up to the Vicarage, where I turned them all into my field to play, and stuffed them with gingerbread, making them race for it, etc. They were as happy as they well could be, and I hope they are not sick this morning." [5]

Before moving to Warwickshire Ernest had suspected that his father and step-mother were not getting on well. Certainly, from time to time they spent a few weeks apart. Like her son, Lady Howe paid occasional visits to Gopsal, a property inherited from the Curzons. She was there in August 1833. Meanwhile Wathen was busy with royal visits in Windsor and London, and as ever kept Thomas up to date with his doings.

"Pope's Villa, Aug[st] 5. Your two letters my dear Boy dated July 8 and sent by Lord Wiltshire arrived here on Saturday last, three days after that dated July 11th & which was peculiarly interesting to me from the political news it contained of the Russians. I sent that part to the King on Saturday at Windsor where I drove down for a couple of hours & returned here to dinner. I told you in my last that I had settled to go to London on the 12th to be present at the Queens Birthday the 13th & shall remain there till after the Kings on the 21st! Then I think I shall visit both Ernest & Anna for a few days, if my <u>pocket</u> will pay the post horses – I shall pay into Hoares before I go to Hastings which I believe will be the 1st week in Nov[r] the £400 for you, reserving <u>only</u> what I have lately <u>expended</u> for <u>you</u> & of which I will send you an account." [6]

Anna's good humour was unmistakable when she picked up her pen two days later. At last she was entertaining friends and family in a home of her own, and thoroughly enjoying the experience:

"Camerton House, August 7th 1833
7 ^OClock in the morning

My own dearest Boy,

   I have risen thus early as we have a large party in the house, and I am determined that I will not be hindered from writing to you today, so here I am established in my dressing gown. Your welcome letter of the 8th of July arrived safe yesterday my Wathen, but the lost sheep which I was deploring in my last has never made its appearance, nor ever will now. It seems so strange (not being used to it) to receive an answer to one letter, having written several since to the same person. I have sent you 3 if not 4 letters, since my return from Town, and have received 3 from you including the short one as touching the Turkey Carpet…… Now to tell you something about ourselves. We (meaning my husband and self) are quite well, and at this present moment are assembled under our <u>tumble down</u> roof: Georgie, Sainsbury and the babes – Lady Elizabeth, Mr Repton and their boy, Mrs Brooke, and Aunty Stephens ⁷ – all in good health thank God! – GG is growing portly, and expects in December to add to her family. The boy is a fine fellow – as active as a greyhound and as bold as a lion. He prattles incessantly now. Missy is a bouncing girl, and <u>they say</u> she is to be <u>good</u> looking <u>some day</u>. Lady Elizabeth is gaining strength after her severe illness. She sends her love, and says she will write soon. The weather is lovely for the harvest, and for our building, which makes a grand show, as the roof is almost completed. It is certainly a beautiful situation, and I long to find myself in it, but there will be much, very much to do as to forming and levelling the ground, before it will be seen to any advantage… Old Driver is quite well, and excepting that he will get to the hay tub more than is either decent, gentlemanlike, or agreeable, is in as high favour as ever…… He sends you as much love as he can spare…… Ernest is at his curacy, very well, very happy, and I trust fully occupied. I have just sent him at his particular request, a little of my <u>experienced</u> advice as to Schools, Penny Clubs &c which he appears to take much interest in, accompanied by a few of my <u>least murderous</u> medical recipes, for the benefit of his parishioners. He says he has already had many funerals! …. Mrs Brooke declares that since the Camerton village has fallen into my dangerous clutches the Church Bell has <u>tolled daily</u> – What <u>some</u> people will say! Oh dear!!! And after the <u>wonderful cures</u> I have effected!" ⁸

   Although Wathen was feeling his age throughout that summer, he did not confide his poor spirits to Anna. She was, in any case, very busy. At the start of September she reports to Thomas that her summer guests are departing. The old manor house had been quite stretched, but she and John had taken great pleasure in playing host, and were looking forward to doing the same on a grander scale when the new house was ready. They had been fortunate with the weather and had enjoyed an excursion to "Cheddar cliffs".[9] Their principal guests, Georgiana, her husband Sainsbury and the two children, and Lady Elizabeth with her husband and son, amount to only seven people, but evidently they travelled with an entourage of their own servants: "Our party is diminishing daily – The Sainsburys, 9 in number, left us on Friday, and the Reptons (5) left us on the following day. Mrs Brooke and Aunty Stephens[9] are now our only inmates, the former goes to Worthing on Tuesday, and the latter to Clifton in the course of the week …"[10]

Anna and John were planning some visiting of their own – a rather lengthy period away from Camerton while the building work was in progress. They had changed their minds about saving money by living quietly in what was left of the old house. There were other and pleasanter ways of living cheaply. John had a large extended family of landed gentry with splendid country houses in landscaped parks, for whom receiving house guests was a way of life. After all, it was in order to entertain in style that such people possessed sumptuous ballrooms and dining rooms, opulent furniture and the finest porcelain dinner services. The Jarretts set off almost as soon as their own guests took their leave. "On Wednesday the 11th [September] we our noble selves, take wing for the Penrices[11] at Witton n^r Norwich, whither we are going to be present at the Festival. I am looking forward to it with great pleasure, and a M^r & Mrs Rhodes James,[12] and John Barnard[13] and his wife are to be guests in the same house with us, I trust we shall be a merry party. From thence we shall proceed on a <u>visiting</u> tour, in Norfolk, Suffolk & Hampshire, so that I think several months will probably elapse ere we again see Camerton, and knowing as I do the cold of this old House, I shall not be very anxious to return during the severe weather."

Although Anna would not be returning to Camerton in the winter, she would not be going to Froyle either, even though her presence there might be a comfort to her sister. She explains her reluctance to her brother, once again feeling slightly guilty that she will not be offering Georgiana any moral or practical support at a time of need. Quite possibly she is hiding the real reason – that she is more distressed than she cares to admit at her own childless state, and cannot bear to be present when her sister gives birth for the third time. "GG is to be confined in December – if I should happen to be there at that time, I should not be sorry, but I said nothing as to making any promises…. God grant that she may do as well as before, and then I shall have no cause for uneasiness & I shall not be grieved to get a holiday myself just now for a little while, for with a very large party in the house, there is much to do and attend to, and when it lasts some time as ours has done, I begin to want a <u>wee bit</u> of rest."

The journey to Norfolk took three days, with Anna very much looking forward to the hectic social life expected at the Penrices; it would be an enjoyable but "fatiguing week of pleasure".[14] By the beginning of October, she has a great deal to relate to Thomas. They still are at Witton House with the Penrices, greatly enjoying themselves. "I must tell you that our festivities have passed off delightfully, and we have had charming weather for them, which considering that we had the trajet to Norwich and back to perform <u>twice</u> a day, and many of the gentlemen <u>outside</u> passengers, was no small addition to our comfort. I did not miss one morning Concert, and only one evening one, which of course we have just heard was the best of the whole. I have been charmed with the Oratorios. The Orchestre was excellent and the Chorusses <u>perfect</u> but owing to our sad deficiency in the vocal performers…. the evening Concerts were certainly very poor – and the selection far from happy. De Berriot on the violin was a splendid exception. I was <u>absolutely enchanted</u>, for I had never heard him before. The Ball in St Andrew's Hall, was I think as beautiful a sight as could be seen of its kind. The Hall was brilliantly lighted with Chandeliers, and most elegant <u>Festoons</u> of Gas. There were 1200 people, many of them in fancy dress, and the remainder in Court or full dress. Diamonds and feathers were sparkling and waving, and the whole end of the Hall, where the Orchestre had been, was <u>lined</u> from the ceiling to the floor with spectators. The whole certainly formed as striking a coup d'oeil as I ever witnessed. Dancing was entirely out of the question, at least for me, as I do not like merely to push through a Quadrille. Quadrilles, Waltzes, and Gallopades however there were in profusion, but I sat like <u>a matron</u>, in the patronesse's gallery. Once I went down and made the tour of the room, but returned with my clothes considerable the worse for the scramble, so I desisted from farther incursions. To night we are going to a Ball at Aylsham, which they tell me, is to be very good. It is <u>18 miles</u> off so I hope it will repay us. On the 16th there is another Grand Ball at Norwich, which I believe we shall patronise, so you see, I am fairly come <u>out of my shell</u>, and am launched on a sea of dissipation." [15]

Thomas has asked Anna to send him a miniature of herself and she is keen to do so, but wants to have it done by a leading painter (as befits a person depicted by both Beechey and Wood before the age of five). "With regard to my portrait dearest, you shall certainly have it, and I will go to the best person I can hear of, that you may have some chance of obtaining a likeness, instead of a scarecrow. …. I believe I must delay it rather longer than you mention, as it will probably be two or three months before I am either in London or Bath." They have mapped out their time away from home for at least the next few months: "We stay here until after the 16th, when we shall go to Tattingstone (Mr Rhodes James's). We then return to the Penrices at <u>Yarmouth</u>, and as they press us very much to stay with them until Christmas, I do not think it improbable that we may do so, and I shall revel in warm sea baths, and long walks on the <u>fine</u> sands, which will make me forget the town of <u>Yarmouth</u>, and if possible the <u>Yarmouthians</u>. I have become such a walker! Mrs

Penrice and I walked to Norwich (5½ miles) the day before yesterday, and shopped afterwards. We did condescend to return in the Phaeton, but I was not in the least tired, and the day after walked another 4 miles. After this, I leave you to guess at the state of my health. I shall certainly end in becoming a <u>female Hercules</u>, only <u>would I were fatter</u> (Vide Julius Caesar)!"

Time and again Anna attempts to counter Thomas's anxieties about his spiritual life with sisterly words of advice. She is much relieved when he begins to respond in evident good spirits. "You cannot think my beloved Wathen, how delighted I am to find you are so well, so cheerful and so happy. God grant you may ever continue so, and <u>you will</u>, my dearest brother, if you continue to cultivate and cherish that inward peace and contentment of spirit, <u>without</u> which, no outward circumstances, however prosperous, can make us truly happy, and in the enjoyment of which, no calamity however grievous, however <u>deeply felt</u>, and sincerely mourned, can make us <u>entirely</u> wretched."

Wathen meanwhile was not happy at the approach of winter. Writing to Thomas from Pope's Villa in mid-October, he gave his son an update on some minor expenditure on his behalf and a watch repair, but soon revealed how he was feeling, and how much he missed his son. "This is as you know always a bad time of the year <u>for me</u>, & the fogs here have been <u>before</u> November <u>this</u> year & very thick & very constant & my face has felt it & I am very nervous but not <u>ill</u> in <u>health</u>……. would to God I could hold you to my heart, it would quickly restore my nerves & dispel every complaint." Despite feeling rather low, Sir Wathen had a very busy time in prospect: "I go from Windsor on Tuesday Morning next to Froyle, remain there Wednesday, & start for Tachbrook on Thursday, but shall only go as far as Aylesbury that night, & get to Ernest on Friday noon, stay with him till the following Tuesday, I then return to Norfolk S[t], see the King on Wednesday & take leave of him, as he starts the following Saturday for Brighton, then return here & pack up for Hastings where I hope to arrive on the 1st of November & remain, occasionally visiting Brighton till the End of March or Beginning of April. The Countess Howe [his step daughter-in-law] is made the <u>new</u> Lady of the Bed Chamber to the Queen [Adelaide]… Prince George with the Duke & Duchess left London on the 1st of October & I have only as yet heard from him from Calais, where he arrived safe & well, on the 3rd. He expected to be at Berlin on the 15th & I therefore suppose I shall not hear <u>again</u> before <u>22</u> or <u>23</u>. News there is none!"[16]

Thomas was concerned about his father's apparent depression, and took to heart the suggestion that his long absence might be the cause. Anna, while reassuring her brother, explains what she considers to be the cause of Wathen's mood changes: laudanum. "Do not be at all uneasy about our dear Father. He is as well as usual from what I hear …You know he is very apt to give way to sudden, and sometimes <u>fancied</u> depression of spirits, occasioned as I have ever thought and shall think, by the quantity of laudanum which he is obliged to take, and which has so <u>completely</u> <u>unhinged</u> his nerves, and if he sat down to write while in this mood his letter would naturally be melancholy, nay its gloom would be increased by the thought that he, whom he was writing to, and whom he so dearly loved, was at such a distance from him, but perhaps a few minutes after the letter was dispatched to the post, someone might come in, or he might enter into society and then his spirits rise again, and he forgets all his sadness. Indeed dearest, your presence would neither prevent, nor decrease these fits of gloom, which I believe are the effects of disease, or rather I should say of its <u>remedy</u>. He would doubtless rejoice (as should we not <u>all</u> – <u>above all</u> your own Anna,) to see your dear face again, but after the first burst of pleasure was over, his mind would return to the same state, and if he could not fret about <u>you</u>, he would fret about something else. Indeed our dear Father has enough to worry him one way or the other, but now that Prince George and his royal parents, are gone to Berlin, I trust that he will be spared much of the anxiety and fatigue, which he has lately endured on their account, and which at his age cannot be undergone, without being <u>felt</u>."[17]

Early in November Anna is able to give Thomas some good news about their father: "I received a most satisfactory letter from our dear Father two or three days ago. He had been down to see Georgie and Ernest previous to his departure for Hastings. He gives a good account of both, but says that the former is <u>such a size</u> that he thinks she can never wait until December. Suppose and suppose that she should have <u>Twins</u>!! What a catastrophe that would be, although the new buildings are completed and Miss Anna Maria <u>walks alone</u>. The boy, having heard Papa called Sir Wathen, insists upon calling himself <u>Sir Langford Sainsbury</u>. What a specimen of <u>early ambition</u>!"[18] Wathen remained in good spirits throughout November; Anna was able to write: "I have this morning received a letter from Papa written in <u>excellent spirits</u>. It is long since I have had such a cheerful and affect[ionat]e letter from him, and it pleased me much, so you see dearest, his fits of gloom are, as I told you, only transitory."[19] John and Anna are about to go to Camerton for a brief visit to supervise the movement of furniture and the dismantling of wainscotting and roofing from the old house. They are to travel by stage coach, quite a novelty for Anna. She has a snippet of particular interest to impart, about Ernest: "he <u>has taken</u> a <u>great fancy</u> to one of the Miss Wises, but I am <u>not</u> to suppose he is in 'love' " – to which Anna adds her own amused, affectionate comment: "Humph!!" – the double exclamation marks are hers. Having survived the trip to Camerton and returned to Tattingstone she is able to report: "Driver is quite well and happy, and looks as <u>sleek as a mole</u>."[20]

Two weeks later Anna announces the "joyful news" that Georgiana's second son has been born: "The babe was born on our Ernest's birthday. May he resemble him in more than in the day of his birth!" [21] The Jarretts will be at Yarmouth for

Christmas and stay till the end of the year, too long for John, who finds the town terribly dull. However, Anna is later able to report that the Penrice family had celebrated Christmas in splendidly merry style, with plenty of entertainment for the children: "Christmas day, we sat down 29 to dinner, out of which number 21 were children and all Penrices. Nine in this house and twelve of the fourteen children of Mr Penrice. He has lately buried a 15th. The Magic Lantern and Blind Man's Buff were the order of the evening, in both of which my dear husband exerted himself to the utmost, to the infinite delight of the children, who as well as the older branches declared him to be the life and soul of the party."[22] John evidently relished a quasi-paternal role, perhaps inwardly regretting not being a father after a decade of marriage. The end of the year encourages a thoughtful mood in both Anna and Ernest, who reflect on their shortcomings of the year past, and their hopes for the following year. Anna, as so often, meditates at length on the Christian message and the need for salvation. Ernest, with his uncomplicated, sincere faith, echoes Anna's thoughts far more concisely: "This is the last time I shall write to you this year. May God shower down every blessing upon you, my dear Brother, during that which will so soon begin. Shall we meet before the next year ends? It is uncertain – shall we ever meet again? God grant we may, even in this world; but thanks be to God, no power shall hinder our doing so in a better, if we be not wanting to ourselves."[23]

Notes

1. WCRO: CR0341/327/26, EAW to TWW, 29 July 1833.
2. WCRO: CR0341/327/29, EAW to TWW, 28 October 1833.
3. WCRO: CR0341/327/36, EAW to TWW, 29 April 1835.
4. WCRO: CR0341/327/40, EAW to TWW, 6 August 1838.
5. WCRO: CR0341/327/36, EAW to TWW, 29 April 1835.
6. WCRO: CR0341/327/5, JWW to TWW, 5 August 1833.
7. 'Aunty Stephens' was John Jarrett's great-aunt, his mother's aunt Anne, the sister of her father James Stephens. Mrs Brooke was the widow of the Revd John Brooke, who had been domestic chaplain to Lady Sligo. She and her brother, Captain Bowen, were good friends of the Jarretts, and were often mentioned in Anna's letters.
8. WCRO: CR0341/327/60, AJ to TWW, 7 August 1833.
9. WCRO: CR0341/327/61, AJ to TWW, 13 August 1833.
10. WCRO: CR0341/327/62, AJ to TWW, 1 September 1833.
11. The Penrices: John's cousin Maria Catherine Penrice (née Jarrett) was married to John Penrice of Witton House near Norwich.
12. William Rhodes James (II) was a cousin of John Jarrett. (His father's half-sister, Rachel Allen Jarrett, married a William Rhodes James, & their first son was named after his father.)
13. Mary Ann Barnard (née Jarrett) was a younger sister of Maria Catherine Penrice. The Barnards were married in 1830; she drowned in a boating accident in 1836.

14. WCRO: CR0341/327/63, AJ to TWW, 15 September 1833.
15. WCRO: CR0341/327/64a & b, AJ to TWW, 2 October 1833.
16. WCRO: CR0341/327/7a, JWW to TWW, 13 October 1833.
17. WCRO: CR0341/327/65, AJ to TWW, 16 October 1833.
18. WCRO: CR0341/327/66, AJ to TWW, 3 November 1833.
19. WCRO: CR0341/327/67, AJ to TWW, 17 November 1833.
20. WCRO: CR0341/327/68, AJ to TWW, 1 December 1833.
21. WCRO: CR0341/327/69, AJ to TWW, 14 December 1833.
22. WCRO: CR0341/327/70, AJ to TWW, 31 December 1833.
23. WCRO: CR0341/327/30, EAW to TWW, 16 December 1833.

Chapter 12

January 1834 to January 1835, a time of change

"it would be foolish to run the risk of having a bad or ill painted likeness, for the sake of a few guineas more or less."

Anna Jarrett

"a married man may live in every respect like a gentleman with a much smaller fortune than I thought was necessary."

Ernest Waller

At New Year 1834, the Waller family was somewhat scattered: Sir Wathen and the Baroness Howe were at their villa in Hastings; Anna and John were about to leave Yarmouth (though they would spend another month visiting Jarrett cousins in Norfolk and Suffolk); Ernest was in his Warwickshire parish, Bishop's Tachbrook; Georgiana was with her husband Sainsbury Langford Sainsbury and three small children in Froyle; and Thomas was in Therapia on the Bosphorus, where the British Ambassador to the Ottoman Court had his temporary residence.

By complaining that Lord Ponsonby was difficult to work with, Thomas had given his father the impression that he was far from happy in Turkey. Wathen needed no further prompting. He set about lobbying King William at every opportunity, unable to rest until he had obtained a more congenial posting for his son. In the meantime, however, Thomas had had a change of heart. Before Christmas 1833 he was feeling so settled and content in Therapia that he was not even thinking of taking a holiday for well over a year. When Anna learns of his plans she is horrified, and tells him so in no uncertain terms: "your letter of December 22nd has sadly destroyed my castle building. You calmly talk of <u>asking leave, next spring twelvemonth</u>!!! To spend a <u>few months</u> in England. Why dearest I had never dreamt that your <u>whole stay</u> at Constantinople, would have extended to that period! I would advise you to leave <u>nothing behind</u> that you <u>value</u>, when you <u>do come</u>, for sure am I that we shall never let you go back to fetch it. I should think even worse of the ingratitude which our Father meets with in a high quarter than I do now (which is scarcely possible) could I think such an event likely, No! No! No!!!!"[1]

Anna's bitter comment about ingratitude reflects her disappointment that King William had not immediately granted Wathen the favour requested – but she had misjudged the King and her criticism turned out to be unwarranted. By February William had prevailed upon Palmerston, his Foreign Secretary, to offer Thomas a new posting and a promotion.

Thomas was to be Secretary of Legation at the British Embassy in the newly created monarchy of Greece, where the young Bavarian Prince Otto had been appointed King Othon. Although her brother would still be far from home, Anna realised that the new posting was a positive step: "Now dearest I must congratulate you most sincerely on your promotion. Everyone tells me it is a very likeable thing, and so I trust it will be agreeable to you. It does not indeed bring you much nearer us to us, but … it is a step in your profession, and brings an increase of salary, as well as of importance. I hear it is a situation of great responsibility and that there will be much to do… I am also told the climate is delightful, the country beautiful, and the society &c far more agreeable than Therapia. I cannot find out exactly where you are to be, whether at Napoli [2] [better known as Nauplia, where King Othon's Court was first established] or at Athens… the dear Dad looked very well but rather aged in the face. He seemed much pleased at your appointment, and looks forward some day to a living for Ernest. I hope he will not look in vain. He ought not!"[3] Anna had no qualms about her brothers' accepting patronage – on the contrary, she was well aware that this was how advancement was achieved. Wathen was relieved and delighted that his negotiations on Thomas's behalf had been successful, expecting his son to be equally happy. Ironically however, Thomas no longer wanted to leave Turkey. Certainly the first few months with Lord Ponsonby had been uncomfortable and rather miserable, but in time he had become well acquainted with the Ambassador and was actually enjoying working with him in Therapia. Anna attempted to counter Thomas's negative view of the new posting, quite rightly reminding him that it had taken him some time to appreciate the merits of Therapia: "after much discomfort you are now so well reconciled to Therapia, I trust that it may prove the same with Athens."[4] She clearly knew her brother very well, for this comment was to prove prophetic.

In her fortnightly letters to Thomas, Anna often returned to the well-established topics – Christian belief, her brother's health, money, the new house – but to these she added three new ones: Ernest's courtship of Louisa Wise,[5] John Jarrett's health, and the miniature portrait that her brother had requested. The need to find a suitable painter was a major preoccupation, so she went to London with her husband to make enquiries among her father's acquaintances. Initially Anna had intended to pay for the miniature herself, but since the cost would be more than she had anticipated, she had second thoughts, and agreed to let Thomas pay for it, warning him it would be expensive. She was adamant, however, that it must be well done: "it would be foolish to run the risk of having a bad or ill painted likeness, for the sake of a few guineas more or less." [6] In her next letter she was able to report some progress: "I have settled about my miniature dearest, and am to have my first sitting of <u>two hours</u> on Monday next. After looking at the miniatures of all the painters in London, I have chosen <u>Ross</u>, who both for likeness and <u>finish</u>, appeared to me the best. Nor is he dearer than others, but alas! my Wathen <u>all</u> are <u>very dear</u>, and I little thought when I told you 25 guineas as the outside price, that I should have to say <u>30</u> is the best I can procure it for…. I think it very probable my Father will have it copied, and John too, if the likeness should prove good." [7] Anna chose well: William Charles Ross was the foremost miniaturist of his day, and was fast acquiring a clientele amongst the highest echelons of society. Unfortunately, her sittings for the portrait were destined to be problematic. She fell ill with a severe attack of influenza towards the end of February, and the first appointment had to be postponed. As she explained to her brother, she was obliged to keep to her room taking opium every 4 hours, and "though I am getting well, yet I fear some little time must elapse before I feel equal to attend to Mr. Ross. Besides I must get up my looks again, and coax a little flesh upon my old bones, for I am a perfect skeleton." [8]

When she recovered, Anna went to visit her sister Georgiana at Froyle for a month, intending to return to her father's London home in Norfolk Street in April to sit for her portrait. However, this plan was also frustrated when John, who had gone to Camerton to supervise the transfer of his wine to the new cellar, was taken ill, and his brother Stephen sent an urgent message that Anna must come at once. She explained in a letter to Thomas that John had collapsed one evening at dinner: "he fell to the ground <u>unconsciously</u> but as if shot. He remained insensible for <u>one minute</u>, not <u>longer</u>, and recovered directly, feeling scarcely any inconvenience but not being well the next morning, he sent for medical advice, when as I have before mentioned he was bled, the inflammation was very great I hear and with good discipline was soon about again … He must for the future be <u>most careful</u> both as to <u>Diet</u> and <u>Medicine</u> … He is alarmed <u>himself</u>, which I <u>must</u> feel grateful for, and if he continues the habits of abstinence, which he has so well begun, the event which <u>seemed</u> a calamity, may by God's blessing prove a mercy to us <u>both</u>." [9] So the sitting had to be postponed once again, and Thomas would have to be patient.

The Jarretts returned to Froyle as soon as John had recovered from his sudden illness. Anna thought it a salutary warning to him to take better care of himself, and with her customary faith thanked God for the positive outcome. Before the couple left Froyle again, Georgiana's baby was christened Thomas Ernest, with his Uncle Ernest and Great-Uncle Joseph Slack as godfathers. John also returned briefly to Somerset in order to prosecute (at the Taunton Assizes) some thieves who had broken into the old manor house in February and stolen hams, bacon and servants' clothes. [10] Anna heartily approved of their conviction and the harsh sentence: "The trial of the three men who robbed the house is terminated to our entire satisfaction. They are <u>all</u> transported for life, <u>and</u> as the evidence of their guilt was so clear, I am truly glad the country will be rid of them. I fear they were hardened men."[11] In view of the items stolen, it seems highly likely that the crime had been motivated by poverty; life was very hard in the 1830s for the rural poor. However, Anna prefers not to consider any extenuating circumstances; in her eyes theft is wrongdoing and deserving of severe punishment.

At last in May Anna was able to sit for her portrait, and with this new pastime added to her usual London life she was very busy. There is plenty to tell Thomas: "This letter will not go until Thursday, but I have taken advantage of a rainy afternoon to write it for do what one will, one always feels in a bustle in London and leisure is precious because scarce. Indeed what with Mr Ross, shopping, visiting, sight seeing (which I have not yet begun), and furnishing, the day is gone, before I have caught it. I shall not close this till the last moment, but do not expect to have any news to add. Good news is a <u>rare</u> article, and I trust bad news will not be mine to tell, though if I began on the West Indies subject, or the Coal Company, you would say <u>things looked very black</u> in <u>both</u> cases. Excuse the pun dearest; it is bad enough to carry the conviction that it was almost involuntary,"[12] – a rare touch of humour from Anna, albeit politically incorrect in twenty-first century terms. Within a couple of weeks she was able to report to Thomas that her portrait was finished: "Everybody considers it wonderfully like me, and I am sure it is, for I see it strongly myself. It makes me fancy I am looking at myself in a glass, and I feel my features assuming the same form, till it fairly makes me laugh. They tell me he has not been <u>flattering</u>, which I am glad of, as I particularly wished to avoid it. You must send me word what is to be done with it. I shall be so anxious to know whether you like it."[13] She also wanted a portrait of Thomas. Ernest had just acquired one – a copy of a portrait belonging to his father; he had hung it in a place of honour in the Parsonage. Anna was rather envious; she proposed to have a copy made for herself as soon as she could afford it.[14]

Wathen's enthusiasm for the annual "Glorious First" royal party had waned considerably over time, and in 1834 he admits he had hoped to escape it altogether, but found he could not avoid it – if only to please his wife. The Baroness set great store by the commemoration of her father's victory, and there was no better pretext for entertaining the monarch and his family. Anna had been allocated specific duties as a member of the host's family and she gave her brother a detailed account: "I must now tell you that the Royal Party on the 3rd went off extremely well. The afternoon was beautifully fine, and the lawn looked lovely. We had some slight showers in the morning, which only served to frighten us, and to lay the dust. The King and Queen arrived about 5 o'clock, and the latter walked about the grounds till dinner. The table was magnificent by day light. I did not see it lighted up, as I dined down stairs…My office was also to receive the evening party, as most had arrived before dinner was over, and even afterwards Lady Howe was engaged with the Queen. The Countess Howe [the Baroness's daughter-in-law] looked lovely…. Our dear Father hit his head against a chandelier which knocked him down, and cut his face sadly. However though much disfigured for the present, I trust that no real mischief will ensue."[15] How ironic that Wathen, adorned with his late father-in-law's medals, and exerting himself to the utmost to offer the Royal Family unrivalled hospitality, should be knocked down and injured by a chandelier – of all furnishings the most magnificent, and symbolic of the sophisticated splendour to which he aspired. Perhaps a fitting touch of farce to deflate the host's pomposity?

After the royal party, the summer social season continued busily, and Anna was delighted to meet Louisa Wise and her family, Ernest's neighbours in Warwickshire, and indulge in a little matchmaking, in a rather Jane Austenish fashion: "On Monday the Sainsburys, 10 in number, are expected at Twickenham – I am to meet them there, and on Wednesday we go to Epsom for the Ascot Races; on Friday however the whole family including ourselves are to arrive at Pope's Villa. The Reptons will also be there, and Mrs Nutcombe [Mr Wise's sister], and M^r and the Miss Wises. These last are just come to Town, and as you may suppose I have not lost any time in making their acquaintance. Half a dozen words made us feel as we had never been strangers. The youngest Louisa, is very pretty, very ladylike and pleasing. I am quite ready to accept of her as a sister in law, as soon as Ernest can accomplish it, but I cannot exactly find out how the inclinations stand on either side. They have been so well brought up, that I think we may feel quite secure as to good principles…. Mrs Nutcombe is a very nice person, and I think we shall shortly become friends."[16] Within a fortnight Anna was able to say of the visitors from Offchurch: "We are no longer strangers, and I like them very much, particularly the eldest [Catherine], and the youngest [Louisa]!" [17]

The Wise family had been the mainstay of Ernest's social life since his arrival in Tachbrook. Henry Christopher Wise, the vicar of Offchurch's son, was a good friend from his university days, and happened to live close by. He had enabled the new curate to feel at home in Warwickshire within weeks. Ernest explained his good fortune to his brother: "Young Wise lives about 6 miles from here, on the other side of Warwick, at a place called Woodcote, so I was not perfectly without acquaintance on my arrival…. nothing in the world could have been kinder than they all have been to me [that is, not just the Woodcote Wises – Henry Christopher Wise and his wife Harriett, with their three small sons – but also the Offchurch Wises – Henry Christopher's widower father, the Reverend Henry Wise, his sister Mrs Nutcombe, and his three daughters]. The beginning of next month, they are all going down together to Dover for sea bathing, and I dare say will make a long stay; this will be a great loss to me, but it cannot be helped."[18]

From the outset Anna was well disposed towards the Wise family and Ernest's tentative courtship of the youngest Miss Wise. In her eyes they were eminently suitable acquaintances. Not only was Louisa's father a clergyman, but her late mother was the daughter of a courtier, Sir Stanier Porten, and so the families had much in common. In fact they were almost related; coincidentally the Reverend Henry Wise's mother had been Mary Wathen before her marriage, the eldest daughter of Dr Samuel Wathen, and a niece of Wathen's step-grandfather Jonathan. Early in 1834 Anna wrote approvingly to Thomas about Ernest: "You need not fear dearest that I shall laugh at him about Miss Wise, for from what I have heard of the family, I should think the daughters are likely to be every thing one would wish for in his wife."[19] A month or so later she returned to the topic: "Ernest is looking very well, but he says he is very lonely, and thinks he must marry. He says if he thought he could support a wife, he should certainly think seriously of it, and he adds that the Miss <u>W's</u> are excellently brought up for clergymen's wives." [20]

However, contemplation of marriage in the early nineteenth century inevitably implied overt consideration of money matters, as readers of Jane Austen are well aware. In her next letter to Thomas, Anna discusses Ernest's financial situation in some detail, and with considerable sympathy: "unless he gets a living, his means are small, for my Father tells me that his fortune [i.e. capital] is £20,000, which even at 4% (which he could scarcely get) would bring him but 800 per annum; say his wife has something which made up the £1000 – still when you look forward (as you must) to supporting a family, the means are not large. With the addition of a living of 5 or 600 a year (if such should drop from the skies) he would do very well. Papa was saying he thought he must try and allow him another £100 per annum <u>now</u> if he could possibly manage it, and I wish he may, for though Ernest says nothing, yet I dare say it will be very acceptable, for he spends but little on himself, books being his chief expense; still, as resident minister of a parish, when you come to clubs & schools, wine, food, clothing and medicines, which must constantly be bestowed on one or another, the articles though trifling in themselves tell upon a small income." [21]

When his father made him the extra allowance of £100 per annum, Ernest at once wrote to his sister that he thought he must look out for somebody to help him to spend it, and Anna expected him to be married within a year, with the approval of all the family.[22] In a long letter principally devoted to conveying spiritual support and encouragement to his brother Thomas, Ernest referred to a discussion they had had some years earlier about the feasibility, financially, of marriage. First, he paid his usual tribute to the Wises; he was greatly missing the "delightful family" as they were in London, and admitted that among them he expected to find "a partner for life." He went on, "as far as I remember, I said I would never marry until

I had <u>ample</u> means to keep a wife properly. Now, dearest Wathen, my words about keeping a wife properly are strangely altered since then, & I am perfectly sure that a married man may live in every respect like a gentleman with a much smaller fortune than I then thought was necessary to keep a wife <u>properly</u>." ²³

Having persuaded himself that marriage was financially possible, Ernest resolved to declare himself to his intended partner, but this proved to be quite difficult. Shortly after her eleventh wedding anniversary Anna painted for Thomas a vivid picture of her younger brother's (non-)wooing: "I do not despair of dear Ernest following in our steps before very long, if his own shyness and timidity does not stand in his way. He is certainly very sincerely attached to Louisa Wise, and longs to tell her so, but cannot find courage. On the contrary, though dying to find out whether she cares for him or not, yet does he take the most sedulous pains to prevent her from supposing that <u>he</u> likes <u>her</u> more than her sisters, and for fear of appearing officious [meaning unduly forward] is scarcely as attentive as civility might demand. In this way they will never advance. In the mean time, the poor fellow is quite unhappy – suspense is at all times a most uncomfortable state, and he is luxuriating in all its miseries." ²⁴ In a later letter Anna could not resist a feeble pun: "Ernest is <u>wooing</u> – whether he is <u>wise</u>? time must show." ²⁵

All did turn out well in the end, and Ernest poured out his delight to Thomas: "Already has a week flown by since the little whispered 'yes' told me I had nought to fear, & confessions which have since taken place show me that I have for some time been nestled very snugly in the young lady's heart. But who is she? Why, Mr Wise's youngest daughter, Louisa. What is she like? Short, small, fair, in every body's eyes allowed to be pretty, in my eyes very pretty, not so much from actual beauty, as a sweetness of countenance, which the more you look the more you own its power. What is her character? I do not believe a sweeter tempered creature walks the earth, sufficiently accomplished to make home pleasant, and above all brought up in the good old way, which makes God's word the foundation of every thing. Her family is universally respected & beloved wherever they are known, and their family circle is one which it does one's heart good to contemplate; one soul seems to animate them all." ²⁶ The wedding would take place in mid-January. ²⁷

In the meantime John Jarrett had suffered several more sudden bouts of illness. Wathen, commenting on them to Thomas, calls them "slight indications of apoplectic & paralitic affections."²⁸ The initial treatment was always bleeding, and he was advised to give up alcohol and to eat more moderately. Wathen himself was not in the best of health either and his spirits were often low: ²⁹ At 65 he felt that death might be imminent, though he was to live nearly twenty more years. Anna, who was often dismissive of her father's depression, for once seemed genuinely worried about him, although remarkably unsympathetic towards his housekeeper who was about to undergo a mastectomy, without anaesthetic, of course, and possibly dying – how terribly inconvenient! "Papa …. looked worried to death. I have not seen him so low for some time. What annoys him now is the illness of poor Agnes, his housekeeper…… independently of the concern he so truly feels for an old servant, it will greatly inconvenience him to be deprived for so long a time of her valuable services, and should it terminate fatally (which too often happens), he says he knows not what he shall do, as nobody else knows anything about all the goods at Pope's Villa. You can easily guess how all this would worry him, of all men in the world."[30]

In August the Jarretts, still without a proper home, returned to Camerton, spending a week "in the cover of an old mass of ruined stone once called Camerton House." They took great pleasure in inspecting the progress of the new house: "I wish you could have seen Darby and Joan trotting about their new House, and their own Domain!! suggesting improvements, making alterations, planning roads &c. We were as happy as birds and as you may infer well also."[31] But Anna spoke too soon on the subject of health. John soon had a further, more serious attack, and had to submit to an unenviable regime of treatments: "Poor, dear fellow! He is quite on the invalid list – cupping, bleeding, leeching, blistering, physicking and starving are his almost daily occupations. He is to get up early (which you know he does not like) and is not to be exposed to hot sun, rain, or wind. All very strong exercise is forbidden, therefore he has ordered his hunters not to be put into condition this winter…… He is most obedient to orders, and certainly throws away no advantage that human skill can afford him."[32] Once he felt better, John took his wife on holiday again. They visited his brother Stephen at Clifton near Bristol, and then embarked on a tour taking in Hereford (for the music festival), Chepstow, and Linton.

Anna was relieved to hear that Thomas's journey from Therapia to Nauplia in Greece would take place in September. She considered that the heat of the summer was particularly conducive to disease, and that it was fortunate that he would "escape the Aguish season." She did not expect him to react positively at first, however, as this would be out of character! "I shall look forward with no small impatience for your first impressions, but I shall not be much disappointed should they prove unfavorable. I scarcely expect that they should be otherwise, but I doubt not things will improve upon acquaintance."[33] In October Anna received two letters from Thomas in the same post. It was fortunate that they arrived simultaneously, as the second proved far more reassuring than the first, which was full of bad news and complaints. Anna replied to both letters together, pointing out the differences between the two accounts: "To know that you are residing in a disagreeable unhealthy place, is of itself sufficient to depress my spirits, but when I add to this, the sensations of uneasiness you mention in your chest, and the actual fever you have been suffering, alone in a miserable hut, without any friend near you, I felt miserable….and yet how grateful should I be, how grateful <u>I am</u>, that thou art mercifully preserved! and according to your second letter <u>well</u> again. Thank God for this his mercy towards us! Indeed I found much consolation, upon calmly re-perusing your letters. Though all your outward circumstances were so uncomfortable, yet how cheerful, how contented, do you express yourself to be!" Although Thomas's indisposition was mercifully short-lived and he would soon move to Athens, Anna urges him not to remain in Greece if his health seems adversely affected. "Above all, my Wathen, should you <u>really</u> find the climate disagree will you, and should you feel any more that you have a <u>chest</u>, pray, pray come home. Leave it all – you have enough to live comfortably in England, and health is before every thing."[34]

As Anna had foreseen, Thomas soon became accustomed to his new posting, and within a few weeks his unfortunate illness on arriving in Greece had been forgotten. Anna was delighted – and all the more so as the Ross miniature had finally arrived at its destination. "To hear that you were well and happy, that you were rejoicing with us at dear Ernest's pleasing prospects, and oh! joy! to know that you had received my portrait safe, that you thought it very like and was altogether <u>more</u> than satisfied with it, all this gave me more pleasure than usually falls to the lot of any body in <u>one</u> <u>letter</u>. My husband also was not a little delighted that you approved it. You are quite right about the mouth. Everybody says the same thing… I would not let him alter the hair. He wanted to make it more in ringlets, but I told him it must be as <u>I wore it</u>, not what would look most graceful in a picture."[35]

In the autumn Anna was excited by the preparations for Ernest's wedding, planned for January at Offchurch. All the family but Thomas would be there. She had already told Thomas how much she liked the eldest Miss Wise, Catherine, and returned to the subject with more detail (having acquired quite a taste for matchmaking after her success with Ernest and Louisa): "she appears from the little I saw of her to be a very nice girl indeed. She is I should say cleverer than Louisa, and her countenance has great intelligence. Her manner is very pretty, and she has just that much of sedateness beyond her years, which would naturally happen when a girl, from the death of her mother, is at the head of her father's establishment. She looks older than I hear she is, having some <u>grey</u> mingled with her dark hair. I thought she must be 30 or thereabouts, but I am told I am mistaken and that she is not so much by some years. Independently of age however I think altogether Louisa is much better suited to Ernest, and I trust there are many years of happiness in store for them."[36] As Thomas was abroad, Anna chose a wedding gift on her brother's behalf: "a very pretty <u>silver butter tub</u>". [37]

At last John and Anna were able to move into the new house, to be known as Camerton Court. Though relatively small in comparison with many grand country houses of the period, it was (and is) a delightful, well-proportioned mansion in the mellow golden stone typical of Bath and its surroundings, ideally situated on a south-facing hillside, with a terrace in front and a large garden running down the slope and then up again towards the parish church. The front has an impressive colonnade in Regency style, and a large orangerie on the left-hand side. To this day, there is an unimpeded view of the house to be had from the church on the facing hill. "We are very busy finishing and furnishing. We have at last got into the upper part of our house. One of the bedrooms we have arranged as a drawing room, and it is <u>very comfortable</u>. We were not sorry to get out of the offices. We were rather cramped for room. We have also got into our own new bedroom, and it is so very comfortable. My boudoir will be ready in about a fortnight, and then I think my little suite of apartments will be perfect. My bedroom is <u>next</u> to the boudoir but not leading out of it, and through the bed room is a <u>small</u> passage which holds my <u>harness closet</u> as John calls it and any thing I may wish out of sight and at the end a <u>private convenience</u> (don't be shocked!) All this is shut from the rest of the house by one door, so that I have a snug corner of the house all to myself, and nicely furnished. The dining room is also all but completed and we talk of dining in it tomorrow for the first time. Your carpet dearest was put down yesterday & it fits very well, and looks extremely handsome."[38]

In his delight at being at last in residence at Camerton, John was keen to plant his garden, but he was still far from well. Strenuous physical work was not good for him, and Anna reported that he had again been taken ill; this time she had coped with the cupping herself. "I grieve to add [John] had another though very slight attack about a fortnight ago. I was unfortunately in Bath, and he independently went into the garden and dug a bed for his tulips. After an hour's hard work, he was seized as before with a sudden dimness of light but this time neither his arm or his mouth were at all affected. He was pale and cold and when his sight returned a violent headache came on. He would not send for medical advice as he was expecting me home, and unluckily I was late. The moment I returned however I cupped him (for I am now an <u>experienced</u> cupper alas!) and took about 6 ounces of blood, after which his head was relieved, and he sat down to dinner, declaring <u>he was very hungry</u>."[39]

As usual, Wathen and the Baroness left Pope's Villa for Hastings in November 1834. It was their custom to spend the winter months in the reputedly milder climate of the south coast, and on this occasion they were delighted to find that the Duchess of Kent and her daughter Princess Victoria had followed suit, settling for a while at St Leonard's, a newly-developed district of Hastings, fashionable among the well-to-do. The Princess noted in her Journal seven occasions during that winter when Sir Wathen called or came to dine, so he was evidently quite well acquainted with the future queen. It was from Hastings that he made the journey to Offchurch to attend his younger son's wedding – and who better to describe the day than the bridegroom himself? Ernest was delighted that Thomas was aware of the date, and had been with him in spirit: "The old proverb says, 'that every dog has his day', these are then certainly my dog days; for a happier dog than your Brother Dolly is, never I think walked upon two legs….The 15th of January shone bright & cheerfully upon us at Offchurch; am I superstitious? I was humbly glad it did so, & just as we were standing at the altar & the service began a bright ray shot through the window upon us: it seemed to speak to me & say 'God has far better things yet in store for you, only you must obey Him & serve Him, & love Him here, if you would enjoy them hereafter'. How I could have longed to have had you with us, had not one known that the wish was hopeless; however I cannot tell you how glad I was to find upon reading your letter, that mine had arrived in time to apprize you of the day: you then, my dearest Wathen were thinking of me, on that day. My dearest Louisa will I am convinced prove a treasure to me; she is – well never mind, you will like her I am sure, although there is not any thing very striking to like at once, but there is a sweet temper, and right good principles to delight and make me love her more & more."[40]

With hindsight, there is a poignancy in Ernest's words, so full of love, hope and optimism. It was indeed a happy marriage, but all too short-lived; on that bright winter wedding day there was mercifully no hint of the sadness to come.

Notes

1. WCRO: CR0341/327/72, AJ to TWW, 30 January 1834.
2. Napoli (di Romania), a port town in the Peloponnese more commonly known in English as Nauplia or sometimes Nafplio. It was the capital of Greece from 1829 to 1834.
3. WCRO: CR0341/327/74, AJ to TWW, 27 February 1834.
4. WCRO: CR0341/327/78, AJ to TWW, 30 April 1834.
5. Louisa Wise was the sister of Ernest's friend Henry Christopher Wise of Woodcote House, Leek Wootton, and the youngest of the three daughters of the Reverend Henry Wise, Vicar of Offchurch in Warwickshire, a village near Ernest's parish of Tachbrook.
6. WCRO: CR0341/327/72, AJ to TWW, 30 January 1834.
7. WCRO: CR0341/327/73, AJ to TWW, 12 February 1834.
8. WCRO: CR0341/327/74, AJ to TWW, 27 February 1834.
9. WCRO: CR0341/327/77, AJ to TWW, 10 April 1834.
10. WCRO: CR0341/327/73, AJ to TWW, 13 February 1834.
11. WCRO: CR0341/327/77, AJ to TWW, 10 April 1834.
12. WCRO: CR0341/327/79, AJ to TWW, 13 May 1834.
13. WCRO: CR0341/327/80, AJ to TWW, 5 June 1834.
14. WCRO: CR0341/327/79, AJ to TWW, 13 May 1834.

15. WCRO: CR0341/327/80, AJ to TWW, 5 June 1834.

16. Ibid.

17. WCRO: CR0341/327/81, AJ to TWW, 19 June 1834.

18. WCRO: CR0341/327/26, EAW to TWW, 29 July 1833.

19. WCRO: CR0341/327/72, AJ to TWW, 30 January 1834.

20. WCRO: CR0341/327/73, AJ to TWW, 12 February 1834.

21. WCRO: CR0341/327/74, AJ to TWW, 27 February 1834.

22. WCRO: CR0341/327/76, AJ to TWW, 26 March 1834.

23. WCRO: CR0341/327/31, EAW to TWW, 10 April 1834.

24. WCRO: CR0341/327/83, AJ to TWW, 16 July 1834.

25. WCRO: CR0341/327/86, AJ to TWW, undated.

26. WCRO: CR0341/327/33, EAW to TWW, 25 September 1834.

27. WCRO: CR 0341/327/34, EAW to TWW, 27 November 1834.

28. WCRO: CR0341/327/9, JWW to TWW, 26 June 1834.

29. Ibid.

30. WCRO: CR0341/327/ 84, AJ to TWW, 31 July 1834.

31. WCRO: CR0341/327/85, AJ to TWW, 14 August 1834.

32. WCRO: CR0341/327/87, AJ to TWW, 10 September 1834.

33. WCRO: CR0341/327/85, AJ to TWW, 14 August 1834.

34. WCRO: CR0341/327/89, AJ to TWW, 27 October 1834.

35. WCRO: CR0341/327/90, AJ to TWW, 26 November 1834.

36. Ibid.

37. WCRO: CR0341/327/91, AJ to TWW, 30 December 1834.

38. WCRO: CR0341/327/89, AJ to TWW, 27 October 1834.

39. WCRO: CR0341/327/90, AJ to TWW, 26 November 1834.

40. WCRO: CR0341/327/35, EAW to TWW, 28 January 1835. Ernest refers to himself by the nickname Dolly – from his second name Adolphus.

Chapter 13

Wathen's *annus horribilis*

"Come home at once, and never will I consent to our separation again… Ambition has lost its power over me… Vanity is I trust much subdued… Throw up everything rather than remain."

Jonathan Wathen Waller

There was of course always a lapse of time between a letter being sent to or from Thomas and its being received, and with parcels the delay sometimes amounted to several months. This happened with a large box of Turkish and Russian textiles despatched by Thomas before leaving Constantinople for Greece in September. The items were intended as Christmas presents for his family and friends, but they reached Anna in mid-January. "Can you fancy the pleasure of unpacking such a box, and eagerly <u>diving</u> to the bottom. John and I had the full enjoyment of it. My Turkish bag & fan are beautiful, so are all the gowns and dressing gowns so beautifully neat, and above all my scarf, which is as lovely a thing as I have seen for some time. But now dearest, will you be very angry with your Anna when she tells you, that it was so very young, so beauteous, and so <u>bride-like</u> that I could not resist the temptation of presenting it to our dear new sister. I knew you would wish her to have something, and that was the prettiest of all – and indeed she deserves it, for a sweeter, more affectionate, natural unaffected little creature cannot exist… I have dedommaged myself for this act of generosity by retaining the 4ᵗʰ Gown for myself. GG has <u>one</u>, I have <u>two</u>, and one I have reserved for Lady Elizabeth. GG has also her Persian silk, and I have divided the other things as equally as I could. I have sent Papa his carpet & his pastilles, and Colonel Caradoc his waistcoat. I have sent Lady Wheatley a blue embroidered bag, and a pair of Turkish slippers to match. Ernest & Louisa were delighted with their butter stand so I hope you will think I have done right. We enjoyed our Warwickshire trip exceedingly."[1]

John had been unwell again before this trip to Offchurch, but Anna had insisted, against the Doctor's advice, that it would do him good. Fortunately, she was proved right. He had been in excellent spirits and thoroughly enjoyed himself – as did Anna. All the Wallers and Wises got on splendidly and the wedding went off "most prosperously". The Jarretts hoped to return to Warwickshire in the summer, but in the meantime Ernest and Louisa were their first house guests in the new house at Camerton.

Anna was still greatly preoccupied with the furnishings, relishing having everything done to her own taste. "I hope by this time you have received the view of this house. We are now almost finished. We have got into one drawing-room, and anything more delightfully comfortable you cannot imagine. Oh! that you could <u>see</u> it. It is handsomely but simply furnished, and the Hall (which I have a great pride in) is quite like a sitting room. It is carpeted, and hung with pictures, and as warm as a toast. The bedrooms are perfect I think, indeed with a <u>few exceptions</u> we are entirely pleased with our new residence, and perhaps these minor inconveniences may be remedied before very long." Knowing that the new house had stretched their finances, Thomas generously offered Anna and John money, but Anna would not hear of it. "No! dearest! That would be unfair indeed. We are <u>idle</u>, and you work hard. <u>Keep</u> my Wathen & <u>enjoy</u> with God's blessings, what you so truly deserve, and do not think we feel your kindness & affection the less, because we do not take advantage of it. I trust we shall get through pretty well. At present the accounts are not come in and therefore we do not know exactly, but we have given up the <u>new stables</u> for the present, and our last accounts from the West Indies are better than we expected. So we have much to be thankful for, and I hope <u>as usual</u> for the best."

Shortly before Christmas, the Court of King Othon had moved from Nauplia to Athens. On his arrival in the Greek capital, Thomas was immediately befriended by an American missionary, John Henry Hill and his wife Frances, who had opened a school for girls there. Mr Hill was a minister of the (Anglican) Episcopalian Church, so he and Thomas were like-minded as regards religion. Anna was delighted that all was going so well: "How I rejoice my Wathen to hear you are so comfortable at Athens, and above all that you have an opportunity of joining in the service of our Church, with a person whom you esteem. I thought of you dearest on Christmas day, though I did not know you were partaking of the same sacred rites as ourselves." She ends with news of Thomas's dog – plus a hint from John for the next box of presents. "Driver is quite well, and sends his best love, so does Driver's <u>master,</u> and he says if you see anything very pretty in marble, or very classical &c and not very expensive, he commissions you to buy it for him. Oh! I must tell you, your <u>fur cloak</u> is the most comfortable thing I ever possessed… I travelled <u>in its folds</u> from here to Warwickshire & back and never felt the cold, although in an open carriage."

When Anna sat down to write to her brother at the end of February, she had quite a task ahead of her. The vagaries of the postal service had landed three of Thomas's letters at her door almost simultaneously, so there were plenty of topics to cover and questions to answer. However, it is obvious that one subject preoccupies her far more than the others, and after thanking Thomas for the letters and a sketch of his house in Athens, she launches into a lengthy diatribe on the subject of a suitable marriage partner for her brother. Thomas had evidently admitted to her that he found Sophie d'Armansperg, a new acquaintance, particularly attractive. Sophie was one of the three daughters of the Count d'Armansperg, leader of the Regency Council, which was charged with ruling Greece during the King's minority. The d'Armansperg family were the current stars of Athenian society, and Thomas's status in the diplomatic ranks assured him of much coveted entry into their circle. Glittering receptions, balls and dinner parties were all part of the routine lifestyle of this select group of privileged individuals, and Thomas clearly relished the opportunity get to know a well-connected and accomplished young woman, who was also a noted beauty. Meanwhile, loud alarm bells were ringing in Anna's head, and she wasted no time in stating her opinion. "You cannot my brother wish more sincerely for a partner to share your feelings, than I do to see one by your side, one whose tenderness, gentleness and virtues, would endear her to your affectionate heart, while her firm moral & religious principles might ensure your esteem, and approve her to your excellent understanding. Without this you could not be happy. I know you could not. Therefore dearest, no Roman Catholic! No (shall I say it) Sophie d'Armansperg! From your description, she may be pleasant as a companion, but could not I am sure satisfy my [Thomas] Wathen's ideas of a wife." [2] Apart from her objection on religious grounds, Anna makes it clear that she would prefer Thomas's wife to be English. She advises him to look around on his next visit home and to find himself "an amiable and virtuous woman" who would devotedly follow him "whithersoever" he might go. Had Anna already a candidate in mind at this stage? Quite possibly.

Having had her say on the subject of Thomas's future wife, Anna moves on to his eventual place of permanent residence. Thomas has hinted that he expects to live abroad for the rest of his life, and is somehow "unfit" to live in England. Anna is appalled as well as bewildered by the very idea. Why should he have such thoughts? After all, he had only gone abroad in the first place because he found his stepmother, Lady Howe, difficult to live with, and Anna suggests that the problem will not last for ever. "Circumstances of discomfort under your father's roof induced you to seek for employment and amusement in a profession you have never loved, and which was no farther <u>necessary</u> for you than for those purposes, and which (should those circumstances change, or any other motive arise) you are surely at liberty to resign at any moment. If you chose to marry and reside in England why should you not be very happy? You would have enough for happiness? If Ernest could afford to marry without imprudence, surely our dear Father will take care of your comforts in a similar situation. With a wife, probably a family, and a small place of your own, I think you would find enough to occupy your mind & time, when you got used to it. But of course dearest you must know best what your feelings are on the subject, and perhaps I only <u>feel</u> as I <u>wish</u>."

The frequent late arrival of Thomas's letters was more than a minor inconvenience; it was a source of considerable anxiety and distress to his father and sister, who dwelt on his every word. They were continually on the lookout for any mention of illness or low spirits, as the notion that all manner of diseases were prevalent in foreign lands was deep-seated in their minds, and they sought constant reassurance that he was well and happy. Lord Byron's death some eleven years earlier had been the subject of immense publicity, and the Waller family, who knew him personally, were only too aware that he died of a fever in Greece. Wathen was also burdened once more by a sense of guilt: he was to some extent responsible for his elder son's "exile" – quite possibly arranged at the behest of Lady Howe, and certainly with the aim of pleasing her. The wrath and judgment of God could be manifested at any moment through disease and disaster; what if something dreadful should befall his beloved son? Thomas did not appreciate the repercussions of any negative comment he made about his health, and was unaware that his father and sister sometimes worried quite unnecessarily for weeks or months over an indisposition that had only lasted a few days. By mid-1835 Wathen could scarcely bear his son's absence any longer, and began to think how he might engineer his homecoming.

The frustration Wathen felt at replying to a letter written two months previously is all too evident when he began to write on May 27th 1835. "For these last seven days my dear boy, have I been every morning making my first anxious enquiry 'Is there no letter from Greece?' In vain twice every day have I repeated my question, & I now have only to answer yours of the 29 of March last, & that did not come here till nearly 3 weeks after the usual time. It is really terrible that I can get no information from, or about you. My last was the 1st of May, & it was not till the 11th of May that I received yours of March 29. Anna had a letter of some days later date than that, she <u>tells</u> me you did not seem in <u>good</u> spirits, but she hoped the little tour you talked of, would do you good. I hope so too, but am most anxious to have it confirmed by yourself." [3] So dispirited is Wathen, that he proposes to abandon his annual custom of inviting the Royal Family to a celebration of his deceased father-in-law's famous naval victory, the "Glorious First" – formerly a great source of pride to him and a tremendous boost to his self-esteem. "I have no 1st of June party <u>this</u> year. Lord Howe has <u>all</u> the advantage of <u>it</u>, & let him have the <u>expence</u> [sic]. I will never do it <u>again</u>. If their Majesties like to come & dine with me when the summer is more advanced & it will not cost me <u>60</u> or <u>70</u> pound for <u>a</u> <u>desert</u> [sic], I have no objection." As usual, he sends Thomas a meticulous update of his bills, promising to add the sum required to the balance of his son's account at Hoares. There is news of the Cumberlands. "I had a very kind letter from Prince George yesterday. He is just the same, & never fails desiring his remembrance to you." Wathen still has royal duties in abundance, but is finding them a strain rather than a pleasure. His weariness is evident in the fractious tone of his letter; earlier he had attended the King's Levée, which went ahead despite the King's bad cold, and later that day he was to be in attendance on the Queen at an "Antient Music" Concert.

After a couple of similarly busy days Wathen resumes writing his letter. Despite feeling exhausted, he is looking forward to a family reunion which is to include Louisa's father, her Aunt Nutty, her brother Henry and his wife, and her sisters Catherine and Mary Patience: "31 May, I returned here [Pope's Villa], on Friday to dinner thoroughly tired out with a Drawing Room [Queen's reception] of 2400 People, a State Dinner at Lord Albermarle's & a Concert at St James & I hoped for my consolation to have found on my table a letter from you, but alas No. So no news have I had of you since March 29…… On Monday the 15 of June however I hope to collect all my family your dear self excepted – & how shall I regret thine absence – to dinner……What would I not give could I but whistle thee here!! alas alas!!! I must bear it – but thy absence will cast a gloom on the scene & give no small pang to your father's heart."

At the end of May Anna is anxious about Thomas's rather depressed state of mind; she often has similar moods. As ever, she reminds her brother that a Christian's life entails trials from time to time, and urges him to overcome any problems by relying on his faith. "No very severe calamities have hitherto been your lot, but still you have had something to endure. In early life you suffered much in health; from Lady Howe's unfortunate prejudice you are almost banished from your home, and living in a foreign land, away from all those dear domestic ties, which sweeten all the joys, and soften all the bitterness of life; once or twice, your heart has been disappointed in its tenderest hopes; you have been through the cholera at Paris… besides the daily crosses & vexations which fall to the lot of all." [4] His latest bout of low spirits may have been occasioned by his acceptance of Anna's advice that Sophie d'Armansperg would not be a suitable bride for him – or indeed she might have rejected him, having set her sights somewhat higher. (Before long she married a Romanian Prince.) Once again Anna takes him to task about his lack of self-esteem and reluctance to live in England: "Why dearest to hear you talk, one might imagine that you were the son of a shoe black, and only tolerated in decent society for a time. Indeed my Wathen you are not just to yourself or to your position in the world. For years at least our dear Father has moved in the first society in England, as you have abroad – and you are by education and situation entitled to continue these when you return to your native country. And what should hinder you from so doing? Look at other young men, who without half your advantages, either of birth, circumstances, talents or manners, find their way without difficulty into good society, stay or visit at pleasant houses, and choose from thence wives, not indeed with large fortunes often, but amiable women, with a little money which when joined with theirs form a sufficient competency for happiness. And why should not you meet thus with an <u>Englishwoman</u>?"

The success of the family gathering depended to a great degree on the mood of the Baroness, and Anna was relieved to be able to reassure Thomas that Lady Howe's temper was "wonderfully improved". "She is <u>stone deaf</u> without her trumpet but appears so much to enjoy being talked to, and grateful for any assistance that we give her towards understanding what is going on, which used not to be the case." [5] Gas, the latest fashion in lighting had recently been installed at Pope's Villa, an unnecessary extravagance in Anna's eyes: "I am sorry because it sinks another £500 in a house which he hates, and which he says he wishes to be rid of – not to mention the disagreeable smell of said Gas." [6] At the family party Wathen had been keen to show off his new lighting, but unhappily a small hitch (reminiscent of the chandelier incident at the royal dinner) rendered the effect more ridiculous than impressive. Anna could not help seeing the funny side: "I must tell you one thing that happened. It was the first experiment of the <u>Gas</u>, which Papa has introduced into Pope's Villa. All did very well, until dessert time, when an unlucky housemaid down stairs, thinking that it was proper to turn the gas on to the library, that it might be ready, mistook the cock (or whatever it may be called) and turned it <u>off</u> from the <u>dining room</u>. So in one moment <u>out popped all</u> the lamps, and we should have remained in darkness, had not some candles been fortunately lighted on the table, about 5 minutes before – I could not help smiling, nor could any body else, although Papa was sorely vexed and angry." [7]

1835 was rapidly becoming an *annus horribilis* for Wathen. He was increasingly overwhelmed by problems, both major and minor, and was missing his son more than ever. "Pope's Villa, July 26th 1835. The 26th is arrived my dear Wathen but no letter from you & I have been looking for it these 6 last days & I am so much in want of consolation that I seize the only one which at this moment presents itself – beginning a letter to my child." [8] He goes on to describe the Baroness's very poor state of health. She had already been suffering from painful erysipelas in her legs when she had a fall whilst visiting her son, "& is now in such a state of inflammation as to confine her entirely to her couch & several small joints have actually mortified & the inflammation is spread so far as to alarm me." The doctors try to reassure him but he apprehends "the worst event…. My anxiety is more than I dare express. God only knows how it will end…. Would to God you were with me, but here I am alone, yet I ought not to murmur for there is one ever near me & who alone can support me under whatever trials he thinks right to ordain for me. Amongst minor evils I have lost one of my front teeth & the other is loose & I had my pocket picked the Wednesday before last & lost my purse with £20 in it…" Finally he comes to something more positive: "the accounts from Froyle & Camerton are all good & I suppose you are not a little pleased to have Sir E Lyons your Chief." (The new

British Minister and Thomas were already well acquainted, having worked together at Nauplia and having toured some of the Greek islands in the Spring. Sir Edmund was a distinguished naval officer and a thoroughly agreeable, decent and honourable man, whose presence with his family in Athens was to enhance immeasurably Thomas's life in Greece.)

When Wathen resumes writing his July letter he is much relieved to have received at last news from Thomas, written on 26th June, his 30th birthday. However, he reports that the Baroness is no better, and her deafness is causing huge problems. He can scarcely leave the house and is struggling to cope. Once again he renews the moral pressure on Thomas: "You would be a great support & comfort were you near me, but He who knows what is best has ordained it otherwise & His will be done." Wathen's only good news is that Louisa is pregnant, and the new grandchild is expected in January.

By the end of August Lady Howe's health had improved enough for her to undertake a strenuous 50-mile return journey to her son's residence at Penn, Buckinghamshire. It is a testimony to her strength of character that she insisted upon it. A week or so earlier she had not been well enough to attend the christening there of her latest grandchild – her ninth – to whom the King and Queen had stood as godparents, but Wathen had attended the ceremony with the royal party, and was violently ill the following day. He was still finding both his domestic and court life stressful when, unwittingly, Thomas added a final straw by mentioning that in the heat of July in Athens he had been feverish. There was no reason to suppose that Thomas's illness was serious; he was already convalescent when writing to his father on 30th July. Nevertheless, when the news reached Wathen four weeks later, he could cope with no further anxieties. He resolved that Thomas must come home, and thereafter remained adamant on the subject.

"My dear boy I beseech you to weigh maturely <u>this</u> event & <u>come home at once</u>, & never will I consent to our separation again." Tired and discontented, Wathen looks forward to spending his remaining years quietly in the company of a supportive and loving son: "I am old & you will find me much altered. Ambition has lost its power over <u>me</u>. Vanity is I trust much <u>subdued</u> & every day retreating from <u>my</u> heart. God has mercifully blessed me with a moderate sufficiency & I can render you in great measure independent of everyone, & <u>humanly</u> speaking 'your <u>bread</u> is certain & your water <u>sure</u>'. I do not think you are ambitious & I believe much more seriously inclined than when we parted, why then should the few years that remain of <u>my</u> life be clouded with needless anxiety & disappointment? The presence & affection of my beloved child will cheer my latter days, & illumine the dark hours. Together we can take sweet council & tho' I do not think, circumstanced as <u>I am</u>, our constant residence under the <u>same</u> roof would contribute to the happiness of either, during the life of the Baroness, yet we could be within the <u>reach</u> of each other & be <u>material</u> comforts & supports. Pray think of all this. I shall talk over <u>this</u> with the King, the first opportunity, & require of Palmerstone [sic] at least your <u>early</u> leave of absence & we can then talk over & arrange future Plans. Your sister Anna has received your letter of the same date as mine, & is if possible more miserable than myself. I conjure you to come to us as quick as possible. Throw up <u>everything</u> rather than <u>remain.</u>"⁹

Sometimes Wathen wrote to Thomas over a period of days or even weeks, so in the course of a single letter, there can be marked changes in his mood, or an alteration to a plan set out in the early pages. So it was in October 1835. Wathen began his letter on the 15ᵗʰ, having just spent a fortnight with his daughters Anna and Georgiana at Camerton, whilst the Baroness was visiting Gopsal. On his return he had immediately seen the King and could report: "He agrees with me that you ought to immediately return home on <u>leave</u> of <u>absence</u> & he promises that you shall then certainly be removed & return no more to Athens. Indeed my dear child I must insist upon it that you come home, as soon as you can after the receipt of this & that you bring home with you or dispose of before you leave Athens, all your furniture etc, for – as you certainly never shall return <u>there</u> – you had better make your final arrangements for a farewell." ¹⁰ Twelve days later, having heard from Thomas that he was in good health and happy, his joy at the news enables him to endorse Thomas's revised plan: "Your argument & reasons for remaining till the Spring at Athens, are cogent & right, & as you are <u>well</u> meet my <u>entire</u> approbation, but I shall look forward to June, if our lives are spared, to the <u>certainty</u> of seeing you in <u>England</u> on <u>leave</u>."

Wathen could scarcely have appreciated how much Thomas's life in Athens had been transformed by the family of the new British Minister to Greece. Sir Edmund Lyons, his wife Augusta and their teenage daughters had welcomed him into their home, and in a very few weeks succeeded in providing him with more warmth, affection and congenial company than he had known in all his life. They took evident pleasure in his visits and he dined with them frequently. He went riding and discussed books with the Lyons' younger daughter, Minna, and gave lessons in German to her older sister Annie. In addition he had begun to help at the Hills' School for girls, where he was appreciated and popular; to his surprise he found he had a real talent for teaching and greatly enjoyed it. He was no longer in a hurry to come home, even briefly on leave, but events and his father's intransigence were to overrule his own thoughts on the matter. Even as he approved Thomas's postponement of his return to the spring, Wathen was relating to his son further setbacks in the Baroness's health: "I was to have gone down <u>to day</u> with the Baroness to Windsor, to take leave of the Queen, but that is <u>now</u> improbable as she has fallen down, & so <u>bruised</u> her <u>knee</u> & <u>elbow</u> that she cannot move, & is confined to her bed. It is a great mercy she did not strike her head, or it would certainly have been fatal. As it is, I fear it will be some time before I can get her again down stairs. She is become <u>very</u> feeble particularly since her <u>last</u> illness, & she will not be assisted or consider herself as an <u>old woman</u>. I must shortly never leave her, for I am never about [i.e. away from home], that something does not occur."[11] Wathen is only too aware of signs of aging in himself too, and, as he contemplates the prospect of his own death and the need to prepare for the afterlife, his own words start to imitate the familiar cadences of the Book of Common Prayer: "I am well in health, but by no means either in <u>mind</u> or <u>body</u> what I <u>was,</u> & each week, as it passes over my head, bids me remember, that the <u>lease</u> of my <u>frail</u> tabernacle is <u>nearly</u> ended, & that I must look now intently forward to that which <u>cannot</u> be dissolved, eternal in the heavens, & withdraw myself more & more from <u>this</u> world, & become more & more made for that inheritance, I hope to enjoy, thro' the <u>obedience</u> wrought out <u>for me</u>, the satisfaction made for me, & the intercession performed for me by the beloved son of God, who took our nature upon him, & effected <u>all</u> for us, who believe in him, & trust <u>alone</u> in his merits." He continues in this vein, all too easily falling into "sermon" mode when addressing his son.

The Baroness died on 3 December 1835. Georgiana, Anna and Ernest at once rallied to Wathen's support, and when the news reached Thomas, he realised that he would have to revise the date of his homecoming a second time, to return to his father's side as soon as his passage could be arranged. Wathen's closest friends, the royal family, wrote letters of condolence which are preserved in the Waller Collection. It is clear that they were written not merely as a formality, but as expressions of their affection for Lady Howe and appreciation of Sir Wathen. Although Queen Adelaide wrote on behalf of the King and his sisters, Princess Sophia and the Duchess of Gloucester also sent him personal letters. The Duchess of Cumberland wrote from Berlin to express the regrets of her husband and son as well as her own; even so, Prince George added a letter of his own. The Duchess of Gloucester's words are typical of this group of letters:

"It is impossible for me my dear Sir Wathen to keep myself from addressing you these few lines – though I am fully sensible I ought not to plague you with a letter at a moment when your mind must be under so much agitation & affliction but the sincere regard & affection I had for dear Lady Howe makes it impossible that I should not beg to express how much I lament the loss of so attached & so kind a friend & also to make my personal enquiries after you <u>who</u> I also have every reason to remember as a most kind friend also – as upon every occasion I have <u>reason</u> to <u>remember</u> & feel greatfull [sic] to you for your <u>attentions</u> to <u>us all</u>, but more particularly to Ernest under his <u>awfull</u> [sic] illness & my poor Brother George the 4th in his last illness – which is deeply engraven on my heart…… The many years friendship that has subsisted from the <u>Howe</u> family & <u>ours</u> makes <u>us</u>

all feel much at the <u>last</u> of <u>Lord Howe's</u> daughters being gone & one who has ever been so kind & affectionately attached to us. It must be a consolation to you to feel that Lady Howe was very <u>sensible</u> of all your attention to her during her illness for she expressed herself so in her letters to the Queen. I beg you will not think of answering this letter but only remember amongst the many friends you also possess you have not one who feels more for you or more anxiously prays for your health & comfort than your friend

Mary Decr 5th Brighton." [12]

The Duchess had evidently written her letter with considerable thought and care, showing concern for Wathen in his bereavement, anxiety about his health, and gratitude for the attentive nursing he had provided in the past for her brothers Ernest and George. Illness in others brought out the best in Wathen. Admittedly he had felt tied to the house when Lady Howe's health was failing, and was in low spirits himself, but he had remained steadfastly by her side, and she had appreciated his attentive, considerate and dependable behaviour.

Notes

1. WCRO: CR0341/327/92, AJ to TWW, 29 January 1835.
2. WCRO: CR0341/327/93, AJ to TWW, 26 February 1835.
3. WCRO: CR0341/327/10, JWW to TWW, 27-31 May 1835.
4. WCRO: CR0341/327/96a, AJ to TWW, 29 May 1835.
5. WCRO: CR0341/327/97a, AJ to TWW, 25 June 1835.
6. WCRO: CR0341/327/95, AJ to TWW, 28 April 1835.
7. WCRO: CR0341/327/97a, AJ to TWW, 25 June 1835.
8. WCRO: CR0341/327/11, JWW to TWW, 26-31 July 1835.
9. WCRO: CR0341/327/12, JWW to TWW, 24-31 August 1835.
10. WCRO: CR0341/327/13, JWW to TWW, 15 and 30 October 1835.
11. Ibid.
12. WCRO: CR0341/136, Mary, Duchess of Gloucester to JWW, 5 December 1835.

Chapter 14

A family crisis

"Our Father's letter is <u>terrific</u>. His state of mind is perfectly <u>awful</u>, and makes me <u>tremble</u> only to think of it. God help him! It appears to me that owing to the constant (though unfortunately <u>necessary</u>) use of so much Laudanum, his reason has been long <u>tottering</u>, and I <u>dread</u> lest some sudden jolt as it were, should <u>entirely overthrow it</u>...... He who gives can alone take away."

Anna Jarrett

Thomas promptly arranged a passage home from Greece to comfort his father, now widowed for the second time. He knew what was expected of him as a loving and dutiful son and that his presence would be the best possible consolation to Wathen. Ironically, setting sail for England in January was the last thing he would have chosen to do. In Athens he was happier than he had been for many years – perhaps in his whole life. At last he felt well able to cope with the various roles he was called upon to play. He was liked and appreciated for the qualities of character he brought to his diplomatic, educational and social duties. Above all he felt accepted by the Ambassador Sir Edmund Lyons and his family, and by Mr and Mrs Hill as a valued member of the diplomatic community and the church; the unexpected warmth of their friendship had enormously boosted his fragile self-esteem. Not knowing whether he would be able to return, he took leave of everyone at Athens regretfully but graciously – leaving letters and presents to be distributed after his departure by his colleague Philip Griffith. In return he received affectionate letters of farewell and thanks, which meant so much to him that he kept them for the rest of his life. Several still exist in the Waller Collection, including one from each member of the Lyons family individually, and a message in Greek from fifteen pupils at the Hills' school for girls. Everyone wished him well and hoped he would come back in a few months. Annie, the elder of the Lyons girls, wrote to him in German to demonstrate her progress in the language under his tuition; Minna, the younger daughter, remained a friend for many years, corresponding with Thomas about her marriage in 1839 to Lord Fitzalan, later Duke of Norfolk, and about the births of her children.

It was March by the time Thomas arrived in London. Clearly the long sea-voyage in the depths of winter was a far from desirable undertaking, and it took some toll on his health. He was unwell for the next two months. Apart from making a brief visit to Camerton, he stayed at his father's London home in Norfolk Street, or in Twickenham at Pope's Villa, which was soon to be put on the market, along with the seaside retreat at Hastings. On 15 April Anna mentions that Thomas still needs some nursing and she is thankful that affectionate "old Fanny" is on hand to take care of him attentively, though she wishes she could look after her brother in person. Her only news of note – mentioned without comment – is that Harriet, Lady Howe, wife of their step-brother Richard, Earl Howe, "is expecting number ten in September".[1]

Six weeks later Thomas is clearly in better health and spirits and able to visit Tachbrook and Offchurch to make the acquaintance of his sister-in-law Louisa, her baby son Ernest Alured Waller, and the Wise family. Anna is delighted to hear how much he likes Louisa and wonders teasingly whether she now has a rival for pride of place her brother's affections. She loses no time in returning to her campaign to get Thomas to follow his brother's example, and marry: "You need not give up your profession. A woman who loved you as you <u>ought</u> to be, and I trust <u>will be</u> loved, would readily and cheerfully follow where your duty led you, and after a few years, should you feel inclined to dwell among us, you would be more likely to be happy, than marrying at a later period in life, not to mention the comfort you would derive from a loved companion, when separated from all other ties, and the consolation it would be to us, to know that you possessed a companion in all your joys, and a soother in all your sorrows. However God forbid that you should marry in haste, and repent at leisure." [2]

Thomas may have met 'Aunt Nutty' very briefly at Tachbrook. Mary Nutcombe was Louisa's widowed aunt and surrogate mother, who had helped her brother Henry Wise to manage the Offchurch Vicarage household after the death of his wife Charlotte in 1827. When Ernest and Louisa married, she had offered them a home in her spacious residence, Tachbrook Grove, as the Parsonage was considered too small for a family. But Mary Nutcombe was seriously ill when Thomas went to Tachbrook, and a few days later she died. Her death prompts Anna to ponder the need for a mother's love, and how a child will instinctively search for a substitute, should a mother die. She explains her thoughts to her brother through an imaginative musical metaphor, and confides that she had been much drawn to Aunt Nutty as a quasi-maternal figure, having known her own mother only very briefly. "Do you know I often think that deprived of a Mother's tender love, there is always a <u>void</u> left in the heart, which naturally impels it towards those, whose age claims honor & respect, while their goodness and gentleness excite our affection. It seems to touch upon that chord of the heart, which death indeed has unstrung, but which planted there by nature, seems ready to vibrate again as soon as there is aught to call forth its tone. So did I feel towards that blessed Saint, who is now gone to perfect in Heaven the life of love and praise, and duty, she has long led on earth. I always longed to tell her all my thoughts, to seek her advice, to ask her guidance; and used almost to envy those dear girls the privilege of so doing."[3]

Gradually Thomas regained his health and strength. He did not expect to spend more than a few months in England before returning to Athens, so he did not take a lease on a property. When not visiting his sisters at Camerton and Froyle, and his brother in Tachbrook, he divided his time between his father's homes in London, Twickenham and Hastings. In July Thomas is with Ernest and Louisa at Tachbrook. Still much preoccupied with her wish to see Thomas married, Anna explains to him that she feels quite justified in praying for this to come about. She admits that she is unsure whether she is praying with adequate faith and devotion, and that indeed many of her prayers are for the power to pray appropriately and sincerely. She continually seeks guidance from the scriptures and commentaries on them, and is well aware that Thomas has similar doubts and concerns in his own spiritual life. "I am sure you are formed for the very sort of happiness you are witnessing. Oh that you could realize it, that you could meet in this wide world with one who would make <u>you</u> as happy as dear Louisa makes Ernest… Indeed dearest, I do not feel I have been presumptuous in praying Almighty God <u>if he sees fit</u> to guide you to such a one. Surely we are encouraged even to ask for <u>temporal</u> mercies if we are careful always to add <u>from the heart</u>, 'Not as I will but as Thou wilt'… In my own case … thank God! I am <u>far far</u> from despair and I hope resigned and <u>willing</u> to wait <u>His</u> time, who alone can bestow the gift."[4] Almost certainly the temporal mercy she has been seeking for herself is a child, although none of her letters contains an overt complaint about having no children after thirteen years of marriage. Comparisons in her own mind with her sister and sister-in-law could scarcely be avoided, however. Georgiana was expecting her fourth child in six years, while John Jarrett's sister, Anne Gooch, had nine so far, and would eventually have fifteen.

Anna's prayers on her brother's behalf were very soon answered. We know nothing about Thomas's courtship of Louisa's sister Catherine except that it lacked all the dithering and procrastination exhibited by Ernest a couple of years earlier. Taking heed of his sister's advice, Thomas proposed to the elder of his brother's sisters-in-law – already recognised by Anna as an eminently suitable wife – and the wedding took place at Offchurch on 20th October. The ceremony was no doubt similar to Ernest's marriage to Louisa, with the bride's father officiating. Just one week later Wathen experiences a sudden, unexpected change of spirits. The joy he had felt at his son's happiness is all too soon dissipated by a "melancholy event at Penn"[5] – the death of his step-daughter-in-law, Harriet, Countess Howe, on 25th October, a few weeks after the birth of her tenth child. Of course Wathen knew her very well, as a member of the family and also at Court where both the Earl and

Countess Howe were major figures. Richard was Lord Chamberlain in Queen Adelaide's Household, and Harriet a favourite Lady-in-Waiting. They were among the closest friends of the King and Queen. Two of King William's sisters, the Duchess of Gloucester and Princess Sophia, describe to Wathen how both the King and Queen were hugely distressed at Lady Howe's death at the age of 39, leaving her husband with a large family of young children. The unexpected blow had left the King quite devastated and unable both physically and mentally to attend to his usual business. "His feelings are deeper than people give him credit for," according to his sister Mary.[6] Sophia comments that he is neither eating nor drinking and has not been in such a state since the loss of his youngest child Princess Elizabeth – his only legitimate child to survive even a few months. Resuming her habitual topics, Sophia gives Wathen the latest report on her eyes, which had been in a very poor state for many years: "I saw [Henry] Alexander yesterday who found the vessels full and advised 4 leeches which I put on this evening – He found the eye had made progress – indeed on Tuesday I hardly saw to paint my face."

By Christmas 1836 Thomas was planning to resume his diplomatic posting to Greece as a married man. His father vehemently opposed this plan, however, having made up his mind more than a year earlier that Thomas's return to Athens was totally out of the question. In the New Year there is suddenly a family crisis: faced with the prospect of Thomas returning to Athens, Wathen has threatened suicide. Both of his sons immediately rush from Warwickshire to London.[7] For years Wathen had suffered from mood swings, involving periods of depression, and both Anna and Thomas were similarly affected from time to time. On the whole, Anna paid little attention to her father's low moods, as they usually passed fairly quickly, especially if he was required to act appropriately at some Court or social occasion. But this time the whole family is shocked and fearful. The Jarretts arrive on a pre-arranged visit to Offchurch soon after the brothers' departure, and Catherine shows Anna the disturbing letter that Thomas had received from his father. Although disappointed not to see her brother, Anna understands that he could not have remained in Offchurch. "You could do no otherwise than you have done, and may God send his blessing on your dutiful efforts, and those of dear Ernest… Our Father's letter is <u>terrific</u>. His state of mind is perfectly <u>awful</u>, and makes me <u>tremble</u> only to think of it. God help him! It appears to me that owing to the constant (though unfortunately <u>necessary</u>) use of so much laudanum, his reason has been long <u>tottering</u>, and I <u>dread</u> lest some sudden jolt as it were, should <u>entirely overthrow it</u>." [8]

The crucial letter from his father, which was to change the course of Thomas's life, is surprisingly absent from the Waller collection. However it created an immensely fraught and delicate situation for Thomas, who, as the elder son, always bore the brunt of trying to live up to his father's expectations. A year had gone by since his step-mother's death, and tensions in the family had relaxed somewhat – or so he had thought. Then, just when his plans seemed to be working out so well, there had been this ironic turn of events, with his father resorting to emotional blackmail of the most extreme kind. Thomas and Ernest attempted to make their father see reason, but they had qualms about challenging his authority, even though the balance of his mind might be in doubt. From their comments and Anna's, scattered throughout the family correspondence, it is obvious that they had always found Wathen demanding and difficult to live with, although the bonds of filial affection, duty, and respect made for a close relationship. Outwardly he was utterly confident, urbane and sophisticated, the epitome of worldly success; in his quieter moments, however, especially as he felt the approach of old age, he was far less sure of himself – often beset by guilt that his behaviour and priorities fell short of a Christian ideal. But in January 1837 introspection had not brought on one of his routine depressions. This time he was in a panic. He could not bear to think that Thomas and Catherine would soon be beyond his reach in Athens. Winter, old age and loneliness had so much afflicted his spirits that he wanted his son close to home at all costs. What he did was emotional and instinctive, rather than thought out or justified – even to himself. Threatening suicide showed just how desperate he had become. It was a last resort, but it could not be ignored. Selfish and unreasonable it might be, but it would prove more effective than any amount of gentle persuasion.

When Thomas turns to Anna for advice on what to do in the face of their father's ultimatum, she takes the matter very seriously, weighing up the two most obvious but incompatible courses of action (to go to Athens or not to go) and endeavouring to find a compromise solution. Her reasoning process is set out eloquently and at great length. Like a judge summing up a case, she examines the pros and cons of the options, their likely effects in the current situation, and their longer-term repercussions. She realises that Thomas desperately wants to return to Greece with his new wife, who is already looking forward to setting up the marital home in Athens and meeting her husband's friends. However, how could he go when he would have no peace of mind? His father, once again overcome with depression, might at any moment take his own life. Anna sympathises with her brother's frustrating dilemma, but is also sharply critical of her father: "Who can say when the storm may rage again, and what havoc it may make. 'His <u>Life or Death</u>', he says, 'is in your hands'. No! thank God! Life and Death are in the hands of <u>no mortal man</u>. He who <u>gives</u>, can alone <u>take away</u>. 'Our times are in His Hand' and in <u>His only</u>." [9] Although Thomas would not be responsible if the worst were to happen, Anna knows he would have an unbearable burden on his conscience. Quite reasonably she suggests a possible middle path: leave of absence for an additional year – if obtainable – might be an acceptable solution.

In this emotionally charged and protracted battle of wills, there could be little doubt who would ultimately prevail. By April, the matter is resolved, and the storm has passed. With King William's help, Wathen has obtained for his son a diplomatic posting within a day or two's journey from London; Thomas is to be offered the position of Secretary to the British Legation in Belgium. Wathen is much placated when Thomas and Catherine give up all thoughts of Athens, and agree to make Brussels their home.[10] The closer location will make the exchange of letters far quicker, and for Wathen the strain of anxiously waiting for news will be considerably lessened. He is greatly relieved that the couple will be relatively near, particularly as by now they are expecting their first child.[10] Shortly before they depart, Georgiana's fourth baby is christened Georgiana Catherine Louisa at Froyle, with her two aunts by marriage, the former Misses Wise, as godmothers.[11] Three weeks later the family welcomes Wathen's sixth grandchild, Ernest and Louisa's second son, to be named Henry after his maternal grandfather and uncle. Thomas is able to resume his diplomatic career with no loss of status, and Princess Sophia arranges for her sister-in-law the Duchess of Kent (mother of Princess, soon to be Queen, Victoria) to put in a good word for him with her brother, the new King Leopold of the Belgians. She continues: "I must now speak for myself & hope I may see my old friend [Thomas] <u>Wathen</u> and that he will bring his wife <u>any day</u> & hour most convenient, Wednesday excepted either at 3 or 4 o'clock as they like best." Sophia reports also that her brother the King is far from well and missed chapel on 14th May. He was pale and his pulse was weak. She concludes her letter: "there is <u>much going on,</u> but I know not what" adding an unexpected note in parenthesis "Burn me pray".[12] Perhaps she feels she has said rather too much.

King William had been contending not only with a rapid physical decline but also with unbearable grief and psychological anguish. His eldest daughter, Sophia (FitzClarence) Sidney, Lady de L'Isle & Dudley, had died in April 1837 after childbirth, within months of the Countess Howe's death in similar circumstances. Sophia was said to be her father's favourite child and had often served as his amanuensis, dealing with his private correspondence. Shortly before her death she completed a watercolour portrait of her father looking frail and elderly. The King was aware that he had not long to live, but at a banquet held on his last birthday, the previous August, he had publicly declared that he hoped his life would be spared a further nine months, until the Princess Victoria came of age. "I should then have the satisfaction of leaving the exercise of the Royal authority to the personal authority of that young lady, heiress presumptive to the Crown, and not in the hands of a person now near me, who is surrounded by evil advisers and is herself incompetent to act with propriety in the situation in which she would be placed." [13] The prospect of a Regency with the much-disliked Duchess of Kent wielding power had haunted the King, and though ailing, he clung to life until Victoria reached her eighteenth birthday, on 24th May 1837. Within a month he died.

By good fortune Wathen had negotiated Thomas's appointment to Brussels shortly before losing his unimpeded access to the monarch – the ultimate position of influence. With the death of William IV, his official role as Extra Groom of the Bedchamber was at an end, and he was no longer to appear in Court circles almost daily. The young Queen Victoria made it quite clear that she would make her own appointments, and even distanced herself – as her uncle had hoped – from her mother, the Duchess of Kent, and Sir John Conroy, Comptroller of her mother's household. Although Victoria became Queen of Great Britain and Ireland, no woman could succeed to the throne of Hanover. Her uncle Ernest, Duke of Cumberland, next in the line of succession, was at last able to employ his energy and talents in a challenging, worthwhile and prestigious role. He set off to claim his Kingdom of Hanover at once.

Notes

1. WCRO: 0341/327/104, AJ to TWW, 15 April 1836.
2. WCRO: 0341/327/105, AJ to TWW, 26 May 1836.
3. WCRO: 0341/327/106, AJ to TWW, 31 May 1836.
4. WCRO: 0341/327/107, AJ to TWW, 19 July 1836.
5. WCRO: 0341/193, Princess Sophia to JWW, 27 October 1836.
6. WCRO: 0341/155, Duchess of Gloucester to JWW, 26 October 1836.
7. Wathen had moved from Norfolk St to 8 New Cavendish St, Portland Place, London.
8. WCRO: 0341/327/108, AJ to TWW, 11 January 1837.
9. Ibid.
10. WCRO: 0341/328/28, Minna Lyons to TWW, 8 April 1837, congratulating Thomas on his appointment to Brussels (though she was disappointed "from a selfish point of view" that he was not to return to Athens).
11. Froyle baptism record, 19 March 1837.
12. WCRO: 0341/194, Princess Sophia to JWW, 15 May 1837.
13. Somerset, Anne, *The Life and times of William IV,* Weidenfeld & Nicolson, 1980, p 209.

Chapter 15

Sir Wathen, King Ernest, Mrs Bankes

"by prudence, caution and good humour I shall succeed in getting things right."
Ernest Augustus, King of Hanover

During the reign of his brother King William, the Duke of Cumberland lived for the most part at his mansion on Kew Green and had plenty of opportunities to meet his good friend Phippy. Once he became King of Hanover, however, the need for letters resumed, and Ernest was soon confiding his first impressions of his new responsibilities as well as his current preoccupations. In the first two letters, both written in July 1837, Ernest mentions how sorry he is – on account of his hasty departure – not to have taken leave of Wathen formally: "I regret very much not having seen you the last day, and shaking hands with you; I trust my sisters expressed this to you in my name – they promised me so to do. I arrived <u>here</u> the Wednesday evening and was received with great enthusiasm, but I have an immensity of business & really am beginning to feel the being unable to get out is fatiguing." He returns to these subjects repeatedly – the volume of work, the necessity of being at his desk all day and the near impossibility of taking exercise, this being particularly frustrating as his custom throughout his life had been to spent several hours each day out riding. However, he has had the satisfaction of being very warmly received in a land long accustomed to the rule of an absentee Elector or King. He enquires solicitously about Queen Adelaide, sympathising with her new situation as Dowager Queen, and realising that she will feel exhausted and dejected once the ceremonies accompanying the death of the King and the accession of Queen Victoria are completed: "pray write to me more news and let me know how Queen Adelaide is, for I own I fear much the <u>first</u> moments of <u>her</u> quitting Windsor, <u>all</u> then will break in upon her, she has been living as it were in an excitement the last six weeks." [1]

The letters sent to Wathen in the early days of his reign in Hanover show Ernest's character in total contrast to the portrayal he had endured in the English press for decades. Even to this day he is widely reputed to have been a "damnable duke", and a "wicked uncle" to Queen Victoria, capable of all manner of unspeakable vices. Yet in his private, unpolished letters to a friend, written with no thought of the wider public, he appears honest, hardworking, and plain speaking, albeit conservative by nature, and convinced that tried and tested principles and policies are most likely to be in the best interest of his kingdom. "I have had plenty to do & shall have enough for some time to come, still I think by prudence, caution & good humour I shall succeed in getting things right; nothing can exceed the enthusiasm and loyalty with which I have been generally received throughout the country, deputations & addresses daily pouring in and I understand my declaration has given much satisfaction for it speaks plain & honest language and in the mildest and least objectionable language, at the same time baldly & openly upholding three true conservative principles which thank God I have always publickly held. Not disavowing or retracting our word. Honesty is the best policy, & gives confidence." [2]

Although busy with affairs of state in Hanover, Ernest clearly misses the daily gossip amongst the royal family and their courtiers in London and Windsor, and he continues to take great interest in the health and welfare of his sisters and of the Dowager Queen, who has retired to her home at Bushy. By August, he is aware that the young Queen Victoria has already taken steps to assert her authority over her mother, the Duchess of Kent, and also Sir John Conroy, the Duchess's reputed lover. He expects Phippy to provide all the details: "I had hoped you would have written again after your visit to Bushy, and have let me know <u>all</u> particulars at <u>both</u> courts. I hear it does not go on very smoothly or harmoniously at Buckingham House, and that the Lady Mother is in great dudgeon & complains loudly how ill used she and her dear Irish man are treated, and the latter is not permitted to put his foot even in the threshold of the door." [3] Ernest also keeps abreast of Wathen's own family news, inquiring how Thomas finds Brussels, and whether the Hastings house is sold. He provides updates about his son George, now known as the Crown Prince, and maintains steadfastly year after year the hope that when the time is right, Dr von Graefe will be able to restore his sight. He is angry that Henry Alexander appears to have mishandled the operation on his sister Sophia's eyes in December 1837, completely sidelining Wathen, even from an advisory role: "it is revolting to common nature to see one who owes so much, nay I may add <u>all</u> to your kindness thus to act." [4] The Princess never regained much sight and was completely blind during her declining years.

Intriguingly, in eight of the surviving letters sent to Wathen by the King of Hanover, there are enigmatic references to enclosures, [5] which are apparently letters from Ernest to be forwarded to a third person, and others received by Wathen for Ernest by way of reply. In his very first letter from Hanover the new King makes the request: "Pray take care of the enclosed that Georgina may get it safe, she desired me to put it under cover to you." Initially there are no clues as to the identity of Georgina, but in subsequent letters we can pick up more information: "I had <u>at</u>

<u>last</u> a few lines from Mʳˢ B. and as I am not certain where she actually is, whether in Dorsetshire or at Sheen, I prefer enclosing my letter to you who will probably know where this may find her." So Georgina is apparently a Mrs B to be found in Dorset or in Sheen, near Richmond, Surrey. Eventually, in a letter dated 1845 Ernest tells Wathen that a Mrs Bankes has sent him news of a "melancholy event", the usual euphemism for a death. With the revelation of her full name, it finally becomes possible to unravel the mystery of the identity of Georgina Bankes, and her connection to the King of Hanover. A most unexpected tale it turns out to be.

By the nineteenth century the surname Bankes and the county of Dorset had been closely associated for at least four hundred years. The family were influential landowners, and had been active in politics since the Civil War. When the constituency of Corfe Castle was abolished in the 1832 reforms, one of the two sitting MPs was George Bankes, the fifth member of his family to hold the parliamentary seat. His wife's name was Georgina. The principal Bankes property in Dorset was Kingston Lacy, a handsome stately home near Wimborne, now open to the public. There, on a side table, displayed just like a family photograph, is a miniature watercolour in a gilded frame, showing Mrs George Bankes and her three eldest children, Georgina, Maria and Edmund. It was painted in 1830 by none other than William Charles Ross, Anna Jarrett's choice of artist just four years later. (Mrs Bankes and her elder daughter wear their hair in ringlets – which Anna refused to do when sitting for Ross.) The miniature rests inside a leather carrying case, and was presumably commissioned as a portable memento by Georgina's husband – or perhaps by her father, who would see her less frequently. The charming, though somewhat idealised portrait shows a young mother and three small children looking blond, pretty and rosy-cheeked, in fact bearing a striking resemblance to the Hanoverian princes and princesses when depicted in their youth. This likeness proves to be no mere coincidence. According to Viola Bankes, a great-granddaughter of Georgina born in 1900, the family had always been aware that Mrs Bankes was the daughter of Ernest Augustus, Duke of Cumberland and later King of Hanover. [6]

This parentage, although acknowledged by the Bankes family and the royal family in private, seems to have been kept secret from the wider public at least during the life-time of Admiral Charles Edmund Nugent, who was recorded as Georgina's father at the time of her christening in 1799 and of her marriage to George Bankes in 1822. Until she married she was known as Georgina Charlotte Nugent, only daughter and heiress of the Admiral – who may or may not have known the truth. They certainly behaved to each other as father and daughter: Georgina lived with the Admiral in London's Bryanston Square in her teens after her mother's early death, and he spent "the closing period of his life" [7] with the Bankes family at Studland Manor, their seaside home in Dorset, where he died in January 1844, aged 85.

The secret of Georgina's birth was remarkably well kept; those intent on vilifying the Duke of Cumberland in the scandal-sheets of the period and in the excoriating obituary in *The Times* were apparently unaware of the existence of his "natural" or illegitimate daughter. Even relatively recent biographers, such as Willis, Fulford, Bird and Wardroper make no mention of her. The Nugent marriage had been childless for eight and a half years when Georgina was born in January 1799, and within a few months it seemed virtually over. Another naval wife, Fanny Nelson, passed on this item of gossip to her husband serving in the Mediterranean: "23 September 1799. I hear Admiral and Mrs Nugent have separated, a difference of temper she says is the cause… Mrs Nugent had a daughter not long ago which I heard had given much happiness to the Admiral. These affairs make [a] little noise for a day." [8] (When her husband, Admiral Lord Nelson, left her for Emma Hamilton a couple of years later, she was somewhat less sanguine in her response.) Lady Nelson gave no hint of rumours or scandal regarding the paternity of Mrs Nugent's child, and at some time between 1800 and 1805 the Nugents were reconciled, or at least came to an accommodation which enabled them to keep up appearances.

We cannot know precisely when Georgina learned the identity of her real father. She may have grown up knowing the secret and certainly knew it before Ernest became King of Hanover in 1837; she was then 38, had been married for fifteen years and was the mother of ten children. Queen Victoria was also aware of the truth. On 5th May 1839 she noted in her Journal a conversation with her Prime Minister Lord Melbourne in which Mrs Bankes's name was mentioned. Melbourne commented that she had been very pretty as Miss Nugent, and very like the royal family: "The King of Hanover's daughter," he added. "I believe so," replied the Queen.[9] The letters forwarded to Georgina by Wathen were clearly part of an on-going correspondence between Ernest and his daughter, and Wathen's role as go-between was to hasten the speedy delivery of the letters and ensure that they were transmitted via safe hands, as Ernest had difficulty in keeping up with her movements between homes in London, Surrey and Dorset. Georgina's royal aunts and uncles also passed on messages to her from Ernest, a few of which survive.

Most of the Duchess of Gloucester's letters to Georgina relate in her characteristic, barely legible handwriting fairly trivial incidents of her daily life; few are fully dated. Among numerous snippets of family news from Hanover, one truly noteworthy item stands out: the announcement that Marie, the wife of Ernest's son George, is expecting a first child.[10] "In case you may not have had a letter from Hanover today I write to inform you of the joyful news – a letter I have had from my brother dated the 13 instant that the Crown Princess is in the family way & there is no doubt that it really is so. My brother desires me to inform all the family of this event & writes in great happiness at this very great blessing. You may judge by your own feelings how overjoyed I am. Pray call tomorrow – about 4 o'clock."[11] The Duchess is clearly excited by the news, delighted to pass it on, and cannot wait to chat about it the following day. The birth of any new baby is a significant event, but this child – if a boy – would be second in line to the throne of Hanover, so the news of the pregnancy was especially welcome. The inclusion of Georgina in the Duchess's notion of "all the family" leaves little room for doubt that she knew she was writing to a niece.

In 1843 King Ernest returned to his native country to pay his respects to Queen Victoria,[12] to seek medical advice, and to visit old friends and family, including, presumably, Georgina and her nine surviving children (there had been eleven, but by this date her fourth son, Frederic, and the rosy-cheeked second daughter portrayed in the Ross miniature, Maria Margaret, had died – aged three and twelve respectively). The following summer Georgina travelled to Hanover to repay the visit, and the Duchess of Gloucester asked her to deliver a "parcel for Ernest which contains souvenirs from Sophy [her sister Princess Sophia] and me for him & George & his wife." [13] It is likely that Georgina made other journeys to Hanover, her father being too old to visit her in England again. At the German Court, according to Viola Bankes, she was greatly admired for her blonde beauty and imposing figure. Evidence of Georgina's closeness to Ernest can be found in the printed text of a sermon preached on the Sunday after the King's death by his domestic chaplain, the Reverend Charles Wilkinson. He refers to "a countrywoman of ours, who was ever admitted to his nearest confidence" – identified in a footnote as Mrs Bankes. She had told him that the King had explained in private to her his profound belief that with the Divine Right and Divine Protection of Kings came the "awful responsibility" of Kings. "So deep was his feeling upon this point, that he never proceeded to take any single step in the settlement of the affairs of the nation without earnest and fervent prayer for the guidance of Divine wisdom; then, after that, he acted to the best of his judgment, and he could never help feeling his heart relieved from a certain weight of responsibility. This anecdote was confided to me as a clergyman in an interesting and serious conversation upon his late Majesty's spiritual state and private devotions, and I believe it was confided to no other living soul. I know it was not even hinted at to his royal son, for I had the pleasure of first communicating it to him, and of witnessing the burst of gratitude to the Almighty with which he received this assurance of his royal father's total dependence upon the direction of heavenly wisdom." [14]

Although Ernest was often thought to be high-handed and arrogant, in private he was capable of humility, and showed a fervent desire to maintain a good conscience. In the strength of his belief in God and his habitual practice of prayer, Ernest greatly resembled his friend Phippy. Separated as the two men were by their stations in life, they were like-minded and totally sincere about religion. For both of them faith in Christ the Redeemer was of paramount importance – indeed the sole path to salvation.

Notes

1. WCRO: 0341/72, King of Hanover to JWW, 6 July 1837.
2. WCRO: 0341/73, K of H to JWW, 21 July, 1837.
3. WCRO: 0341/74, K of H to JWW, 21 August 1837.
4. WCRO: 0341/76, K of H to JWW, 28 December 1837.
5. Enclosures are mentioned in the following letters from the King of Hanover to JWW:

    WCRO: CR0341/72, 6 July 1837

    WCRO: CR0341/73, 21 July 1837

    WCRO: CR0341/74, 21 August 1837

    WCRO: CR0341/75, 23 October 1837

    WCRO: CR0341/76, 28 December 1837

    WCRO: CR0341/80, 8 July 1838

    WCRO: CR0341/81, 30 August 1838

    WCRO: CR0341/92, 28 April 1845.
6. Bankes, Viola, *A Dorset Heritage*, Anthony Mott Ltd, 1986 (2nd edition), p 180.
7. The phrase comes from the epitaph on the Admiral's grave in St Nicholas's churchyard, Studland. It mentions his naval career lasting over seventy years, and ends: "with affection of relatives who caused this stone to be erected".
8. Naish, George, (Ed.) *Nelson's Letters to his wife, and other documents 1785 – 1831*, Routledge & Kegan Paul, 1958, p 533.
9. Royal Archives VIC/MAIN/QVJ (W), 5 May 1839, Lord Esher's typescripts.
10. The letter was written on 18th March, year unstated, but must be 1845; the child was born on 21st September 1845, and named Ernest Augustus William Adolphus George Frederick.
11. Dorset History Centre, Bankes Box 8C/100, Folder 5, iii.
12. Willis, G M, *Ernest Augustus, Duke of Cumberland and King of Hanover*, Arthur Barker, London, 1954, p 345. "The King of Hanover proposed a toast to Queen Victoria at a Dinner and Concert at Buckingham Palace 14 June 1843: 'I have the honour to propose the health of Her Majesty Queen Victoria, and I beg to state distinctly that I do so as one of her Majesty's subjects, and as I have frequently said in the House of Lords that she has not a more faithful subject than the individual who addresses you now and I am delighted to drink her health in her own palace. Kindly accept these wishes of your old uncle, and God bless you, my dear niece, with many years yet!' "
13. Dorset History Centre, Bankes Box 8C/100, Folder 5, iii.
14. Wilkinson, The Reverend Charles Allix, *Reminiscences of the Court and Times of King Ernest of Hanover*, Hurst & Blackett, London, 1887, p 311.

Chapter 16

Births and deaths in a new reign

"the dear pet don' yet know <u>how to manage her large eyes</u>, and they sometimes look so <u>wondrous wise</u>, and sometimes so <u>wondrous foolish</u>, that it is impossible to help laughing. I think there is <u>mischief</u> in them too, please God she lives to perpetrate it."

Anna Jarrett

1837 brought not only a change of sovereign, with the accession of Queen Victoria, but a considerable change of lifestyle for Wathen. Now twice widowed and retired from Court life, he was no longer obliged to entertain lavishly or to keep up a country mansion and a seaside retreat. He disposed of Pope's Villa and the Hastings house as soon as practicable after Baroness Howe's death and maintained a comfortable London home in the heart of the West End, where he was looked after by a small staff of servants he had known and trusted over many years. Life was much less hectic: paying and receiving calls, and dealing with correspondence were his principal activities. The Duchess of Gloucester, also widowed, and her almost blind sister, Princess Sophia, remained close friends and he was often requested to call, or invited to dine. From time to time he spent a few days with the sisters at Bagshot Park, the Duchess's country home. Choosing a christening gift to welcome each addition to the family became a more than occasional pastime and pleasure. In the first decade of the Victorian era, the tally of Wathen's grandchildren rose to nineteen with the arrival of thirteen new babies to join the six born under King William.

With Thomas married and settled in Brussels, Wathen was relieved of much of the anxiety he had experienced when his elder son was alone in distant foreign lands, prey to all manner of fevers and political upheavals. Letters could be exchanged far more frequently and there were no more lengthy and frustrating delays. As Secretary of Legation, Thomas was second only to Her Majesty's Envoy and Minister Plenipotentiary, Sir George Hamilton Seymour, and was called upon to deputise for the Minister on several occasions (as chargé d'affaires), much to the delight of his father and siblings. They all anticipated that a permanent promotion to the pinnacle of diplomatic status was only a matter of time. (A couple of years earlier when Wathen had received "a handsome gift of plate" from King William he had immediately commented to his son: "it will do for you when Ambassador hereafter".[1]) Meanwhile there were family affairs to attend to. In September Thomas and Catherine delightedly announced the birth of a son, to be called George Henry.

Soon afterwards Anna had some special news of her own to impart. After fourteen years of marriage she had nearly given up hope of becoming a mother, but at last her fervent prayer had been answered, and she was expecting a child. Almost overwhelmed with excitement, she wrote to her brother and sister-in-law of "the feelings of deep and fervent gratitude, with which my heart overflows, when I think of all the many, great and undeserved blessings already bestowed upon me and <u>this</u>, the crowning one of all…… at times my heart feels bursting, and it is almost too much for me." Mindful of the possibility of self-deception and wishful thinking, Anna had kept her pregnancy secret even from her husband until it was confirmed beyond doubt, and she is rapturous when finally able to reveal the joyful news and to plan for the great event. "I am to be confined in Town, and my dearest & kind friend Lady Elizabeth has promised to be with me, in my hour of trial. This will be the greatest delight and comfort to me, for nowhere could I find a better <u>human</u> support. Sir Charles Clarke [Queen Adelaide's physician] or Mr Stone will attend me, and Lady E. has written to secure me an excellent monthly nurse."[2] The child is expected at the end of February and the Jarretts intend to travel to London early in January, and will rent a property within easy reach of Wathen's home.

Of course Anna was well aware of the potential danger of childbirth to all women, and especially to "older" mothers. Had not Harriet, wife of her step-brother Earl Howe, died just over a year ago within weeks of delivering her tenth child? Like Anna she was in her thirties. A first pregnancy at the age of 34 was something of a rarity in the Victorian era, and unsurprisingly Anna was caught up in a turmoil of mixed feelings – a combination of joy, apprehension and faith. Attending the Christmas Day service in St Peter's Church at Camerton was an emotional experience for her, and she lost no time in describing it to Thomas: "We are just come from Church, and from the Sacrament. To me the whole ceremony has been more than usually impressive. This is the last time I shall worship God, in our <u>own</u> <u>little</u> <u>church</u>, and probably the last time I may have an opportunity of partaking of the Sacrament, before my confinement. God only knows, whether I shall ever visit the one, or partake of the other again <u>on earth</u>! Do not think me gloomy or out of spirits dearest, no! Nor out of courage. I am none of these, and I have reason, and I <u>do</u> look forward with joyful hope, to a happy termination of my approaching trial. But these more serious thoughts <u>must</u> and <u>ought</u> to occupy my mind at times, and you know mine is not a heart, that can be cheerful from <u>want of thought</u>, or from driving away serious reflection. No I would humbly hope that the calm peace and cheerfulness I enjoy, has a more Christmas foundation, namely that I have placed my trust, where help and strength can never fail me, and knowing that I am under the Merciful Protection of one who <u>loves me</u>, and who will order all things as deemeth best to His all perfect wisdom."[3]

Not all goes to plan, however, and it falls to John Jarrett to provide Thomas with a graphic description of events, in a letter brimming with excitement, and revealing at first hand far more of his character and sense of humour than has been apparent elsewhere: "Rejoice with me, our dear Nannie [Anna] is safe in bed with a perfect, healthy strong <u>little girl</u>. Now for the detail: she was grumbling all yesterday morning about some little pain in her back but we thought nothing of it. Capt. Bowen came to see her and she was in high spirits and enjoyed thoroughly a new pianoforte which had come from Broadwood. Having a nasty little hacking cough, Stone ordered her to dine earlier and at half past five I saw her eating boiled chicken and oyster sauce. I went to dress to dine with your father to meet Ernest and afterwards I went to the Olympic to see Puss in Boots, when lo and behold on my return I found <u>Puss in Bed</u>." [4] As the baby was not expected until the end of February John had had no qualms about leaving Anna in their rented house in Grosvenor Square for the evening of 24th January. No-one realised that there had been a miscalculation of the birth date. "I came home about twelve and found Lady Elizabeth, the Nurse and Mr Stone in full conclave assembled. Symptoms had appeared well known to the trusty Bevan [Anna's maid] who summoned Stone & Co; the pains *veritable* began about half past ten and at nineteen minutes after two I heard what – why the squall I wanted to hear."

Although John had waited a long time to become a father, he probably had no idea quite how he would feel when the baby arrived. He is spontaneously overjoyed on first meeting his daughter – and not at all disconcerted that she has had to be content with a makeshift cradle: "I am quite delighted with the little darling. I could not have supposed it possible to have been so fond of a stranger already. She has dark eyes and dark hair and they say a very tall child – thank God both are doing as well as heart can desire. Stone was kindness itself. Being taken rather by surprise, the little dear was shoved into a washing basket, and there it slept as comfortably as in the most superb cot. You see every body calculated (I suppose according to the <u>old</u> fashion) that the 24th of February was to be the Day, this was erroneous, as according to the new system of arithmetic we say take one from one and two remain." Anna and John are particularly grateful to Lady Elizabeth Repton who fulfilled her promise to be with her friend during the birth, despite the death of her father Lord Eldon a few days earlier. "Dear Lady Elizabeth got out of her bed to come and staid with her the whole night notwithstanding all she has had to do in her affliction. Her husband and young George started yesterday morning for Encombe to attend Lord Eldon's funeral; they return on Saturday. I never can repay her for such real kindness to my sweet Anna." John is not above gossiping about the details of Lord Eldon's Will, which will make the Reptons quite well off: "Bye the bye I do not know why you should not also rejoice in the good prospects of the Reptons. The Old Peer has left them one way and another a clear income of nearly three thousand a year and two thousand five hundred pounds, by way of a what do you call it besides, to be paid within a month of his decease <u>all</u> legacy duty free, this will enable them to live really comfortably." Among his many bequests, Lord Eldon left £8 per annum to provide for his much-loved dog, Pincher.

Anna soon turns her attention to naming the baby. Her first thought is to give the child her own names, Anna Eliza, but in the end she decides on Anna Mary. Sir Wathen is to be godfather, and John's sister Annie Gooch godmother, together with his aunt Stephens. Anna has the baby vaccinated before leaving London, and is rather pleased when the physician Sir Charles Clarke "offered to lay me a bet of 2/6 that I shall have a boy this time twelvemonth. I should not be sorry if he were to win his wager though he is rather sharp upon me." [5]

In August 1838 Ernest Waller pays a visit to his brother Thomas and his wife in Brussels. Catherine is seven months into her second pregnancy; her father, Henry Wise, and her unmarried sister, Mary Patience, are already in Belgium but are to return home with Ernest. For all of them this is the first opportunity to see the baby, George, and to experience a little of a rather alien milieu – the social life of Her Majesty's diplomatic corps. When finalising the arrangements for his imminent arrival, Ernest includes a tongue-in-cheek self-portrait, a verbal caricature of an unsophisticated country curate, summing himself up as "shabby genteel". "Please to let me have a passport waiting my arrival in London on Tuesday 21st of this month, that I may find free admission into the dominions of his Belgic Majesty on Friday the 24th when I emerge from this corking vessel where fishes food is prepared by steam, & distributed by natural organic high pressure power. Personal appearance – bald at the top of the head quite, hair on the side, colour pepper & salt, nose, long, tinged at the end with snuff doubtless; mouth large dimensions of vast capability for reception or emission, chin, placed below his mouth & above his neckcloth – general appearance shabby genteel; deportment, somewhat country bumpkinified – there that will do – & what you are to conclude is that your brother such as he is, will be with you and among you all before long – to see the laddy, the house, the wife, the brother, the father in law & the sister in law, all very dear persons, except the house, & I dare say that is a very dear thing, so God bless you all."[6] Thomas and Catherine's new baby – born in October – is another son, and is named in Ernest's honour with his second name, Adolphus. The following year there are three more grandchildren for Wathen: the first of Thomas's four daughters, Catherine Mary, a third son – Edmund – for Ernest, and a fifth and last child for his sister Georgiana, a boy named Waller at his baptism at Froyle in October 1839.

Sir Charles Clarke did not quite win his bet, but Anna did have a second child, Emily Elizabeth, born in Albemarle Street, London, early in December 1840. This birth was not as melodramatic as the first, but its aftermath was far worse: Anna fell dangerously ill with scarlet fever and the doctors feared that she would not survive. All was well until three days after the birth, and John Jarrett had already written cheerfully to his brother-in-law Thomas that his new daughter "has left off bawling and is settling down into a squarefaced, sharp nosed, black eyed, longfingered fat squab," while the elder child had assumed a patronising attitude to the new arrival: "she says she shall whip it, feed it, and give it her plaid frock. Two to one in favour of kindness at all events." [7]

But John's jaunty frame of mind was not to last long. Soon he and Anna's father were distraught. Wathen moved the two children to his house in New Cavendish Street, but took care not to see them himself, as he visited Anna twice a day and feared cross-infection. He was happy, albeit a little frustrated, to hear "little Birdie's feet trotting"[8] over his head, and to know that she, the toddler Anna Mary, and the baby were well looked after. A flurry of letters survives from this worrying time, as Wathen wrote daily to Thomas in Brussels. Fortunately the emergency is soon over, and on December 12th Anna is pronounced out of danger. However, her convalescence lasts several weeks, and John writes to Thomas of the care they must take that complications do not set in: "I am well aware of the consequences of such a malady as Scarlatina at such a time. The usual consequences unless taken the greatest care of are dropsy or consumption – depend upon it my dear Wathen I shall not throw a chance away, for which reason I have D[r] Watson in conjunction with Stone to look her over and I shall continue to do so, until they <u>assure</u> me that all is safe. I need not tell you what she feels at not being allowed to see her Chicks and how grateful we both are to your dear father for his fatherly care of them. They have told her today that if all goes on well, they think she may without danger see them on the 5th of January. We must have a stick and notch off the days as we used to do at school." [9]

Faced with a real crisis – his daughter's life in danger – Wathen, who had tried the patience of his immediate family so often, had responded quite splendidly. He organised the doctors, supervised the care of the infants, wrote numerous bulletins to his absent children, and even concocted a medicine which appeared to effect an improvement. Anna, who on many occasions had been critical of her father, was almost overcome with gratitude: "I must speak of our dear father. He has been kindness & affection itself. Twice in every day has he come to see me, and to meet Sir C Clarke & Mr Stone, and (since the former's departure) Dr Watson. Indeed I think often, that under providence I owe my rapid recovery greatly to him, for he proposed his own lotion for my throat, which tho' at first rejected, was afterwards adopted, and the effect was <u>marvelous.</u> Mr Stone quite exclaimed with astonishment, and if you had seen the dear man's face, when after finding the good it had done me, he used to trot up to my bedside, with his silver probe & bottle, you would have been as gratified & pleased as I was."[10] She concludes with a juxtaposition surely worthy of Jane Austen: "My dear sister Georgiana and Lady Elizabeth are to be the Godmothers of our new darling. Will you my Wathen be the Godfather? Mrs Blunt [Sainsbury's Aunt] is dead at last and he will have an addition of £10,000 at least, probably more."

It was not until the second week of January that Anna was at last able to be reunited with her two-year-old daughter, nicknamed Birdie, and the new-born baby. She describes the emotional moment to Thomas: "after having embraced my dear Father, you may imagine the delight with which I hastened to the nursery to press my treasures once more to my heart. My Birdie hung her head and was shy, for the first few minutes, but perhaps my crying (which I could not help) frightened her. She soon knew me quite well, and would not leave me afterwards for a moment all day, sitting on my knee, and every now & then stealing her little arms round my neck & kissing me."[11] As for the baby, to be named Emily Elizabeth: "the dear pet don^t yet know <u>how to manage her large eyes</u>, and they sometimes look so <u>wondrous wise</u>, and sometimes so <u>wondrous foolish</u>, that it is impossible to help laughing. I think there is <u>mischief</u> in them too, please God she lives to perpetrate it."

When Anna is well enough, she and John spend a week in Richmond, with her husband so attentive and tender that she fancies it a honeymoon. "<u>He</u> says he never spent a happier week in his life, no small comfort to <u>me</u> after 17 years & ½." In March the Jarretts are back in Camerton, and Anna delights in seeing the children installed in her own home: "You cannot think how <u>imposing</u> it looks, to see <u>the two children</u> and their nurses walking up and down the terrace. I watched them yesterday, and could not half believe they could be mine… who never (for many years past) could hope for such a blessing. I could not help feeling a little <u>proud</u>, but I trust it was <u>smothered</u> in deep gratitude to the Gracious Giver."[12] Yet in spite of her overwhelming thankfulness for the blessings bestowed on her, Anna feels that her response as a Christian, by way of faith, prayer and meditation is still inadequate. She describes her dissatisfaction with herself at great length to her brother, who has often been afflicted with similar self-doubt, and has shared his own anxieties with her. Neither of them seems able to attain the level of spirituality which their father had insisted from their earliest childhood was a prerequisite of salvation. "<u>How fervently</u> I wish to pray as I ought … I do not allow myself <u>willingly</u> to offer mere lip sacrifice, which can be only mockery to God, and yet… how often do I rise from my knees, with the dreadful consciousness of not having offered up one prayer which could be accepted by an All-seeing God. No one can guess my wanderings, my inattention, my listless coldness! And yet there are times, blessed times, tho' few alas & far between, when I feel quite <u>otherwise</u> – when by God's grace I can lift up my heart in prayer, and then I weep bitter tears to think that I cannot do so oftener."

When eventually she turns from her troubled reflections to the latest news, Anna tells Thomas of a major change anticipated in the parish. There is to be a new Rector at Camerton, appointed to succeed the Reverend John Skinner, [13] a difficult and unhappy man with whom the Jarretts had struggled to get on socially, whilst respecting him as a man of the cloth. His replacement is to be none other than John's cousin and good friend, Wilfred Lawson Jarrett, recently married to Marianne Wightwick Knightley of Offchurch Bury, a manor in Warwickshire. A former neighbour of Anna's sisters-in-law Catherine and Louisa, Marianne will be a welcome and eminently suitable companion for Anna in socially isolated Camerton.

During the winter of 1840-1841, when Anna suffered her sudden and acute illness, Queen Frederica of Hanover was beginning a slow decline, gradually losing her strength and energy over a period of six months. On 29th June she died, leaving the King overwhelmed by grief. After 26 years of marriage, he finds it hard to imagine life without Frederica, and he pours out his emotions to her brother: "You know how much I loved that adorable woman… For me she was everything in the world, for me all is lost, for I can say that I lived only for her; in her I found the tenderest wife, the most sincere amie, whom I consulted upon everything, and who always gave me the best advice, for it was always <u>disinterested</u> … my misery is great, the world holds nothing more for me."[14] Intriguingly, it was this quality of disinterested affection that Ernest had so much appreciated in his former love, Mrs Nugent (see Appendix). Replying to Wathen's letter of condolence, King Ernest expresses both his gratitude for the mark of friendship on the dreadful occasion no earthly comfort could cure, and also his trust in the Almighty to provide the strength to submit respectfully to His Divine Will – a sentiment he knew his friend would share.[15]

Thomas and his brother Ernest both welcomed new daughters in 1841: Sophia Harriett Waller was born in Brussels, and her cousin Louisa Mary in Warwickshire. Thomas's third daughter, Charlotte Louisa – named after her maternal grandmother and youngest aunt – arrived early in 1843. But in the same year came tragedy. A second daughter was born to Louisa and Ernest and given the names of their much loved aunt, Mary Nutcombe, who shortly before her death had been so overjoyed at the birth of their firstborn child, Ernest Alured. Mary's namesake was to survive only a few months. Ernest's touching letter describing his daughter's dying days is written from his father's house in London, where the parents had gone to seek the best medical advice. His anguish is unmistakable:

"My dearest Brother
  The account you have had of late of the anxious state in which dearest Ludi [Louisa] & myself have been kept by the illness of our beloved Babe, will in some measure have prepared you for the sad sequel. After a week of suffering, our dear

Babe is released – her sufferings are over, & she is now most assuredly where suffering can never in any shape touch her again. No – No – No – There is fullness of joy, and pleasures for evermore. Her little span of this life is past, & she is entered into the joy of her Lord, who when on earth suffered little children to come unto Him, & took them up in his arms & blessed them. We have indeed, Dearest brother, passed an anxious week. This very day last week, the convulsions just came on, & nearly at the same time this very morning she breathed her last – so calmly, so tranquilly, that for a long, long time we could not tell whether she were alive or not. In appearance she has suffered much, in reality I believe but little during her illness, for distressing as it is to contemplate, I am told the suffering is not great."

Having re-lived the dreadful experience whilst describing it to his brother, Ernest can eventually turn his thoughts away from his daughter, and realise how great a toll the last few days have taken on him. "Now that all is over, I feel the constant watching & want of rest tell upon me, & today my nerves feel shattered; but I hope a good night's rest will put me all to rights again. Thank God, my beloved Ludi bears up admirably, & we have this instant returned from seeing our dear child put into its coffin.… May the choicest blessing of Almighty God rest upon you, my Beloved Brother, & upon your dear Wife, & all your sweet little brood, & may He who never afflicts but in mercy, if it seems good to His unerring wisdom, shield you from that bitter pang – the loss of a dear child."[16] Unlike Thomas and Anna, Ernest appears to suffer no crisis of faith, and, as befits a clergyman, accepts the sad loss of his daughter as the will of a merciful God.

This is the last letter from Ernest to Thomas in the Waller Collection; it may have been the last that he wrote, though there was probably an exchange of letters in the summer of 1844 to mark the birth of Ernest and Louisa's youngest child, Stanier – named after Louisa's maternal grandfather, the courtier and diplomat, Sir Stanier Porten.

In April 1845, Sir Wathen again had cause for desperate anxiety about the health of one of his children; once again he provided all possible support, and was, in the words of Louisa Waller, "kindness and sympathy itself". The Tachbrook Wallers had come up to Wathen's home in New Cavendish Street, to seek the best medical advice to be found in London. This time it was needed for two invalids: Ernest himself, and his four-year-old daughter Louisa, known as Lucy. Before long the little girl rallied, but there still remained much concern for Ernest's condition. Louisa realised that his painful and swollen stomach indicated a serious disease, though she tried to make light of it. In a letter to Thomas and her sister Catherine,[17] she confides that the doctor has told her to keep Ernest up and "not make the most of his case to him" in order to save him anxiety. She tries hard to keep her tone calm, stoically believing that God will answer their prayers in the way He deems best. Having been taught from her earliest childhood to recite "Thy will O Lord be done," she prays that the words will come from the heart, and that she will meekly submit to "whatever His wisdom appoints." Clearly she fears that the illness may prove fatal. Vapour baths and rest have been recommended by the doctors, but there is no diminution of the swelling in his stomach. Mr Pearson, a Warwickshire priest, has agreed to undertake Ernest's parochial duties at Tachbrook for a couple of months at least. The family are gathering at New Cavendish Street. Anna and John arrive from Camerton; Louisa's father and sister Polly (Mary Patience) are expected shortly from Offchurch, and her brother Henry and his third son William will call on Monday.

Two days later, Ernest died. He was 37. Louisa, a widow at 35, was sole parent to five surviving children under 10 – the two older boys already away at school, and the youngest some months from his first birthday. Thomas set off from Brussels immediately to support his sister-in-law and his father. It was Georgina Bankes who sent the King of Hanover news of this "melancholy event" – rapidly confirmed to him by his sister the Duchess of Gloucester. Now it was the King's turn to express condolences. The early death of Wathen's younger son, his godson and namesake, came as an enormous shock to him, and he was prompt in proffering the only moral support possible. "Though no words of condolence can cure the natural grief and misery occasioned at the time, still it is a sort of alleviation and soothing to one's mind when one knows one has friends who are anxious as far as they can to prove their friendship on the occasion. This you must well know must be ever my feeling towards you. Religion is the only and best support one can have on such an occasion. You have always been a truly religious man and therefore know that the Almighty always acts for our best, and with this persuasion must we bow down submissively to his will."[18] Wathen was indeed of like mind, and Ernest Waller would not have disagreed. A well-intentioned, good-humoured family man of steadfast faith, he is commemorated to this day by a plaque erected to his memory in St Chad's Church, Bishop's Tachbrook.

To the Memory of
The Rev[d] Ernest Adolphus Waller
(second son of Sir Jonathan Wathen Waller Bart)
For nearly 12 years Curate of this Parish
In the hope that his labours may be blessed to the
Flock over whom he so faithfully watched, by Him
whose Servant he was, these, nearly his last words
are here recorded for their comfort
"Believe in the Lord and verily thou shalt be saved."
It is as true as the goodness of God.

Louisa was supported by the affection and assistance of all the family, and particularly by Thomas, who was doubly related to her by marriage: he was her sister's husband as well as her deceased husband's brother. Eight years previously, shortly before Thomas had left for Brussels, Ernest had drawn up a Will, naming Thomas an executor and trustee (along with his closest friend, Henry Barton, and Henry Christopher Wise, Louisa's brother). They were charged with managing the income from a trust fund, invested to produce an annual income of £200 for Louisa, the remaining interest to be applied to the children's "clothing, maintenance & education as the guardians [the trustees] think proper." At 75, Wathen was still a practical man, adept at logistics and financial planning. Immediately he re-wrote his Will, re-distributing Ernest's share of the legacies pending after his own death, under the provisions of the Wills of Thomas Slack and Jonathan Wathen.

So touched was Louisa by the exemplary behaviour of Thomas towards her family that she wrote a letter to her eldest son to be read after her death. "I desire to express with all thankfulness the true comforts I have derived from the many dear relations & friends by whom I am surrounded, who have each & all showed me such loving affection & kindness – but to your dear Uncles who were appointed by your Father to be your Guardians do I owe a debt of gratitude <u>never</u> to be repaid. Your Uncle [Thomas] Wathen most kindly took the active part in this Guardianship, & if through God's infinite mercy I have been guided aright in your education & professions, to his <u>sound counsel</u>, <u>good advice</u> & never varying <u>kindness</u> & <u>thoughtfulness</u> do I in great measure attribute this. He has indeed acted a true Father's part by you all, & may you ever feel towards him the affection he so fully deserves." [19]

Wathen was to survive his younger son by more than six and a half years, but his health and energy diminished rapidly, and for much of this time he was virtually housebound. By 1846 his sight was failing, and – in an ironic twist of fate – the renowned oculist was obliged to undergo surgery to remove cataracts twice. After the first operation the Duchess of Gloucester wrote to Thomas hoping that his father might soon "be restored to the blessing of sight & <u>rewarded</u> for all he has gone through & suffered." [20] Henry Alexander had expressed his customary optimism about the outcome of the surgery – as in the case of Princess Sophia – but Wathen soon became totally blind, and reliant on his faithful valet James Payne to take care of him, and also to write letters at his dictation. A few of these survive. All his life Wathen had lived in fear of an apocalyptic event, so it is not surprising that in his old age, after losing his sight and his independence, news of natural disasters and political upheavals should greatly upset him. He had always taken very literally biblical references to a Day of Judgment. An earthquake in Leghorn (Livorno) in August 1846 prompts the comment that "the times are full of events that seem to me proving the Approach of the early Fulfilment of Prophecy."[21] And when in February 1848 he learns of yet another Revolution in Paris, during which his old friend Louis-Philippe has been deposed, Wathen is appalled, but not surprised: "I have been for months as you know expecting an explosion as warnings appear to me to have been given on every side; at length the storm has burst, and where it will end He alone who directs the whole can alone determine. His word will be fulfilled to the Tittle, we are permitted to watch and pray but not to pry into the future with vain curiosity."[22] The revolutionary spirit of 1848 spread across much of Europe, through Germany, Poland, Denmark, Italy and the Austrian Empire. Louis-Philippe was once again exiled to England, and he spent the remainder of his life at Claremont in Surrey, the former home of Princess Charlotte of Wales and Prince Leopold. In Hanover, King Ernest, though far from well, resisted the uprising with courage and determination, at one point standing on a chair in the Palace doorway to address the mob. [23] He retained the respect and loyalty of the army and emerged unscathed, indeed even strengthened politically.

Physically, however, King Ernest was frail, and the deaths of his close friends and relations depressed him. In November 1851, at the age of 80, he died. Thirty thousand of his subjects, virtually the whole population of the capital, filed silently past their late King as he lay in state at the Leine Palace for two days. Unpopular in his native land, he had earned the respect and affection of the Hanoverians. On silk cushions close to the body lay the Crown and Sceptre of Hanover, his English Field Marshal's staff and the chains of the Order of the Garter and St George. Finally his body was transferred in a night-time procession to Herrenhausen, with 500 citizens carrying torches. He was buried in a new Mausoleum, to which his wife's coffin had also been conveyed. The mourners were headed by the King of Prussia leading Ernest's blind son, now King George V of Hanover, on his left arm, with Queen Marie and the nine-year old Crown Prince on his right. The funeral was conducted according to the liturgy of the Anglican church.[24]

In December 1852, Wathen dictated to James Payne his last letter to Thomas. He was well aware that he had little time to live and ended "my days are drawing to a close. With love and blessings to you all. Your affectionate Father." [25]

He died at his home on New Year's Day 1853, aged 83.

Notes
1. WCRO: CR0341/327/13, JWW to TWW, 15-30 October 1835.
2. WCRO: CR0341/327/109, AJ to TWW, 23 October 1837.
3. WCRO: CR0341/327/110, AJ to TWW, 25 December 1837.
4. WCRO: CR0341/327/119, JJ to TWW, 25 January 1838.
5. WCRO: CR0341/327/111, AJ to TWW, 12 February 1838.
6. WCRO: CR0341/327/40, EAW to TWW, 6 August 1838.

7. WCRO: CR0341/327/120, JJ to TWW, 8 December 1840.
8. WCRO: CR 0341 327/16, JWW to TWW, 10 December 1840.
9. WCRO: CR0341/327/121, JJ to TWW, 18 December 1840.
10. WCRO: CR0341/327/114, AJ to TWW, 25 December 1840.
11. WCRO: CR0341/327/115, AJ to TWW, 15 January 1841.
12. WCRO: CR0341/327/116, AJ to TWW, 8 March 1841.
13. Skinner, a genteel intellectual – a writer and amateur archaeologist – was somewhat irascible by temperament, and was tragically out of place for nearly forty years in the agricultural and coal-mining community of Camerton, quite unable to empathise with his uneducated, hard-drinking parishioners, many of whom were brutalised by poverty. So desperate had he become after the deaths of two infant children, then his wife, his daughter Laura and son Joseph, that he had taken his own life.
14. Willis, G M, *Ernest Augustus Duke of Cumberland and King of Hanover*, Barker 1954, p 334-335, quoting a letter from the King of Hanover to the Grand Duke of Mecklenburg-Strelitz, 29 June 1841.
15. WCRO: CR0341/89, King of Hanover to JWW, 19 July 1841.
16. WCRO: 0341/327/42, EAW to TWW, undated but probably May 1843.
17. WCRO: 0341/327/48, Louisa Waller to TWW, 17 and 18 April 1845.
18. WCRO: 0341/91, King of Hanover to JWW, 28 April 1845. This is the last letter from the King in the Waller Collection.
19. WCRO: 0341/322, Louisa Waller to Ernest Alured Waller, opened after her death in 1871.
20. WCRO: 0341/328/22, Duchess of Gloucester to TWW, 18 May 1846. The Duchess takes the opportunity to express her thanks for Wathen's service to the royal family over fifty years in a spontaneous testimonial: "The number of years friendship that the Duchess of Gloucester has had for Sir W Waller, founded upon the courtesy, assistance and devotion he has shewn first to her father George the 3rd, secondly to George the 4th, thirdly to William the 4th & lastly to her beloved sister, Princess Sophia, makes her feel a gratitude as well as regard for Sir W Waller that makes her take an immense interest in whatever befalls him & those belonging to him."
21. WCRO: 0341/327/23, JWW to TWW, 29 August 1848.
22. WCRO: 0341/327/24, JWW to TWW, 28 February 1848.
23. Willis, G M, op.cit. p 368.
24. Willis, G M, op.cit. pp 411-412.
25. WCRO: 0341/326, JWW to TWW, 9 December 1852.

Epilogue

On his father's death Thomas inherited the Waller baronetcy and nearly all of his material assets. Wathen had changed his Will when his younger son died, in order to provide for the five surviving children of Ernest's marriage to Louisa Wise – dividing a legacy from step-grandfather Jonathan Wathen so that £1400 could be invested for each of them after his death. Wathen made no mention of his daughters, Georgiana and Anna, since the settlements made on their marriages ensured that they would never have to face poverty in the unlikely event of their husbands failing to keep them in the comfort to which they were accustomed.

Both Sainsbury Langford Sainsbury and John Jarrett were men of substantial means, though not without occasional anxieties over their finances. Georgiana and her husband had moved from Froyle to Beckington in Somerset in 1842 as the patronage of that parish – a manorial rectory – had come to Sainsbury on the death of an uncle, whom he promptly succeeded as Rector and Lord of the Manor. After Sainsbury died in 1849, Georgiana remained at the Rectory, now her permanent home, with the younger children; a curate took care of the souls of the parishioners until her eldest son could be ordained and in turn become Rector.

Wathen's two Jarrett grandchildren, pious, intelligent and capable women of independent means, remained unmarried and devoted their lives to improving the lot of those less fortunate than themselves. After the deaths of John and Anna Jarrett in the 1860s, Anna Mary, their elder daughter, inherited the Camerton estate, and the Jamaican plantations were divided between the two sisters. Anna Mary threw herself wholeheartedly into the role of lady of the manor, with one thought in mind: to follow in her father's footsteps and live among the people of the Camerton estate – the tenant farmers, agricultural and colliery workers – doing good to all. In her mother's eyes the miners had appeared "troublesome and wrong-headed", but Miss Jarrett saw them in a better light: she managed to empathise with them, and to show her appreciation for their hard work and loyalty. In particular she saw it as her duty to promote religion and education in the neighbourhood and she used her considerable talents as a musician and composer in the service of both. On an outlying part of the estate she created the ecclesiastical district of Peasedown St John, building there an Iron Church, School and Parsonage in the 1870s. Miss Jarrett was daily church organist in all weathers and in varying states of health, and she trained the choir at Peasedown and at Camerton. With her sister, she undertook major re-building of St Peter's Church in Camerton, where she donated an organ, still in use, and the two ladies largely funded a stone church at Peasedown, dedicated to St John the Baptist and consecrated amid great celebrations on the saint's feast day, 24th June, in 1893. (The first high altar frontal was made from their mother's wedding dress, and it is preserved and used in the parish to this day.) In November of the same year an explosion at one of the Camerton pits killed two miners, and the resultant distress may have hastened Miss Jarrett's death on 8th December. A hundred and twenty years later her philanthropy and benevolence are still remembered in the village.

The second Miss Jarrett, Emily Elizabeth, on inheriting her sister's estates and role in the community, took over the management of the colliery and lands, continuing the tradition of "good works" for a further eighteen years and teaching at the school and Sunday school on a weekly basis. The sisters, known personally to most of their employees, were remarkable for their independence and hands-on approach to running their businesses, in an era when women played largely subordinate roles. Despite their obvious commitment to the neighbourhood they lived in, the Misses Jarrett had no vote and were ineligible for any of the public offices previously held by their father: magistrate, Sheriff and Deputy Lieutenant of the county. Nevertheless they were greatly loved and appreciated. The whole community turned out at their funerals to express affection and gratitude for the dedication they had shown to their neighbours and workers. A local newspaper devoted three columns to Emily's death and funeral, describing the mining village as a changed place in its garb of mourning, a throng trudging through the countryside "to pay their last tribute of respect to a lady whose personality and open-handed generosity had endeared her to their hearts." Emily left the Camerton estate to her first cousin once removed, Amy Maud Gooch, a granddaughter of her father's sister Anne Gooch, but Amy never lived there. The Jamaican estates were left to sons of her third cousin, Herbert Kerr, on the condition that they added Jarrett to their name. One son, Herbert the younger, was in India at the time and interpreted the request by putting Jarrett first – thus founding the family of Jarrett-Kerrs. The other son, Francis Moncrieff Kerr, was in Jamaica, and he added Jarrett after his own surname – his descendants being known as the Kerr-Jarretts.

Louisa Waller, widow of Sir Wathen's younger son Ernest Adolphus, brought up her family of four sons and a surviving daughter in Warwickshire with the help of her brother Henry Christopher Wise of Woodcote, Leek Wootton, and her brother-in-law Thomas Wathen Waller, who were co-guardians with her of the children. The boys were educated at Marlborough College, and the eldest, predictably perhaps, emulated his father by going up to Oxford and subsequently into the church. He was for many years vicar of Little Packington in Warwickshire, and became an honorary Canon of Worcester Cathedral. His wife Mary was the daughter of his father's best friend, Henry Barton, and they had ten children – four boys and six girls. Ernest and Louisa's daughter, another Louisa, married a clergyman, Daniel Goddard Compton. The second and third sons, Henry and Edmund, became officers in the Royal Navy and the Army respectively, both dying on active service in their early thirties. The loss of the two young men in their prime was a terrible blow to their mother, who barely outlived them. She did not witness the long, varied and distinguished career of her youngest son, Stanier, named after her courtier grandfather, Stanier Porten. He spent thirty-eight years in the Royal Engineers, reaching the rank of Colonel. Like both of his grandfathers he enjoyed a close association with the royal family, serving as Equerry to Queen Victoria's son Leopold, Duke of Albany, for five years, and subsequently as an extra Equerry to the Queen herself.

Sir Thomas, the second baronet, remained at his diplomatic posting in Brussels for five and a half years after his father's death. The focus of his anxiety soon turned from the older generation to the younger, when his elder son George, barely out of Harrow and with minimal training, was sent to the Crimea as a commissioned officer at the age of seventeen. Well aware that his parents pored over every word from the front, George kept up a stream of letters, playing down as much as possible the horrors of war and relating anecdotes of how he and his fellow officers passed the time whilst laying siege to Sebastopol. He describes how they had great fun making a plum pudding "worthy of any English cook" to celebrate the first Christmas.[1] The fighting was intermittent; harder to bear was the harsh Russian winter and the incidence of "Crimea fever". In August 1855 George fell ill with the fever that killed far more soldiers than the battles. During a brief stay in Scutari he met Miss Nightingale, who had managed to bring some order, cleanliness and discipline into the chaotic military hospital. Later that year he was injured in a steeplechase; his eyesight was affected and he reluctantly spent a further period in hospital, at the Monastery, a haven for convalescents. Peace was confirmed in January 1856, whilst George was still recuperating. He was relieved and delighted to go home, but had served courageously and earned a knighthood of the Légion d'honneur. Far from being put off the military life, he embraced it – serving nearly four decades as an army officer and reaching the rank of Major-General.

In 1858, when Thomas decided to retire and return from Belgium, he revealed his disillusionment with his diplomatic career in an exchange of letters with the Foreign Office on the subject of his pension. As he was a wealthy man, the amount of his pension was not crucial to his standard of living, but he was also a proud man and had hoped for an upgraded pension as a mark of recognition for his unblemished record. (He had remained on the same grade, Secretary of Legation, for well over twenty years, apart from a few months as acting Chargé d'affaires in the absence of the Ambassador.) Thomas was informed that he would receive £700 per annum, the pension to which he was entitled, and the letter ended with a few platitudinous compliments. The faint praise, condescendingly bestowed, provoked an angry, resentful and bitter reply, significant enough for Thomas to have retained a draft in his collection of letters. Echoing the words addressed to him, he wrote sarcastically of his gratification that there had been "no occasion for Her Majesty's Government to express dissatisfaction with my public conduct or to find fault with me in any way." [2] He had the consolation of knowing, after thirty-two years' service, that "the unusually ill success of my professional career is not to be attributed to any fault or misconduct on my part." The authorities were not swayed; the next official letter confirmed that Her Majesty Queen Victoria had been graciously pleased to grant him a diplomatic pension of £700 a year.

The marriages of the Waller brothers Ernest and Thomas to the Wise sisters Louisa and Catherine had ensured that the two families were forever entwined, and in the next generation their fortunes were further merged, when Major-General George Henry Waller, Thomas's elder son, came into a substantial inheritance in property from his cousin George Wise, eldest surviving son of his mother's brother Henry Christopher Wise.[3] In 1888 the Major-General, with his wife and children, moved to the Wise estate, Woodcote, in Leek Wootton, Warwickshire, where they took on the community activities and charitable good works expected of a lord and lady of the manor. The family became known as "the Wallers of Woodcote". In January 1892, George briefly became the third baronet Waller, but he survived his father by only eleven days, and the title as well as the Warwickshire estate passed to his elder son, Francis Ernest Waller, then a twelve-year-old pupil at Harrow School. While Francis remained a minor, his mother – Beatrice, Lady Waller – took responsibility for Woodcote and maintained her role in the community. Her death coincided with Francis's coming of age, but the heir had determined on a military career, and on leaving Sandhurst he was deployed in the Boer War, not returning to Woodcote until 1902. Only on his retirement from the army in 1908 was he able to fulfil his duties as lord of the manor and in the community, becoming a magistrate, Deputy Lieutenant and High Sheriff of the County. The outbreak of the first World War ended Francis's peaceful and gracious way of life. He re-enlisted at once, and was killed within months – in October 1914. His brother, fellow-officer and heir, Sir Wathen Arthur Waller, the fifth baronet, resigned his commission when peace was restored in order to carry out his public duties. He was too old for active service in the second World War, but like many owners of country houses, he and his wife Viola vacated their home, and Woodcote became a Red Cross hospital for convalescents. The couple were about to resume residence in 1947, when Sir Wathen Arthur Waller died. They had no children to inherit the baronetcy, so it passed to descendants of Ernest Adolphus Waller, and in two generations became extinct. As for the property, Lady Waller sold Woodcote to Warwickshire Council, and various other parcels of land to local individuals and authorities.[4]

Around the same time, Viola Waller, Sir Wathen Arthur's widow, deposited on loan to the Warwickshire County Record Office the combined manuscript archives of the Wise and Waller families, some 1700 items, of immense interest to historians, both amateur and professional, in Warwickshire and throughout the country. Sixty years later the WCRO acquired the archives when they were put up for sale by Lady Waller's heirs. The collection encompasses a wide variety of documents, including deeds and leases relating to ten counties and spanning the twelfth to the twentieth centuries. Some of them touch on major events on the national stage, such as the fate of the Priory at Warwick after the dissolution of the monasteries. Others, more domestic, are rare survivors: an eighteenth-century recipe book handed down in the Wise family has proved invaluable to social historians. Most personal and intimate of all are the royal and Waller family letters, idiosyncratic first-hand accounts of court and private life from the latter years of George III's reign to the Victorian era. The new light shed on the controversial character of Ernest, Duke of Cumberland and King of Hanover, is an unanticipated bonus, but it is his friend and confidant, Phippy, Sir Jonathan Wathen Waller, who dominates the chronicle. His is the pivotal role, astride two parallel worlds, as courtier and as father.

Notes

1. WCRO: CR0341/324/8, George Henry Waller to TWW, 6 January 1855.
2. WCRO: CR0341/316, Draft of letter from TWW to Edward Hammond, 5 August 1858.
3. The circumstances could scarcely have been foreseen. At the time of the two Wise/Waller marriages in the 1830s, the Reverend Henry Wise, Vicar of Offchurch, owned the Priory estates in Warwick, which his great-grandfather of the same name (landscape gardener to Queen Anne and George I) had bought in 1709. When the Vicar's son, Henry Christopher Wise, inherited the Priory and its lands in 1850, he sold the house and its immediate grounds to a railway company, and bought Woodcote, the mansion and park adjoining the Wise lands, which he had been renting as a family home for twenty years. There he had brought up ten children with his first wife Harriett (née Skipwith), and after the main purchase he gradually expanded his estate into the village of Leek Wootton. He still held unsold Priory lands stretching westwards to the canal at Warwick and intended to pass on the two combined estates as a substantial inheritance for his eldest son, Henry Christopher the younger, an army officer. Then, in 1854, came news that Captain Wise had been fatally wounded during the gold-miners' riots in Ballarat, Australia, aged only twenty-six. His mother Harriett died just three years later. It was George Wise, the second son, who inherited the Priory and Woodcote estates, some thirty years after his elder brother's death. He was then a bachelor in his fifties and had established his home in Sussex, visiting his Warwickshire properties only occasionally. Few of his siblings had reached middle age, but there was a son and a daughter from his father's second marriage. When he bequeathed Woodcote, George Wise disregarded his half-brother, preferring to name someone of his own generation, his cousin George Henry Waller, as his heir.
4. Eldridge, Paul, *The History of Woodcote,* Leek Wootton History Group, 2011.

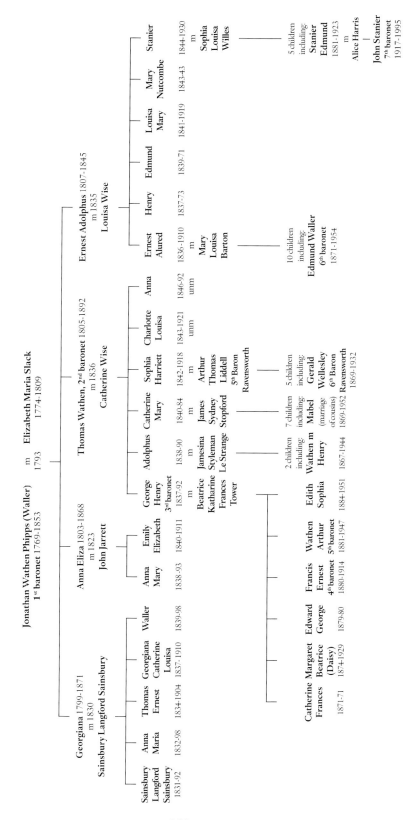

THE WALLER BARONETCY
(simplified family tree)

Appendix

Flashback: the Duke's secret love affair, 1794-1813

"no-one was happier than me with the agreeable prospect of passing a short time at the house of and in the company of one who I know loves me, but I must go on in the old humdrum manner, today, tomorrow & ever more."

Prince Ernest, 1794

Although she was brought up as the daughter of Admiral Nugent, Georgina Bankes may have known her real father for most of her life. Ernest's affection and concern for her is evident in his sending of letters via Wathen, and in the visits Georgina made to Hanover. The timing of the first visit – after the death of Admiral Nugent – suggests a measure of tact and sensitivity towards the Admiral on Georgina's part. Ernest met her mother Mrs Nugent in the 1790s, before he became Duke of Cumberland, so a major step back in time is required to consider how their love affair began. And who was the woman as yet identified only as the Admiral's wife and Georgina's mother? Fortunately, her identity can be easily discovered, since the marriage of Captain Charles Edmund Nugent in July 1790 warranted an announcement in *The Gentleman's Magazine*: the bride was (Deborah) Charlotte Johnstone, a young widow. Her life story turns out to be a fascinating tale.

Charlotte was born in Lisbon in 1756, the youngest daughter of the British Vice-Consul, James Dee. Her early life was spent in Portugal, where her family "kept the best company".[1] In 1775, when rumours reached the British Embassy in Madrid that she was to marry the Consul in Lisbon, Sir John Hort, she was already famous for her striking good looks[2] and was a favourite with portrait artists of the day. (Such a marriage may have been considered, but did not come about.) A portrait painted in Lisbon by Thomas Hickey in 1781 shows Charlotte Dee as a charismatic dark-haired beauty with a serene, restrained expression, and the fashionable "high hair" much favoured by Queen Charlotte and the Duchess of Devonshire.

The following year Charlotte married her first husband in Lisbon. He was a man twice her age, Commodore George Johnstone, a Scottish naval officer, former Governor of West Florida and MP. (George already had a family of four surviving children with a long-term mistress, Martha Ford.[3]) The Johnstones settled at Taplow near Windsor soon after arriving in England in 1782. There Charlotte and her older sister and companion, Leonora Dee, both intelligent, well-educated and accomplished women, made the acquaintance of Mary Harcourt and her husband General William Harcourt, and also of William's brother Earl Harcourt and Elizabeth his Countess, with whom they formed a strong friendship. All four of the Harcourts were on the closest terms with the royal family, and they introduced the sisters to Court circles. There was only one child of the Johnstone marriage: a son, John Lowther Johnstone, born in 1783. Before long George Johnstone became seriously ill with cancer of the throat; both of the sisters nursed him attentively during his lengthy decline. He died on 24 May 1787, leaving Charlotte a widow at the age of 31 – with a very modest income for her station in life. Mary Harcourt, who was both kind and gregarious, at once invited Charlotte to stay at her spacious home, St Leonard's Hill, near Windsor, and to join her in the autumn at Deal in Kent, for sea-bathing.[4] It was through her friendship with Mrs Harcourt that Charlotte was to meet Prince Ernest some seven years later. Meanwhile, Lord and Lady Harcourt recommended Leonora Dee to George III as a highly suitable governess/ companion for his niece, Princess Sophia Matilda, daughter of the Duke of Gloucester; the appointment proved so successful that it lasted for forty years.

The widowed Charlotte Johnstone may have had a brief affair with the Prince of Wales in 1788-9.[5] We cannot know the truth of the matter, but they were certainly friends and exchanged letters for well over a decade. No doubt exists, however, about the affair she began in 1794 with Prince Ernest, whom she met during the war in Flanders. General Harcourt was then second-in-command of the Allied troops under the Duke of York. His wife had decided to accompany her husband to the theatre of war, and her friend Charlotte, by now Mrs Nugent, joined her there. Mary maintained that she found it less stressful to be close to the action than at home in Windsor, as at least she knew what was going on: "Anxious I must be, but here I have opportunities of having my anxiety relieved and I would not take millions to be back in England. I shudder when I look back to the misery I used to feel; listening to every creaking door that opened, expecting letters, and afraid to read them when they came… and if good news arrived knowing that time enough had elapsed since its date to have followed it with bad. Thank God, I now know he is safe and well." [6] Mary fully recognised that she was in an unusual and rather bizarre situation, describing to her sister-in-law the agreeable social life which continued unabated whenever there was no actual fighting: "I write it you mixing Fighting, Dinners, Drums, Trumpets & Plays all together as it is in War so mix'd, to give you some idea (though almost impossible) of what our Life is, which cannot however drown the heartache I feel from morning to night at the approach of the campaign, the event of which is certain." [7]

In his early teens Prince Ernest had known Mrs Harcourt at Windsor, and he was surprised and delighted to come across her in the unlikely setting of the Flanders war. Mary greatly enjoyed the company of the young Prince Ernest. He was 23, and she thought him very handsome. "[He] never comes to Tournay without calling upon me; we din'd together at the General's quarters yesterday, had a very merry party, the Prince is belov'd, & thought a good officer; … I have many visitors, & it is impossible for any body to be more in their element than I am; I know indeed that there are Cannon Balls in that odious French Camp but, I know too when they are not firing, & at St Leonard's they were ever in my imagination…… the more I see of Prince Ernest the more I like him, in good hands he might be made a charming young man, I never knew a better temper, or a kinder heart." [8] Clearly Mary was kindly disposed towards Ernest and recognised in him some admirable qualities. In later life he was rarely, if ever, described in such complimentary terms. In the spring of 1794 Mary Harcourt invited Charlotte Nugent to spend some time with her at the Château de l'Hermitage, near Valenciennes and not far from Tournai, while Captain Nugent was on naval duties in the West Indies. Writing to her sister-in-law Elizabeth Harcourt, on 30th March 1794, Mary describes her temporary residence as "a most delightful house, full of comforts we have no idea of in England…. We dined with Prince Ernest on our way here." [9] This may have been the occasion when Charlotte Nugent first met the Prince.

Charlotte remained in Flanders for five or six more weeks[10] and it seems certain that she met Prince Ernest several more times; however, it was in the summer back in England that they began their affair. The first mention of Mrs Nugent in Prince Ernest's published letters occurs when he writes to his brother, the Prince of Wales, on the 11th May 1794: "Mrs Nugent being gone to England I cannot fulfil your commission [probably just to give her his regards], but beg in return you will give her my respects & tell her how sorry I am not to have seen her before her departure." [11] Unfortunately for Ernest, Charlotte's departure early in May coincided with his being wounded in combat – as described in Chapter 2 – and he confided to his brother how frustrated he was by the inopportune timing: "I wish'd (as I must have got this curs'd wound) that it had taken place 3 days before so I should have seen her. Mrs Harcourt is at Brussels; I shall probably write to her today & shall not fail mentioning her to your kind remembrance, which will flatter her, for so often she talks to me of you it is with a degree of enthusiasm." [12] Initially, the Prince underestimated the gravity of the injuries to his arm and his eye, but Mrs Harcourt realised that they were getting worse rather than better. "I fear Prince Ernest's arm is a bad business… I wish him to go to England, but not to stay there long." [13] In the circumstances the King had to agree, and he granted his son leave to come home for the first time in eight years. The injuries were real enough, but the few months in England would also provide Ernest with opportunities to renew the acquaintance of Mrs Nugent, or so he hoped. However, the King insisted that his son was to join the family on their traditional summer holiday in Weymouth, something Ernest greatly resented. To the Prince of Wales, his only confidant, he complained: "Nothing in my eyes so terrible than a family party. No-one loses more than I do, for no-one was happier than me with the agreeable prospect of passing a short time at the house of and in the company of one who I know loves me, but I must go on in the old humdrum manner, today, tomorrow & ever more."[14] From Weymouth in August he wrote to the miniaturist Richard Cosway to order a copy of an existing portrait of himself, the new version showing him with an injury to his arm. Perhaps a gift for the one who loved him? In this romantic gesture Ernest was surely following the example of his favourite brother. Had not the Prince of Wales and his unacknowledged "wife" Mrs Fitzherbert exchanged miniatures by Cosway? [15]

There is little doubt that Charlotte Nugent was the person Prince Ernest was missing whilst marking time with the family in Weymouth, and that he did manage to spend some time with her before returning to his regiment in late October. She was constantly on his mind that autumn. Whilst awaiting favourable conditions to undertake the sea crossing he wrote to thank his brother for all he had done for him, ending: "My best compliments to Lady Jersey [the current mistress of the Prince of Wales]. All I hope is that you may both be sincerely happy. If you see Mrs Nugent remember me most kindly to her. Adieu."[16] He seems to be emphasising that he too has found himself a mistress. Despite postponing the channel crossing for several days, he endured a dreadful voyage and was "dead sick". Yet as soon as he disembarked in Holland, he sent a further message: "give my compliments to Lady Jersey and Mrs Nugent."[17]

Within a year, Prince Ernest wrote to his father begging for permission to return to England again, this time to consult "Dr Wathen", as his injured eye showed no sign of healing. The King was not easily persuaded, fearing that Ernest would form an alliance with his recalcitrant eldest son, the Prince of Wales. When Prince Adolphus, serving in Flanders alongside his brother, added his weight to the plea,[18] the King at last relented, and accepted that Ernest's return was absolutely essential on medical grounds. What he did not know was that Ernest was delighted to take up residence at St James's Palace and at Kew, where he would find opportunities to resume his relationship with Mrs Nugent. During the period of rest and recuperation recommended by Wathen, a close friendship was established between oculist and patient, and Phippy probably knew of Ernest's clandestine love affair from this time onwards.

By April 1798 Charlotte Nugent was expecting her lover's child, probably with very mixed emotions. When thanking the Prince of Wales for a Christmas present that year, she is clearly apprehensive about the very real possibility that she might not survive the imminent birth. "Ten thousand thanks for your remembrance, which I am more flatter'd at & grateful for than I can express, so much so that I shall never part with it while I exist, & lose no time in leaving it to my son [John Lowther Johnstone] as a monument of your kindness (if an event should happen that the impression of my mind suggests not to be distant) and I should at this moment feel happy if I could persuade myself that I should have the pleasure of ever seeing you again and of thanking you de vive voix."[19] Although Charlotte destroyed nearly all of the Prince of Wales's letters, the few that remain are testimony to an enduring friendship between them. A week after Christmas, and three weeks before Georgina was born, the Prince wrote declining an invitation to dinner on Sunday, assuring her: "I will make a point of calling upon you & arranging a day for a quiet party with you. Best compliments to the Admiral. Ever dear Mrs Nugent's very sincere friend."[20]

The Prince of Wales made sure that everything possible was done to ensure the safe delivery of Charlotte Nugent's baby, providing his own physician, Christopher Pemberton, to supervise the event. Ernest passed on to his brother Charlotte's thanks, along with his own: "I received yesterday evening a few lines in which a recapitulation of thanks, and the firmest gratitude to you for your goodness in writing. I also thank you for your goodness. Pemberton has assured me today the babies is [sic] perfectly well."[21] We have Lady Nelson's word for it that Georgina's birth gave Admiral Nugent much happiness, and there is no doubt that throughout his long life a close father-daughter relationship existed between them, whether or not he knew the truth.

After her separation from the Admiral within months of Georgina's birth, Charlotte was clearly in some distress and unsure about what to do. She was in a difficult position socially, despite having many influential and royal friends. She and Ernest had decided that their relationship was to remain secret, possibly for Georgina's sake, and that the child would be brought up as Georgina Nugent. Perhaps Charlotte went abroad for a time; she clearly considered the possibility, and wrote to Ernest's brother Frederick, Duke of York, for advice. He replied: "[I] beg to assure you how truly sorry I am that you have not as yet been able to make such an arrangement as would relieve you from the continued state of alarm in which you live at present and preclude the necessity of your going abroad. If you have determined to go abroad and remain till some arrangement has taken place there is no Town which will in my opinion answer your purpose better than Osnabruck, and you may depend upon not being molested there."[22]

In her Christmas letter of thanks to the Prince of Wales in 1798, Charlotte had spoken excitedly of Prince Ernest's forthcoming elevation to the rank of Royal Duke, news she had heard about in confidence from Mr Pybus, Lord of the

Treasury, one of her many contacts in the corridors of power. The peerage brought with it a seat in the House of Lords, plus a separate income and establishment. In addition it symbolised the King's new confidence in Ernest after years of treating him with suspicion and disdain. The Duke's maiden speech in the Upper House (on 23rd May 1800) was on the unlikeliest of topics, but perhaps his motivation could be guessed at by a few of his closest confidants. He spoke in opposition to a Bill drawn up to discourage adultery by preventing the marriage of guilty parties of a divorce, and pointed out that to deprive a woman of future marriage and the common comforts of life was not only extremely cruel, but designed to reduce her to the most abject state of misery, and take from her whatever nominal rank she enjoyed. She would not even be able to marry the man with whom she had committed adultery. He was well aware, of course, that in his own circumstances this was not an option; he needed the sovereign's permission to marry, and – even if Charlotte obtained a divorce – marriage to a divorced woman, a commoner, would never be approved by George III.

Although the Duke could not set up home with Charlotte, the relationship continued and he endeavoured to protect her interests whenever he could. Perhaps inevitably, he became involved in the affairs of her son, John Lowther Johnstone. The boy had been educated in Scotland from the age of 6 on his father's express instructions, but the arrangement did not turn out well. John grew up showing little affection for his mother, and Charlotte found her son wilful and headstrong from his early teens. He took no notice of her wishes or her advice. Early in 1802 she was much preoccupied by John's increasingly dissolute behaviour. He was 19 and an ensign in the Coldstream Guards, but apparently was absent without leave in Edinburgh, and addicted to gambling and alcohol. Ernest enlisted the help of an old friend in whom he had complete confidence, General Vyse, a fellow cavalry officer and veteran of the Flanders campaign, now in command of the troops in Scotland.[23] Without revealing to Charlotte his involvement in the appointment, the Duke prevailed upon Vyse to take "young Johnstone" on as his aide-de-camp – but John continued to do exactly as he pleased. He had fallen for Charlotte Gordon, youngest daughter of Charles Gordon of Cluny, and his mother was afraid that her son would "run away with the girl". Neither family approved of the match. The Gordons were wealthy landed gentry of considerable pedigree, with an ancestral castle to their name, but as far as Charlotte Nugent was concerned they were not good enough for her son.

True to form, John married Charlotte Gordon on 18th January 1804 in defiance of his mother's wishes. He was 21, heir to a title and a fortune, and not disposed to take advice or instructions from anyone. Nor did he have to wait long for his inheritance: his father's elder brother, Sir William Pulteney (formerly Johnstone) died the following year, and the Johnstone baronetcy plus the

Westerhall estate in Dumfriesshire were rightfully his. Just three years later he came into a further inheritance – including vast tracts of land in New York State – from Sir William's only daughter, Lady Bath. With her properties in Dorset came the patronage of the constituency of Weymouth and Melcombe. Sir John Lowther Johnstone was returned unopposed as its MP in 1810, but his parliamentary career was to be exceptionally brief. He collapsed in the House of Commons, suffering from *delirium tremens* in March 1811 and thereafter remained mentally and physically incapacitated until his death on Christmas Eve that year, aged 28. His widow was left with three small children, two girls and a boy. The son and heir, Sir Frederick Johnstone, 7th Baronet, had just reached his first birthday.

John Lowther Johnstone had been a wealthy man, though his lands in America were the subject of legal tussles for decades after his death. He had had the foresight to leave a Will, naming the Duke of Cumberland as one of four trustees and guardians to his children – Charlotte Nugent's grandchildren. Ernest took his responsibility seriously, but it was to prove sadly detrimental to his own interests and well-being. Among other things, the trustees were charged with looking after the Johnstone family interests in the Weymouth and Melcombe constituency. The way the Duke went about this was probably clumsy, but he endeavoured to fulfil the obligation, and his resultant unconstitutional behaviour caused an uproar, a full-scale parliamentary row, as described in Chapter 4. Of course it was the Duke's involvement with Charlotte Nugent that had led him to become embroiled in her son's affairs and the Weymouth election, but he was unable to explain openly his motivation. As a peer, a member of the Upper House, he knew he had no right to interfere in an election to the Commons. To avoid jeopardising Lord Liverpool's Tory administration, which he had helped to set up, the Duke decided to withdraw from politics and leave the country for a while. The Napoleonic wars were still on-going, and it made sense for him to resume his military career, even though active service on the continent would separate him from Mrs Nugent – at least for a while. He left Yarmouth on 3rd May, to seek command of a Hanoverian regiment with the rank of Lieutenant-General. He little thought that within three weeks Charlotte Nugent would be dead.

We can only conjecture whether the Weymouth constituency *débâcle* and Ernest's subsequent departure for the continent contributed to Charlotte Nugent's sudden ill-health, but the timing of her rapid decline, starting in the first week in May, certainly suggests a connection. Lady Charlotte Campbell Bury, one of the Princess of Wales's ladies-in-waiting, quotes an unnamed woman friend who called at her home in Upper Brook Street, London, and at once realised the gravity of the illness: "Today I went to see Mrs Nugent. She is more like a corpse than any thing can be that is not one. I have paid her several visits. Her conversation is sensible and composed. Whatever scandal may have formerly said against her, must I conclude, now be silenced." [24] On another occasion she had "witnessed gloom at Mrs Nugent's", adding: "I only saw her daughter, for she herself is too ill to see any one." [25] Charlotte Nugent died at her home on 20th May 1813, in her fifty-seventh year. The news of her death came as a complete shock to Ernest. From the start of his relationship with Charlotte, the Duke had taken very few people into his confidence on the subject, so it was once again to his brother George, now the Prince Regent, that he turned in his immense distress:

"Strelitz, 7th June 1813
I have been so much knocked down by a piece of news I received in my last letters from London that I have hardly been able to collect my thoughts except on that subject, for believe me I have never had such a friend or ever again shall meet with one so highly honourable and disinterested, having never had any object in view but my honour and character; as the blow was unexpected, so much deeper is the wound inflicted by it. Excuse my having mentioned this much to you, but as you are the only brother with whom I have been in the habits of talking freely what concerns myself I have not been able to conceal my feelings from you. To describe all the misery I have felt and with a lacerated heart to appear quiet and undisturbed has been no great soother. However a man must act like a man, and I must exert myself especially at a moment when it appears to me that things are in a very ticklish state."[26] In December his mind was still in turmoil, and he described himself as "borne down with grief and misery". Returning to England was out of the question in the short term: "You know I have met .... with a disaster, which has left a sore which time alone can cure, and to return would only rip it up again."[27]

Although often represented as inhuman and unfeeling, Ernest had loved Charlotte Nugent for nearly twenty years. Throughout that time he showed no sign of seeking a marriage partner, and his grief at Charlotte's death is evident. In an age when flowery phrases and elaborate images were the norm, he prided himself on plain speaking, so his reference on this occasion to "a lacerated heart" is all the more striking. Ironically, however, it was on the very day that Charlotte Nugent died, that Ernest first set eyes on his cousin Frederica of Mecklenburg-Strelitz, with whom in time he would have a second long-term loving relationship. Despite the implacable opposition of his mother, two years later Frederica became his wife.

Notes
1. Bodleian MSS, Harcourt Papers, D.3880, 105/6.
2. Bedfordshire & Luton Archives & Records Office: Wrest Park (Lucas) MSS, L30/17/2/105, Letter from Frederick (Fritz) Robinson (Secretary to the British

Ambassador at Madrid, his brother Thomas Robinson, Baron Grantham) to his sister Anne Robinson, 6th February 1775:

"We have heard but I do not quite give credit to it, that Sir John Hort was going to be married to a Lisbon beauty a Miss Charlotte Dee. I fancy it would not be a good match. We have seen her picture so often that I should certainly know her. Lelu the painter of whom we [have] often spoken, had taken all his ideas of beauty from her." The French painter Pierre Lelu lived in Portugal for more than 40 years.

3. George Lindsay Johnstone, Sophia Johnstone, James Primrose Johnstone, Alexander Patrick Johnstone. Another son, John, had died in 1780. Rothschild, Emma, *The Inner Life of Empires*, Princeton University Press, 2011, pp 337-8.

4. Carter, Elizabeth, *Letters to Mrs Montagu 1755-1800*, Letter CCLXVI, Deal, 19 October 1787. Mrs Carter lived in Deal.

5. Camp, Anthony J, *Royal Mistresses and Bastards: Fact and Fiction 1714-1936*, Camp, 2007. Also, "the Prince is in full pursuit of a new Beauty, Mrs Johnstone, Widow of the Governor of West Florida." The words of Lord Abercorn, quoted by James Munson in *Maria Fitzherbert, The Secret Wife of George IV*, pub Constable, 2001, p 211.

6. *The Harcourt Papers*, Vol. V. p 184.

7. Bodleian MSS, *Additional papers of the Harcourt family*, B4 3661.

8. Ibid.

9. *The Harcourt Papers*, Vol V, p 423.

10. Ibid, p 437. In April 1794 Mary and Charlotte stayed briefly at the Prince de Coburg's château at Jallaix, where they agreed to house two injured officers overnight. Mary reported that one of them, "Mr Estridge, a boy of 17, was so much wounded that the blood streamed from his leg when he was lifted from the cart…. Mrs Nugent, whose activity and benevolence on such occasions know no bounds, helped me to nurse them."

11. Aspinall, A (Ed), *The Correspondence of George, Prince of Wales, 1770-1812*, Letter 827, Vol 2, p 430, Prince Ernest to POW, 11 May 1794. From the 1930s onwards for many years Professor Aspinall had unprecedented access to the correspondence of George III and George IV in the Royal Archives, selecting items he considered of historical interest for publication. In a footnote, he comments on Prince Ernest's mention of Mrs Nugent: "Apparently a respectable person: she was habitually at the Queen's Drawing Room."

12. Ibid.

13. Bodleian MSS, Additional papers of the Harcourt family, B4 3661.

14. Aspinall, A, op.cit. Letter 852, Vol 2 p 446, Prince Ernest to POW, 24 July 1794.

15. Despite the long estrangement between Mrs Fitzherbert and George IV, when he died in 1830 he was wearing the Cosway miniature she had given him.

16. Aspinall, A, op.cit. Letter 877 Vol 2 p 471, Prince Ernest to POW, 25 October 1794.

17. Aspinall, A, op.cit. Letter 881 Vol 2 p 475, Prince Ernest to POW, 30 October 1794.

18. Willis, G M, *Ernest Augustus, King of Hanover*, p 48, Prince Adolphus to King, 24 December 1795.
19. Aspinall, A, op.cit. Letter 1403 Vol 3, p 492, Mrs Nugent to POW, 25 December 1798, in reply to his letter of the previous day.
20. Aspinall, A, op.cit. Letter 1417 Vol 3, POW to Mrs Nugent, 1 January 1799 (originals at Dorset History Centre: Bankes Box 8C/100, Folder 2, vii).
21. Aspinall, A, op.cit. Note to Letter 1421, Prince Ernest to POW, Vol 4, p 11, 4 February 1799.
22. Dorset History Centre, Bankes Box 8C/100, Folder 2, iii, letter from Frederick, Duke of York, to Mrs Nugent, 19 November 1799.
23. Centre for Buckinghamshire Studies: Letter D-HV/B/32/23, Duke of Cumberland to R. Vyse, 10 February 1802. This paragraph is based on the letter referred to and others from this collection.
24. Campbell Bury, Lady Charlotte, *Diary illustrative of the times of George IV*, ed. John Galt, Lea & Blanchard, Philadelphia, 1839, Vol 1, p 133.
25. Ibid. Vol 2, p 97.
26. Aspinall, A, *The Letters of King George IV, Vol 1, 1812-1830:* Letter 282, p 255, Duke of Cumberland to the Prince Regent.
27. Ibid. Letter 356, pp 341-342.

Bibliography

Manuscripts

The principal manuscript source is The Waller Collection (CR 0341) in the Warwickshire County Record Office (WCRO).

Others

Bedfordshire & Luton Archives & Records Office: *Wrest Park (Lucas) MSS.*

Bodleian Library, University of Oxford: *Harcourt Papers and Additional papers of the Harcourt family.*

Centre for Buckinghamshire Studies: *Letters from the Duke of Cumberland to R.Vyse.*

Cornwall Record Office: *Extracts of letters from the King of Hanover to the Revd D.C. Delafosse.*

Dorset History Centre: *Bankes Boxes.*

East Sussex Record Office: *Letter from Lord Sheffield to Lord North.*

Lewisham Local Studies and Archives: *Account of the fire in which Thomas Cartwright Slack died (1815).*

Richmond Local Studies Collection: *Pope's Villa File.*

Royal Archives, Windsor: *Queen Victoria's Journal* and *Letters from the Duke of Cumberland, Georgian Papers.*

Surrey History Centre, Woking: *Ware, James, Journal of Transactions while in London, 1773-77 and General Notes and memorandum during my stay in London, 1775-1777.*

The National Archives: Chancery papers, *Baroness Howe v Richard Curzon; Wills.*

The National Art Library, Victoria & Albert Museum: *William Wood's papers.*

The National Library of Ireland: *Westport Estate Papers.*

Wellcome Manuscripts: *Letter from Sir Jonathan Wathen Waller.*

West Sussex Record Office, Goodwood Archives: *Correspondence of the Duke of Cumberland and the Duchess of Richmond.*

Newspapers & periodicals

The Bookman
The European Magazine and London Review
The Gentleman's Magazine
The London Journal of Medicine
The Royal Lady's magazine, and archives of the Court of St James's
The Times

Transactions of the Society Instituted at London for the Encouragement of Arts, Manufacture and Commerce

Books

Anon, *Biographical Memoirs of Louis-Philippe the first, King of the French, with a Sketch of the Revolutions of 1830 and 1848*, Cradock, London, 1848.

Aspinall, A (ed), *The later correspondence of George III*, Cambridge, 1962-1970.

Aspinall, A (ed), *The Correspondence of the Prince of Wales*, 1770-1812, London, 1963.

Aspinall, A (ed), *The Letters of King George IV*, Cambridge, 1938.

Bankes, Viola, *A Dorset Heritage*, Anthony Mott, 1986 (2nd edition).

Barrow, Sir John, *Life of Richard, Earl Howe, Admiral of the Fleet*, John Murray, 1838.

Berkley, Grantley Fitzhardinge, *My Life and Recollections*, Hurst & Blackett, 1865.

Berry, Mary, *Extracts of the journals & correspondence of Miss Berry, 1783-1852*, ed. Lady Theresa Lewis, Longmans & Green, 1865.

Bew, Jon, *The Ambulator*, London, 1820.

Bird, Anthony, *The damnable Duke of Cumberland*, Barrie & Rockliff, London, 1966.

Burke, John, *A General and Heraldic Dictionary of the Peerage and Baronetage of the British Empire*, H. Colburn and R. Bentley, 1832.

Camp, Anthony J, *Royal Mistresses and Bastards: Fact and Fiction 1714-1936*, 2007.

Campbell Bury, Lady Charlotte, *Diary Illustrative of the times of George IV*, Lea & Blanchard, Philadelphia, 1839

Carter, Elizabeth, *Letters to Mrs Montagu 1755-1800*, London, 1817.

Cliffe, Leigh, *Anecdotal remembrances of distinguished literary and political characters,* London, 1830.

Cobbett, R S, *Memorials of Twickenham*, Smith, Elder & Co, London, 1872.

Cooke, George Wingrove, *The history of party: from the rise of the Whig and Tory factions,* J. Macrone, London, 1837.

Eldridge, Paul, *The History of Woodcote,* Leek Wootton History Group, 2011.

Farington, Joseph, *Farington Diary*, London, 1923.

Foreman, Amanda, *Georgiana, Duchess of Devonshire*, Harper Collins, London, 1998.

Fraser, Flora, *Princesses, The Six Daughters of George III*, John Murray, London, 2004.

Fulford, Roger, *Royal Dukes*, Penguin, 1933.

Godsall, J R, *The tangled web*, Troubador, Leicester, 2008.

Greville, Charles, *Journal*, Longmans, Green & Co, London, 1875.

Gurney, W B & Seabury, S, *The Trial of Josiah Phillips for a Libel on the Duke of Cumberland*, J. Hatchard & Son, London, 1833.

Harcourt, E W (ed), *The Harcourt Papers*, Oxford, 1880.

Hardy, Thomas, *The Dynasts*, London, 1908.

Henry, David, *A historical description of Westminster Abbey, its monuments and curiosities*, Newman & Co, 1827 edition.

Hemlow, Joyce, *The Journals and Letters of Fanny Burney* Oxford, 1972-84.

Hibbert, Christopher, *George IV, Regent & King, 1811-1830.*

Hilton, Boyd, *A Mad, Bad and Dangerous People? England 1783-1846*, Oxford, 2006.

Hobhouse, John Cam, later Lord Broughton, *Recollections of a long life*, Murray, 1909.

Kerr, William James, *The Genealogical Tree of the Family of Jarrett of Orange Valley, Jamaica, and Camerton Court, Co. Somerset,* Southampton, 1896.

Kerry, Charles, *The history and antiquities of the hundred of Bray,* 1861.

Leslie, Shane, *George the Fourth,* Little & Brown, Boston, 1926.

Low, Sampson, *The Charities of London,* Low, London, 1850.

Marryat, Joseph, *A history of pottery & porcelain, medieval and modern*, John Murray, 1868.

Mitford, John, *Royal Intrigues and Amours of Many Illustrious Persons related to the Court of St J[ames]'s,* by a distinguished Courtier, London, 1830.

Munson, James, *Maria Fitzherbert, The Secret Wife of George IV*, Constable, 2001.

Naish, George (ed), *Nelson's Letters to his wife, and other documents 1785-1831,* Routledge & Kegan Paul, 1958.

Oulton, W C, *The Authentic and Impartial Memoirs of her late Majesty, Charlotte, Queen of Great Britain and Ireland*, 1819.

Overton, Grant, *American Nights Entertainment,* New York, 1923.

Peach, R E M, *Historic Houses in Bath and their Associations,* Simpkin, Marshall & Co London, 1883.

Roberts, W, *Sir William Beechey, RA*, Duckworth, 1907.

Robinson, Lionel G (ed), *Letters of Dorothea, Princess Lieven, during her residence in London, 1812-1834,* London, 1902.

Rothschild, Emma, *The Inner Life of Empires*, Princeton University Press, 2011.

Saunders, John Cunningham, *A treatise in some practical points relating to diseases of the eye,* Longman, Hurst, Rees, Orme & Brown, *London,* 1811.

Smith, E A, *George IV*, Yale University Press, 1999.

Somerset, Anne, *The Life and times of William IV,* Weidenfeld & Nicolson, 1980.

Strachey, Lytton, *Queen Victoria,* Harcourt Brace & Co., New York, 1921.

Sweetman, John, *Oxford Dictionary of National Biography*, Oxford, 2004.

Thomson, Mrs M T, & Wharton, Philip, *The Queens of Society,* 1860.

Thorne, James, *Handbook to the environs of London,* 1876.

Tomalin, Claire, *Mrs Jordan's Profession,* Viking, 1994.

Twiss, Horace, *The public and private life of Lord Chancellor Eldon,* Carey & Hart, Philadelphia, 1844.

Wardroper, John, *Wicked Ernest*, Shelfmark Books, London, 2002.

Waring, E J, *A Manual of Practical Therapeutics*, J.Churchill & Co, 1866.

Watkins, John, *The life and times of "England's patriot King", William IV*, 1831.

Watson, J Steven, *The Reign of George III*, Oxford, 1960.

Wellesley, Gerald, 7th Duke of Wellington (ed), *Wellington and his friends*, Macmillan, 1965.

Wentworth, G (ed), *The poetical note book and epigrammatic museum*, 1824.

Whyman, John, *Aspects of holidaymaking and resort development within the Isle of Thanet, with particular reference to Margate, c1736 to c1840*, published in *Dissertations on Economic History*, 1981.

Wilkinson, The Revd Charles Allix, *Reminiscences of the Court and Times of King Ernest of Hanover*, Hurst & Blackett, London, 1887.

Williamson, George C, *The Miniature Collector, a guide for the amateur collector of Miniatures*, 1921.

Willis, G M, *Ernest Augustus, Duke of Cumberland, King of Hanover*, Arthur Barker, London, 1954.

Woodham-Smith, Cecil, *The Reason Why*, Constable & Co, 1953.

Yonge, Charles Duke, *The Life and administration of Robert Banks, second Earl of Liverpool*, Macmillan & Co, London, 1868.

Zeigler, Philip, *King William IV*, Collins, 1971.

Abbreviations
used in Notes and Index

JWP for Jonathan Wathen Phipps 1769-1813; JWW for Jonathan Wathen Waller
    1814-1853; JWP/JWW for periods overlapping his surname change in 1814
TWW for his son Thomas Wathen Waller
EAW for his son Ernest Adolphus Waller
AJ for his daughter Anna Jarrett; JJ for her husband, John Jarrett
SLS for his son-in-law Sainsbury Langford Sainsbury
POW for the Prince of Wales

Index

The children of (Jonathan) Wathen Phipps, later Waller, are listed under their first names: Georgiana, Anna, Thomas, Ernest.